WHEN CRIME WAVES

WHEN CRIME WAVES

WITHDRAWN

Vincent F. Sacco
Queen's University

SAGE Publications
Thousand Oaks ▪ London ▪ New Delhi

For information:

Sage Publications, Inc.
2455 Teller Road
Thousand Oaks, California 91320
E-mail: order@sagepub.com

Sage Publications Ltd.
1 Oliver's Yard
55 City Road
London EC1Y 1SP
United Kingdom

Sage Publications India Pvt. Ltd.
B-42, Panchsheel Enclave
Post Box 4109
New Delhi 110 017 India

Printed in the United States of America

Library of Congress Cataloging-in-Publication Data

Sacco, Vincent.
When crime waves / Vincent F. Sacco.
    p. cm.
Includes bibliographical references and index.
ISBN 0-7619-2783-2 (pbk.)
  1. Crime. 2. Criminology. 3. Criminal statistics. 4. Mass media and crime. 5. Criminal justice, Administration of. I. Title.
HV6025.S23 2005
364—dc22

                          2004026393

This book is printed on acid-free paper.

05 06 07 08 10 9 8 7 6 5 4 3 2 1

Acquisitions Editor:	Jerry Westby
Editorial Assistant:	Laura Shigemitsu
Production Editor:	Denise Santoyo
Copy Editor:	Kris Bergstad
Typesetter:	C&M Digitals (P) Ltd.
Indexer:	Kathy Paparchontis
Cover Designer:	Janet Foulger

Contents

Preface

We live in very interesting times. The world, it seems, is becoming a very complex place. Weather systems and outbreaks of disease in countries many of us might not even be able to locate on a map have profound consequences for our economic life and for our food supply. "Distant wars" now seem a lot less distant than they once were. Constantly changing and rapidly diffusing technologies profoundly affect the ways in which we relate to each other and how we perform even the most mundane tasks.

As the world becomes a more complicated place, the need for a critical understanding of contemporary social problems becomes paramount. Ironically, however, several different kinds of factors conspire to impede that understanding. Perhaps most important is the fact that we experience so much of the complexity of social life in vicarious ways. Various forms of mass media and related technologies become the principal sources of information about the world around us. Unfortunately, for reasons relating to the economics and the conventions of media production, the images and narratives presented to us are too often simplistic and melodramatic when what we really need is comprehensiveness and sober assessment. This observation is no less true with respect to crime than it is with respect to any other aspect of the social world.

Crime waves, which are the subject matter of this book, are a case in point. It is noteworthy that while the term *crime wave* is commonly used by journalists and political speechmakers, the concept has received scant attention from academic criminologists. At first glance, crime waves might appear to be simple matters—simple in form and simple with respect to causes and solutions. The chapters that follow challenge this view in that they proceed from the assumption that the social phenomena we call crime waves are complicated indeed.

As we will see, when crime wave episodes are under way, the problem of crime can dominate the media, occupy the time of lawmakers and distract all of us from other (perhaps more pressing) problems. Private citizens and their governments direct scarce resources toward efforts intended to offer protection against new and burgeoning crime threats. But too often such efforts produce no tangible benefit. For these reasons we need to think carefully about the complexities of crime waves. It is important that we understand where they come from, how they develop, and what their consequences are. The following chapters attempt to accomplish these objectives.

Three important aspects of the approach employed in *When Crime Waves* require comment. First, it will become clear to the reader that as one attempts to make sense of crime waves one needs to draw on many of the lessons to which the student of criminology may already have been exposed. The study of crime waves, it will be seen, is the study of media images of crime, public reactions to crime, crime measurement, theories of crime causation, and policy assessment.

Second, the arguments about crime waves are built around a variety of historical and contemporary cases. The diversity of the examples is intended to encourage the reader to derive some common lessons from what, on the surface, often appears as dissimilar events. The Wild West, hip-hop music, the career of Al Capone, the development of the drive-by shooting, the McDonaldization of criminal justice, the "monkey man of New Delhi," the power of gossip, and the current focus on terrorism, along with a host of other topics, are discussed in order to help the reader understand what crime waves are and why we respond to them as we do.

Third, as a supplementary text for undergraduate criminology and sociology of crime courses, the book is intended to help students appreciate how the analytical skills they are developing can be applied to real-world situations. In this sense the approach is hands-on, as students are asked to assess critically much of what popular culture makes available to them. By definition, crime waves intrude on our consciousness, and *When Crime Waves* gives the reader an opportunity to think skeptically about real-world situations.

The book consists of eight chapters. Chapter 1 develops a conceptualization of crime waves as social constructions. In this framework, a crime wave can be said to be under way when large numbers of people come to believe that one is under way. The chapter also overviews a theoretical perspective, known as social constructionism, within which most of the arguments in the book can be situated.

Chapter 2 deals with what in many ways is the most fundamental question of all: Why do crime rates suddenly go up and down? Summarizing much of the relevant research, the chapter argues that three kinds of abrupt social shifts—dislocation, diffusion, and innovation—help us to answer this question.

In Chapter 3 we discuss issues and problems relating to the ways in which crime is counted. Of course, one of the key indicators that a crime wave is under way is a dramatic shift in our counts of crime. The problems raised here are different from those raised in the previous chapter. The key issue in this chapter is how the social process of counting crime might change abruptly over time, irrespective of how the things we are counting are distributed in time. The chapter also discusses what happens when crime statistics become news stories.

Chapter 4 looks at the relationship between crime waves and mass media. For some analysts, crime waves are really best conceptualized as media waves. This chapter explores the images of crime that "nonfiction" media make available to the very large audiences that attend to these media. What is the content of contemporary crime media? What sorts of organizational and economic factors explain the patterns we observe? Why does the amount of crime news and information found in the media change over time?

The mass media are not the only sources of crime news and information to which most of us have access. Of at least equal importance is the kind of information that comes to us through our informal interpersonal networks. Rumors, gossip, and urban legends, which are often crime narratives, are the subject of Chapter 5. More to the point, many of the stories we hear about crime from friends (or read about in their e-mails) are stories about new and burgeoning problems. Like statistical practices and mass media reporting, informal storytelling constructs crime waves.

Chapter 6 focuses on a much studied type of public reaction to crime waves—the fear of crime. Fear of crime is defined, and its major correlates are discussed. Of central relevance are questions relating to the relationship between shifting crime levels and shifting levels of fear.

When we come to believe that crime waves are under way, we usually seek to do something about them. These efforts are addressed in Chapter 7. How can we stem the rapidly developing problem? The intention of this chapter is not to review the very large number of studies dealing with the hundreds of solutions to the crime problem that have been advocated over the years. Rather the emphasis is on more general issues. How does the need to do something quickly promote a kind of crisis thinking, which is often counterproductive? How do our socially constructed images of the problem at hand shape our responses? How do the politics of crime waves undermine serious prevention efforts? How might efforts to control crime problems actually make the problems worse?

The final chapter of *When Crime Waves* offers a summary of the book's main arguments in a "how to" format. Readers are given practical advice about how to diagnose crime waves. How do we know crime waves are under way? What kinds of questions do we need to ask in order to behave like responsible and skeptical consumers of crime information?

Acknowledgments

I am grateful to a large number of people for their generosity during the time this volume was a "work in progress." I am thankful to my friend and colleague Les Kennedy, with whom I originally discussed this book and who offered me those critical initial words of encouragement. I also owe a huge debt to Jerry Westby at Sage for his guidance and especially for his patience. I extend my gratitude as well to Laura Shigemitsu; Denise Santoyo, my production editor; and to everyone at Sage who lent advice and support. I am especially indebted to Kristin Bergstad for both her careful copyediting and her good humor on even the coldest and bleakest December day. Reviewers Gregg Barak, Eugene Bouley, Stephen J. Brodt, Lisa Broidy, Dick De Lung, Stephen Demuth, Kristine Empie, Stephen C. Richards, and Carl Russell provided critical and thoughtful commentary that helped me clarify and extend the arguments I was trying to make.

Several people—friends, colleagues, and especially students—at Queen's University provided practical and moral support. My friend and Department Head, Roberta Hamilton, encouraged me to make the book a priority even when administrative and teaching obligations seemed to dominate my professional agenda. Adriane Bilous provided helpful library assistance. The Administrative staff of the Department of Sociology—Michelle Ellis, Lynn O'Malley, Kathleen Umanetz, and Joan Westenhaefer—assisted in a number of ways; I tried to keep track of how many but lost count. I owe a particular debt to the large number of undergraduates with whom I have had the privilege of interacting over the past few years. It was in connection with my sociology of crime courses that I first started to think and talk about crime waves. I have learned a great deal from these students about what is and what is not good pedagogy and about a number of other things as well. As a group they are without equal in my 25 years of teaching experience.

In any list of acknowledgments, there is always a group of people whose connection to the project in question is obvious to no one but the author. The present case is no exception. Terry Boyle, Tara Carnochan, Athena Elafros, Ron Gillis, Reza Nakhaie, Wendy Regoeczi, and Bob Silverman deserve my gratitude. I owe a special thank-you as well to Nick Sacco. Nick is one of the best read and most sharply critical people I know. Over the past couple of years, we argued about and discussed (but mostly argued about) the nature and value of what is often called "skeptical inquiry." Nick's diatribes (I am sure he wouldn't mind me calling them that) led me to rethink a number of issues.

Of course, my family was, during this project, what they have been throughout anything I have ever attempted—supportive and loving and with humorous barbs at the ready. I am very appreciative of the work our daughter Katherin did on the manuscript at a very crucial point in the process. I am also thankful for her insistence that I really should try listening to Tupac and Biggie because I would find them interesting (she was right). While our son Daniel did not work on the manuscript directly (despite offers to do so), he was my constant source of information about the most arcane elements of popular culture. He was also a constant source of welcome distraction (when at least one of us didn't feel like working). Finally, I am so grateful to Tiia, who took time out from everything else she had to do to read and comment on the manuscript. She is a clear thinker and a calming influence, and she is philosophical about the fact that I am often neither of these things. All in all, this is one terrific family.

Of course (even though I really don't believe it), any errors or omissions in the chapters that follow are my fault and not anyone else's.

1

What Are Crime Waves?

The Black Hand Strikes Again—*Most New Yorkers first learned about the crimes of the "Black Hand" in September of 1903. First the* New York Herald *and then other city dailies began an extensive coverage of what seemed to be a growing crime problem. For the residents of New York's Little Italies, however, the papers said nothing they didn't already know. For decades the members of the rapidly growing Italian immigrant communities in New York, New Jersey, Philadelphia, Buffalo, and elsewhere had been victimized by gangs of extortion artists who often identified themselves as members of various Black Hand societies.*

To be sure, there was nothing particularly sophisticated or complex about the typical Black Hand crime. A prosperous member of the Italian community might receive a letter in the mail or find it attached to the front door of the home or business. It would demand that a certain sum of money be paid to the sender by a particular date and under very specific conditions. The letter would describe, often in explicit detail, the dire consequences that would follow if the payment were not forthcoming. The victim or the victim's family might be threatened with violence. Alternatively, the letter might warn ominously that fires and explosions would occur unexpectedly and with devastating results. Typically, the letters were signed with a black handprint—a sure sign of terror to those who knew its meaning. Sometimes victims ignored the letters, in which case, a second or third might follow, escalating the threat or even reducing the amount of payment demanded. All too often, however, to ignore the demand was to risk serious harm. By the time the New York papers had begun to report on the Black Hand, crime, bombings, murders, mutilations, and beatings were becoming routine occurrences in most—if not all—cities with sizable Italian American populations. The victims, often alienated from and afraid of police departments that had no Italian members, were easily and increasingly exploited by the growing Black Hand menace.

While the extortionists tried to present an image of themselves as members of a single powerful criminal organization, most expert observers agreed that Black Hand gangs were small-time, often solo operations that required little more than ready access to victims and some coal dust into which to dip the hand used to sign the letter. The Black Hand reign of terror would continue until the dawn of World War I. Before it was over, though, it would result in the development of a specialized policing squad in New York City, prompt the formation of citizen crime organizations in Chicago and elsewhere, and forge an indelible relationship in popular culture between Italian immigrant communities and violent criminal conspiracies.

The Lawless Years—*On a hot July night in 1934, the City of Chicago witnessed one of the climactic acts in a long-running crime wave that had gripped much of America. In the presence of a crowd milling around the Biograph Theater on North Lincoln Avenue, federal agents shot down one of the most notorious desperados of the era—John Dillinger. Dillinger and his gang, along with other celebrity bandits who sported media-friendly names like "Baby Face" Nelson, "Pretty Boy" Floyd, "Machine Gun" Kelly, and "Creepy" Karpis, commanded headlines for months as they robbed banks, broke out of jails, and took hostages. The publicity machine of J. Edgar Hoover and the FBI had been largely responsible for turning these rural Midwestern bank robbers into figures of national notoriety, and each time one fell or was captured, the status of Hoover and his agents climbed markedly.*

It was perhaps the passage of the Eighteenth Amendment in 1919 that should be seen as the logical starting point of the crime wave that would occupy Americans between the two world wars. Prohibition had turned every social drinker into a criminal, and many observers argued that the widespread lack of respect for the laws prohibiting the sale of alcohol translated into a more general disrespect for the law itself. Importantly, Prohibition provided the first real sustained market opportunity for the multiethnic urban gangs that existed in all major American cities. With a continual source of profit from the sale of illegal alcohol, these gangs grew larger and more powerful and established important protective links with corrupt urban politicians.

However, as the gangs sought to resolve conflicts that arose between them, violence was an inevitable result. The Illinois Crime Survey estimated, for instance, that in just 2 years (1926 and 1927), 130 unsolved gangland murders occurred in the City of Chicago. By the end of the decade of the 1920s, the nation and indeed much of the world would be shocked by an event that suggested how badly crime had spiraled in few short years. The so-called Saint Valentine's Day Massacre occurred when seven members of a rival gang were machine gunned in the early morning hours of February 14, 1929, most probably by members of the Al Capone mob. Within a few years, not only would Dillinger be killed, but Capone and many of the other famous crime figures between the wars would be dead or in prison.

Crime in the Streets—*Olympic Park in Irvington, New Jersey, was once known as one of the finest amusement parks in the eastern United States. By the 1960s, however, its better days were behind it. The fate of the park was sealed on the first day of May 1965 when a group of several hundred Newark youth went on a destructive rampage inside the park. When chased out of the park, they continued to destroy and vandalize property and to threaten residents of nearby neighborhoods. For many who witnessed or later learned of the event, the riot was just one more example of a general breakdown in law and order, which had been under way in America for some time.*

The 1960s saw the century's most massive increase in street crime. In the 12 years between 1959 and 1971, rates of street crime reported to the police more than quadrupled. Total violent crime rates more than tripled. The rate of robbery, perhaps the most feared and the most powerful symbol of crime in the streets, almost quadrupled between 1958 and 1970. Crimes against property, such as theft and burglary, also showed dramatic increases over the period.

The effects of the postwar crime wave were pervasive. Most generally, cities were perceived as steeped in crime, poverty, and violence. Those who could flee the city for the relative safety and security of the suburbs did so. As this more affluent, largely white population fled, a largely southern, rural, African American population became increasingly dominant in many urban areas. Detroit, for example, at the end of the Second World War was mainly a "white city." By the end of the 1960s, however, African Americans made up about half of the population. The civil disorder that emerged out of the racial and economic inequality of urban social structures only added to the fear and trepidation of many city dwellers.

There were also consequences for political discourse. For the first time, presidential politics were dominated by the problem of crime and urban disorder. "Crime in the streets," "victims' rights," and "law and order" emerged as potent campaign slogans.

The Devil Made Them Do It?—*The television documentary drew record audiences for a show of this type. The host, journalist Geraldo Rivera, warned viewers that America was in the midst of a satanic crime wave. "Every hour, every day," he told them, "their ranks are growing. Their crimes are vicious and bizarre and include child abuse, the production of child pornography, animal mutilation, grave desecration and grisly satanic murders."*

The television special, Devil Worship: Exposing Satan's Underground, *aired in October 1988. By this point, concern and anxiety about satanic crimes and criminals was almost a decade old. Since about 1980, a loose coalition of conservative religious groups, anticult organizations, politicians, and tabloid journalists had been spreading alarm about the threat that the growing level of satanic crime represented. Their claims almost defied belief:*

- *As many as 1,000,000 children are kidnapped each year and used in satanic ritual sacrifices*
- *In excess of 40,000 Americans are killed each year by satanists*
- *Satanists have taken over a large number of day care centers and are working to actively influence the content of music, television, and other forms of popular culture*

But how was it really possible, critics asked, for such activity to go unobserved by those in a position to prosecute the offenders? The response was disturbing. Satanists, we were told, were highly organized in order to escape detection. More important though, it was suggested, many police, judges, reporters, and prosecutors were part of the conspiracy.

Reliable evidence in support of the claims about satanic crime was hard to come by, and many of the claims simply defied logic and common sense. How could satanists be killing 40 to 50 thousand people per year without anyone noticing? What evidence could be offered that as many as 1,000,000 children were going missing every year? Nonetheless, the response to the crime wave in many sectors was swift and certain. Policing agencies developed special "cult cop" squads. A large number of psychotherapists began to specialize in helping patients "recover" earlier memories of child abuse. Parents' groups moved to pressure record labels to control the satanic imagery in music. Before the decade was over, the concern about the rise in satanic crime was a preoccupation not only of Americans but also of Canadians, Australians, Norwegians, the British, and the Dutch.

Bad Company—*To her fans, Martha Stewart was the epitome of good taste and homemaking ingenuity. In 2002, however, many came to think of her instead as a corporate criminal. Media outlets as diverse as the* Wall Street Journal *and* People *magazine reported allegations that Stewart had benefited from insider information that had allowed her to sell stock shares at a high price before the stock was to fall dramatically. Media interest in her possible criminal involvement was in large part a reaction to her celebrity. In March of 2004, a jury found Martha Stewart guilty on four counts of obstruction of justice and lying to investigators about a curiously timed stock sale. Of perhaps equal importance, though, was the wider context of the allegations.*

America in 2002 appeared to be in the middle of a "corporate crime wave" and when the allegations surfaced against Stewart, she was merely the most recent—if the most notable—offender. The corporate crime wave first came to public attention with the case of Enron, a very large energy company that declared bankruptcy in December of 2001. Subsequent investigation revealed that the kinds of crimes in which Enron executives had been involved lacked many of the subtleties that are sometimes associated with corporate offending. It was alleged, for instance, that they deliberately hid company losses and the degree of indebtedness from investors, and with full knowledge of these problems encouraged company employees to buy Enron stock.

In the months that followed, it became clear that Enron was not an isolated case, and a number of other financial scandals quickly surfaced. The companies involved in these scandals included Tyco, Global Crossing, Quest, WorldCom, Xerox, Adelphia, and others. The consequences were of course severe for investors and the employees of these companies. More generally, though, the scandals weakened the stock market and contributed to a general lack of confidence in the economic and moral order. The media had never really used terms like crime wave *or* crime spree *to describe corporate offending, but all that seemed to have changed.*

These Black Hand extortionists, prohibition-era gangsters, marauding street gangs, satanic conspirators, and corporate criminals are all actors in the kind of grand social dramas that this book explores. We refer to these dramas as *crime waves.* In the popular media, the rhetoric of politicians, and the proclamations of criminal justice officials, however, they are often known by other, related names including criminal crises, epidemics of crime, or crime panics. Whatever the name given to them, their essence is easily understood. What such dramas involve is a collective understanding that some crime problem is getting a lot worse. Sometimes, these crime problems are old and familiar and appear to be just reasserting themselves. Juvenile crime might be a good example of the kind of problem that seems to intrude into public consciousness with some degree of regularity (Gilbert, 1986). At other times, the problems seem new and different. The concern with serial killers in the 1980s (Jenkins, 1994) and cyberstalkers in the 1990s are good examples (Best, 1999).

In this book we use the term *crime wave* because it is preferable to many of the alternatives. *Epidemic* and *crisis* seem too sensationalist to serve as useful analytical categories. While the term *panic* is popular with many observers, it has its own problems (Cohen, 1972; Critcher, 2003; Goode & Ben-Yehuda, 1994). For one thing, it seems to suggest a kind of psychological model of why things happen during such episodes. It is important to emphasize, though, that events unfold as they do not because people somehow "panic," but because of larger social forces. Indeed, according to sociologist Lee Clarke (2003) scholars, policy makers, and journalists have all exaggerated the degree of public irrationality or the tendency on the part of people to panic under extreme circumstances. In addition, the term *panic* implies that the fear people experience during such episodes, or that the precautions they take to protect themselves, are an "overreaction." In other words, when we speak of a moral panic we tend to speak of situations in which there is a response to some problem—like rising crime—that lacks proportionality.

Some observers have said, for instance, that after the attacks on the World Trade Center and the Pentagon on September 11, 2001, there was a moral panic in America about terrorism (Chapman & Harris, 2002). Many people refused to fly on airplanes or take vacations. Others became increasingly suspicious of anyone from the Middle East, and increasingly willing to suspend certain civil liberties in the name of security. The problem with the use of the label moral panic in this and related episodes is that we can't say with any degree of empirical precision how people *should* react or how afraid they are *supposed* to be. The concept of moral panic really gives us no guidelines regarding what is and what is not a proportionate response. Do people and governments sometimes overreact to threatening situations? Most observers would agree that they sometimes do. But it is difficult to determine whose perspective we are supposed to employ in judging what is and what not an overreaction.

Defining Crime Waves

The concept of crime wave avoids these problems. It also forces us to recognize that since these episodes behave in wave-like fashion, they are of limited duration. But what, more precisely, is a crime wave? This might seem like a simple question given the casual way in which the term is used by politicians and headline writers. After all, doesn't the term just imply some rapid upward and downward movement in the level of crime? Actually, the matter is somewhat more complicated.

What if the level of crime was to escalate rapidly, but aside from those who committed the crimes and those who were victimized by them, no one really noticed? Suppose in this case most people don't even know about—let alone feel concerned about—the increase. There are no demands that the police take any special action, and there are no widespread feelings of anxiety related to crime. Further, suppose that whatever increases do occur in crime levels are not even reflected in crime statistics because victims decide not to report these crimes to authorities. In these circumstances, do we really have a crime wave? This extreme scenario reminds us of the proverbial tree falling in the woods with no one around to determine whether or not it makes a noise.

At the other extreme, what if people act as though crime levels are escalating, even though an objective examination of the rates at which crimes occur would seem to indicate that crime levels are stable. Suppose they believe that crime is increasing and that the streets are becoming more dangerous. They demand that the police "do something" to make them safe from the tide of rising crime. What's going on here? It may be that as people become less willing to tolerate crime, their perceptions of the problem intensify. This decreased tolerance could result in more victims coming forward to report crimes to the police. As a consequence, even the police statistics would register an increase. In contrast to the previous scenario, this one suggests a situation in which a tree is heard to fall in the forest although it hasn't actually fallen.

These examples suggest that the social phenomena of crime waves have multiple dimensions. While they are often about rising crime levels, they need not be. Indeed, rising crime levels in and of themselves may be neither a necessary nor a sufficient condition for crime waves to occur. In a useful review of cross-cultural and historical research on the circumstances under which city-dwellers come to define their communities as dangerous, Sally Merry (1981) argued that while rising crime rates mattered in this regard, they were not the whole story. Most typically, the perception that crime waves are under way is also affected by other social conditions, such as rapid urban growth and the escalation of conflict between the diverse economic and cultural groups who call the city home. Her analysis revealed that we need a way of thinking about crime waves that can take into account shifts in both actual crime levels as well as in perceptions of and feelings about crime levels. A theoretical perspective known as social constructionism provides such a framework.

Social Constructionism

Social constructionism is a broad theoretical perspective that is useful for understanding a wide range of social problems (Holstein & Miller, 2003; Loseke, 1999; Loseke & Best, 2003; Spector & Kitsuse, 1977). As an approach, it contrasts with more "objectivist" perspectives that dominated the study of social problems for decades.

Objectivist approaches to social problems focus rather narrowly on the material conditions of problems (Loseke, 1999). Researchers working within this tradition might ask, for instance, "What sorts of neighborhood factors are associated with high levels of crime?" or "What causes poverty?" or "What kinds of people are most likely to engage in racist behavior?" Such questions assume that we know what the problematic conditions in society are and that all we really need to do is just investigate their objective dimensions. As an approach, objectivism is pretty unconcerned with how the members of a society at any particular point in time come to understand some conditions rather than others as troubling.

For constructionist writers, it is precisely these subjective perceptions of social conditions as problems that demand investigation (Spector & Kitsuse, 1977). As a result, they are led to ask a different kind of question: What are the social processes through which we come to understand what our social problems are? Constructionist writers warn us against naively assuming that it is simply the nature of the objective conditions themselves that drive this process.

In other words, what we see as our most urgent problems at any point in time are not necessarily those that produce the most harm (however this is defined). As the example at the beginning of the chapter demonstrated, satanism came to be seen as a significant social problem in the 1980s even though there was virtually no evidence to substantiate the claims that were made about its social problem status (Jenkins & Maier-Katkin, 1992; Richardson, Best, & Bromley, 1991).

We can say then that social constructionism is concerned with the study of the subjective meaning of social problems (Best, 1995). Why do some conditions rather than others seem to demand our attention? Why have we, as a society, been so much more worried about street crime historically than about corporate crime? Why do we become excited about the violent content of rap music but seem to have little to say about the violent content of country music? Why do we continue to believe that we are threatened most by the actions of strangers when it is actually the murderous rage of people we know best— friends and family—that is most likely to do us in? Social constructionism argues that the answers to these questions reside not in the objective circumstances themselves but in the meanings we assign to them.

Conditions come to be seen as problems not because they somehow demand it but because processes of collective definition confer the designation of "social problem" upon them. It is this process, and in the interests behind it, about which social constructionist writers are concerned. They argue that our collective view of social problems emerges out of a process of "claims-making" in which those who are interested in doing so, try to convince the rest of us that condition X is a problem and that something must be done about it (Spector & Kitsuse, 1977). It is to the study of such claims, the people who make them, and the conditions that affect their success that constructionist writers direct our attention.

An important aspect of this process concerns the manner in which social problems are "framed" (Loseke, 1999). The point here is that any particular social problem can be understood in many different ways, none of which is inevitable. Gambling, for instances, as a social problem can be seen as a crime, as a sickness, or as a moral failing. These problem frames have very different implications for how urgent we think the problem is, how it should be dealt with, and who should be given the resources and responsibility for ensuring that something is done (Gusfield, 1981). In a similar way, poverty might be understood as a problem that results from capitalist exploitation or as a problem that results from a lack of motivation of poor people. In a similar way, a "crime wave" can be thought of as a kind of social problem. The term implies that crime levels are escalating rapidly and that, as members of society, we face increasing threats to our values or to our personal safety.

As sociologist Mark Fishman (1978) has written,

When we speak of a crime wave, we are talking about a kind of social awareness of crime, crime brought to public consciousness. It is something to be
remarked upon at the corner grocery store, complained about in a community meeting and denounced at the mayor's press conference. One cannot be
mugged by a crime wave but one can be scared. And one can put more police
on the streets and enact new laws on the basis of fear. Crime waves may be
"things of the mind" but they have real consequences. (p. 531)

It would be wrong, however, to suggest that crime waves specifically or
social problems generally are only subjective matters—or "things of the mind."
Claims-making about social problems always occurs in a social context. The
social context shapes and limits the manner in which the process of problem
definition unfolds. Importantly, sometimes—but not always—that context
includes rising rates of the behavior about which claims are made. This means
that any comprehensive discussion of crime waves must pay attention to questions about how and why crime levels change *and* about how and why crime
levels come to be seen as particular types of problems (Sacco, 2000a). Because
we live in both a physical and a symbolic world, we need to make use of explanations that place both subjective and objective aspects of our social worlds on
the agenda for discussion (Loseke, 1999).

In many ways, this argument parallels the types of arguments that "labeling theorists" writing in the 1960s made about crime and deviance (Becker,
1963). These writers were interested in the study of how people come to be
seen as "deviant" and what implications the deviant label has for the ways in
which other people respond to them. As labeling theorists argued, it makes
sense to think about the labels separate from the people and the behavior that
is labeled. Sometimes deviant labels are "deserved" in the sense that the labeled
person has actually engaged in the behavior the label directs our attention
toward. In other cases, though, people are falsely labeled. Of course, in one
sense whether or not the label is deserved becomes irrelevant. What is common
to both cases is the way in which the label excites particular reactions.

In a parallel way, we can think of "crime waves" as a kind of episodic labeling. In this sense it is a label applied not to particular kinds of discrete acts or particular kinds of people but to particular kinds of social episodes. For the purposes
of our discussion, therefore, we can state simply that *a crime wave is under way
when there exist widely shared perceptions that a crime wave is under way.* Such perceptions do not develop in random fashion, but are influenced by a range of social
factors, including rising crime levels and the actions of police, politicians, journalists, and even victims and offenders. But such influence does not just flow one
way. The widespread belief that a crime wave is under way also has implications
for how police, politicians, journalists, and victims and offenders behave.

This means that there is some sort of dynamic interaction between the objective and subjective dimensions of crime waves (Sacco, 2000a). Increases in crime can promote decreases in levels of tolerance for crime. As tolerance decreases, people might be more likely to report crime to the police or to fight back against the threat in any number of ways. The implication is an important one. It is not just crime but also social control and tolerance that behave in wave-like fashion. That crime waves might be produced by shifts in our willingness to arrest and prosecute offenders (rather than more directly by shifts in the behavior of offenders themselves) is an important theme to which we will return at later points in the book.

The relationship between the subjective and objective dimensions of crime waves is reminiscent of a very important distinction made many years ago by the sociologist C. Wright Mills (1959). Mills wrote that we experience social problems—crime included—as both private troubles and as public issues. To be a victim of crime, or even to be an offender, is to experience crime as a private trouble. The difficulties that the episode might create for us in terms of loss or injury or trouble with the law can have very personal consequences. However, our individual, personal experiences with crime provide the raw materials out of which crime as a public issue is built. This happens when effective arguments are made by academics, journalists, politicians, and advocacy groups that our personal experiences form a particular kind of pattern and when that pattern is successfully labeled as a "crime wave."

The Criminal Content of Crime Waves

Interestingly, of all our social problems, crime is the only one—with the obvious exception of "heat waves" (Klinenberg, 2003)—that is discussed in terms of its wave-like properties. We never read or hear, for instance, of poverty waves, homelessness waves, or war waves. The selective use of the term *wave* in journalistic and political discussions of social problems probably tells us more about popular culture than about the properties of the problems themselves.

While, in principle, any kind of crime might be said to be at the center of a crime wave, in reality our usage of the term tends to be restricted in some ways. First, the term tends to be used in describing more serious rather than less serious crimes. The examples given at the start of this chapter, for instance, all suggest quite consequential forms of crime and victimization. When we use the label crime wave, we seem to be implying that something of substance is occurring—that these changes relate injuries sustained, property damaged, and lives lost. While we could speak of crime waves involving "jaywalking" or "littering," we almost never do.

Second, the term *crime wave* tends to be used most commonly to describe changing patterns of common crime such as theft, murder, burglary, or robbery. The usage of the term to describe crimes of corporations or businesses is much less common. Of course, one important exception to that was the wave of corporate crime that so many journalists and politicians have spoken and written about in recent years and that was summarized at the beginning of this chapter. Even in this case, a theme that ran though much of the coverage was the irony and novelty of using the term crime wave to describe the kinds of activities it is not typically used to describe.

Third, we tend not to use the term crime wave when we are attempting to describe crimes involving people who have some sort of intimate connection to each other. While we might find the term useful to describe trends in robbery or murder or burglary, we tend not to use it to describe shifts in the patterns of, for instance, wife assault. We rarely read a headline that describes upward shifts in levels of wife assault as a "crime wave" sweeping the nation. Of course, this is consistent with a more general tendency, in our society, not to think about such acts as crimes in the first place (even though they are).

Crime waves can be characterized in at least four different ways. Each way brings to the foreground some aspect of criminal events while it assigns others to the background.

VICTIMS

Some crime waves are identified principally in terms of the categories of people who are victimized. M. Dwayne Smith (1987), for example, has examined the argument that the decades of the 1970s and 1980s saw the emergence of a "new female victim." In essence he sought to determine whether changes in the content of women's roles during this period might have resulted in dramatic increases in victimization levels or in shifts with respect to the kinds of crime that victimize women. While he did find an increase in the likelihood that women would be victims of property crime (especially robbery), the rates of violent crime experienced by women during the period were very stable.

In most cases, those who seek to argue that a crime wave is under way tend to stress the innocence and vulnerability of victims. In the 1970s, for instance, there was considerable public discussion about a "crime wave against the elderly" (Cook & Skogan, 1990). Increasingly, during this period, lawmakers, police, and journalists argued that the rate of crimes against older Americans was escalating rapidly. Crimes against the elderly came to be understood as a new national crisis, and policy measures intended to deal with the problem were quickly mounted (Fattah & Sacco, 1989). Police formed special squads, Congress held numerous hearings, and community groups sought through myriad ways to stem the rising tide of criminal danger. By the decade's end, the problem of crime against the elderly seemed to have gone away. As we will discuss later, there is serious reason to question whether the wave of elderly victimization ever happened.

A decade later, the concern was with the safety of children rather than the elderly (Best, 1990). The 1980s saw a number of claims expressed about the ways in which children in American society were at risk—especially at the hands of dangerous strangers. These threats included the contamination of Halloween treats, the growing problem of satanic day cares, child molestation, and, most notably, child abduction (Forst & Blomquist, 1991). As in the case of the crimes against the elderly, much of this wave seemed to have more to do with changes in the ways in which people felt about and experienced the dangers of the world than with changes in those dangers themselves.

Whether or not a crime wave is under way may depend very much on the perspective that victims and non-victims bring to the situation. According to an old expression, "A recession is when your friend is out of work, a depression is when you are out of work." In a similar way, the acceptance of the view that that a crime wave is (or is not) under way probably bears some relationship to how victimization is distributed in society.

Of particular relevance in this respect is the issue of "repeat victimization" (Farrell & Pease, 2001). Increasingly, in recent years researchers have come to realize that some people (and households) seem much more likely to be victimized repeatedly than other people or households. Indeed, having been victimized in the past is an important risk factor for being victimized in the future. This might seem counterintuitive. Most of us tend to think that once we have been victimized, we have more or less gotten the experience out of the way. As a result, we should be safer rather than less safe. Research suggests otherwise, however. British researchers Ken Pease and Gloria Laycock (1996) reported that about 4% of surveyed victims suffer about 44% of the victimizations. Clearly, some people are victimized repeatedly and most people are not victimized at all.

The implications of such an unequal distribution of victimization can be quite profound for the study of crime waves. This is shown in an analysis undertaken by Tim Hope (1995), another British researcher. Hope was able to show that when one looks at the overall rate of crime, it is possible that very little change will be observed over time. Yet when we focus on the problem of repeat victimization we might see that even though the overall rate is stable, there can be a redistribution of victim experiences within the victim population. In such a scenario, roughly the same number of victimizations can be concentrated within a much smaller group of victims. This situation is comparable to an economic pattern in which the overall indicators are stable while the gap between rich and poor increases. Who thinks a crime wave is under way and who does not might depend very much on the character of one's own victim experiences.

OFFENDERS

Sometimes crime waves are identified with reference to the offender rather than the victim. When we talk about the wave of "juvenile crime," for instance, it is those who commit the crimes who draw our attention.

Coincident with the wave of crime against the elderly in the 1970s was a concern about huge increases in the number of elderly offenders (Fattah & Sacco, 1989). Journalists and others began to use the expression "geriatric crime wave" to describe the phenomenon. While prior stereotypes had pictured the elderly offender as someone who engaged in isolated and sporadic acts of shoplifting (prompted perhaps by need), it was argued that the elderly were committing both more crimes and more serious crimes. Magazine feature writers and others saw this as an interesting new twist to the by-then familiar story about elderly victims of crime. An analysis of national arrest data for a 15-year period (1967-1982) revealed, however, that the elderly crime wave was much more about rhetoric than about substance (Cullen, Wozniak, & Frank, 1985). During the period in question, and for a variety of crimes, elderly Americans constituted less than 1% of arrestees. Moreover, these data indicated that older Americans' pattern of criminal involvement remained remarkably constant during the period.

The serial killer crime wave of the 1980s provides a useful example of how offender-centered crime waves are defined (Jenkins, 1994). During this period, the serial killer almost became a national preoccupation. There were movies, television dramas and "documentaries," and a limitless number of "true crime" books and memoirs of "profilers." We were told that the number of serial killers had reached epidemic proportions and that serial murder made up as much as 25% of all homicides. While the serial killer might have particular social and demographic characteristics (they tended to be white men), they could be anyone who had these characteristics. Moreover, we were warned that the serial killer seemed to be a uniquely American problem. At the heart of the serial killer problem, of course, was the issue of "random violence" (Best, 1999). Serial killers, we were advised, could strike anyone at any point. While we learned very little, and can probably recall even less about their victims, the names Ted Bundy, Joel Rifkin, and Jeffrey Dahmer, among others, are emblazoned on our collective consciousness.

CRIMINAL EVENTS

Crime waves are sometimes described with reference to the uniqueness of the event rather than with reference to the uniqueness of the offenders or the victims. The "Black Hand" crime wave discussed at the beginning of the chapter, for instance, was about a particular kind of criminal transaction. It was the nature of the extortion, but especially the powerful symbolic elements of an ominous handprint, that gave the crime wave its defining feature (Sacco, 2003). This is evidenced in part by the tendency of journalists of the time to create words that conveyed the essense of the offense. So, being "blackhanded" meant being the object of extortion, "blackhandism" was the practice of extortion, and of course a "black hander" was one who practiced extortion.

In a similar way, the garroting crime wave in Boston in 1865 referred to a new kind of crime (Adler, 1996). While garroting was a form of robbery, it had some unique and elaborate characteristics. One of the assailants would grab the victim's throat from behind and pull the victim backwards over the assailant's knees. A second attacker would hold the victim's knees to prevent him from kicking back and a third would quickly rifle through the victim's pockets. Needless to say, the crimes were committed quickly, under cover of darkness, and typically in public places.

More recently, we have heard about crime waves involving "carjacking," "home invasion," "stalking," and "hate crime." In its historical context, each represents a new kind of crime and a new kind of victim—at least as far as the labels are concerned (Best, 1999). While many of the behaviors predate the labels, these crime categories were all largely inventions of the 1980s and 1990s. In a sense, each category suggested a new way in which the world was getting worse and a new and more serious strain of the crime problem that required attention.

PLACES

In some cases, we speak of crime waves in terms of the places in which they occur. In other words, it is the setting, rather than the participants or trans-actions, that identifies and describes the problem. In this way, we speak, for instance of "workplace" crime or "domestic violence." More broadly, we some-times talk about "urban" crime waves, implying that whatever problems do exist have less to do with the more rural regions of the country than with the cities.

One of the places that has been at the center of crime wave construction in recent years is the school (Chandler, Chapman, Rand, & Taylor, 1998; Toby, 1995). Owing in large part to a number of high-visibility incidents, school vio-lence has come to be seen as a major problem. The best known such incident, of course, occurred on April 20, 1999, when two fully armed students entered Columbine High School in Littleton, Colorado. The death toll from this one incident was 13, in addition to the two shooters, and the nation was shocked. What made the event all the more frightening to many, though, was the feeling that the incident was part of a larger, worsening pattern (Fox & Levin, 2001). Other deadly incidents occurred in Pearl, Mississippi; West Paducah, Kentucky; Jonesboro, Arkansas; and elsewhere. In March of 2001 a shooting at Santana High School in Santee, California, left two people dead and 13 more injured and gave new life to the worries and anxieties that parents and others felt about the "epidemic" of school violence.

In the wake of these high visibility offenses, the view that a school violence crime wave was under way seemed pretty evident. As with many crimes waves, though, this one seemed to have more to do with perceptions than with objective realities. A number of different types of research suggest that, overall, violent school deaths were actually decreasing rather than increasing during this period (Best, 2003). As well, surveys of students indicated that many non-lethal forms of violence were also in decline. This is consistent with the more general decline in crime rates that was evident during the 1990s. While the media frenzy about unsafe schools continued unabated during the last decade of the century, the empirical evidence continued to support the idea that the risks of violence in schools, for most students, most of the time, were extremely low. According to Best (2003), for every million children who attend school, there is less than one violent school-related death per year. Moreover, only about 1% of children killed by violence are hurt at school, even though they spend such a large amount of time there.

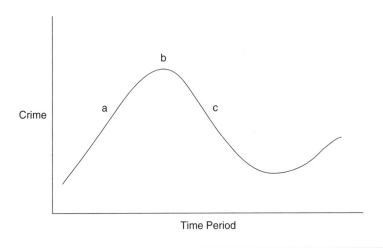

Figure 1.1   Standard (Crime) Wave Graph

The Nature of Waves

The concept of "wave" is usually employed to describe natural phenomena, and it generally conjures up two kinds of visual images. The first is pictured in Figure 1.1. The figure graphs some phenomenon y over some time period measured along the x axis. The y variable in which we would be most inter-ested, of course, would be the level of crime. As the wave unfolds, we see the level of crime rise sharply, reach a kind of peak, and then decline. Figure 1.1 sug-gests that the hypothetical crime wave has three key points—a rise (a), a peak (b), and a decline (c). While placement in any one of those regions would suggest we are "in a crime wave," our colloquial use of the term tends to be restricted to the rise. We are unlikely ever to hear anyone say that there is a crime wave under way when the levels are falling. Of course, criminologists, particularly in recent years, have become very interested in the study of falling crime levels, but these declines are often described as occurring after rather during the crime wave.

Gary LaFree (1999) and other scholars who focus on the study of crime waves as objective phenomena emphasize that crime waves have several properties that require investigation. One such property is "wave length." We can argue that crime waves suggest phenomena at some intermediate position between two extremes. At one extreme are riots. In riots, the escalation and de-escalation of, for instance, violence or vandalism are very rapid (Locher, 2002). Within perhaps hours or even minutes, the number of incidents increases and then declines. A riot is a crime wave within a very condensed time frame. At the other extreme are long-range trends. How do crime levels change across the centuries? Historian Eric Monkkonen (2001) argues that it is important to distinguish short-term changes from "the long sweep of big events." In his analysis of New York City homicides over two centuries, Monkkonen identifies three distinct "waves" of about 60 years each. The first two waves crested in 1864 and 1931, and the most recent crested in 1991. Troughs occurred in the 1820s to 1830s, around 1890 to 1900, and in the late 1940s to early 1950s. While there is again no precise rule, in general we are interested in somewhat more short-term and episodic phenomena. The long sweeps that Monkkonen describes are perhaps best understood as tides rather than waves.

Another property discussed by LaFree is "wave shape." Do waves rise as rapidly as they fall? We might also ask, for instance, whether or not crime waves are symmetric or asymmetric with respect to the kinds of factors that affect their rise and fall. In other words, if a worsening economy drives crime rates up, does it follow that the crime rate will fall in equal proportions when the economy improves? To assume that it will, is to assume that the relationships are symmetrical. While some kinds of causal variables might relate to crime-level changes in this way, it would probably be an error to think that they all do.

A third property of crime waves identified by LaFree is the degree of "linearity." Again, we might be tempted to assume, for instance, that as the economy worsens, changes in the crime rate will be proportionate and consistent. It is possible, however, that the relationship will indeed be linear until the economy reaches a particular level, after which the rise in the crime rate will be much more rapid. Garland F. White (2001) has shown, for instance, that the relationship between rising crime and home ownership is characterized by such a "tipping" process. In other words, rising rates of crime can reach a level at which their impact on home ownership is especially profound. A point is reached at which larger numbers of people than we would expect, given observed effects of crime on ownership, decide to move to another neighborhood. Such large-scale shifts in population further contribute to what are by now rapidly deteriorating neighborhood conditions.

Finally, LaFree says we need to ask if crime waves are synchronous or asynchronous. In other words, when crime waves are under way, how far do they extend? Is a particular crime wave an urban phenomenon? Or is it regional or national or even international in scope? A study by Morton D. Winsberg (1993) of violent and property crime rates in American states during the period 1971 to 1991 found that a majority of the states experienced equivalent fluctuations. This was true even though the states differed from each other in terms of key socioeconomic indicators and even though some states had far higher crime rates than others. In a different way, Martin Killias and Marcelo F. Aebi (2000) compared crime trend data from 36 European countries with rates for the United States for the period 1990 to 1996. Their analysis showed that the European and American trends exhibited different rather than similar patterns over the period.

How much crime and how much change does it take to have a crime wave? As stated, crime waves are often about more than the behavior of aggregate crime levels. When we think about crime waves in terms of fear, anxiety, and the intensification of public concern and public interest, it may be meaningless to talk about some sort of necessary minimum. There is, of course, no rule about the number of people who must be involved before the press or other claims-makers label an episode a crime wave. For instance, what are we to make of the episode that involved the victimization of tourists in Florida during the 1990s (Greek, 1993)? In a single year, 10 tourists were killed and the media were quick to label this a "crime wave." Many people cancelled travel plans and Florida communities engaged in very active advertising blitzes to convince potential travelers that Florida was actually a safe place to visit. As well, new and special precautions were taken at highway rest stops and hotels and other places in which tourists would likely find themselves.

We can debate whether 10 killings of tourists in a single year constitutes a crime wave. Perhaps in absolute numbers it would seem so. At the time of the attacks, however, context was quickly provided by the Florida Department of Law Enforcement. According to data posted on the Department's Web site (http://www.fdle.state.fl.us/fsac/archives/visitor_crime.asp), Florida hosted an estimated record *42 million* visitors in 1995—up from approximately 40 million in 1994. In 1994, only seven-hundredths of one percent (0.07%) of these visitors were victims of crime. And, from the total of visitors, only six-thousandths of one percent (0.006%) were physically injured. Of the total reported victims of crime in Florida in 1994, less than 2.5% were nonresidents. The vast majority of Florida's visitors, the Web site advises, "do not become victims of any criminal activity during their stay." Certainly, though, in terms of the ways in which people were thinking and acting, a crime wave was under way.

Even more interesting in this respect is what journalists and even law enforcement officials sometimes call the "one-man crime wave." Offenders differ from each other, of course, with respect to how "productive" they are. Some commit a very large number of crimes over the course of a criminal career while others commit far fewer. The phrase "one-man crime wave" is used to describe the kind of offender who is very actively and very consistently involved in the commission of crime. As an example, an offender by the name of Eric Edgar Cooke, who was active in Perth, Australia, in the early 1960s, is often referred to this way (Kidd, n.d.). In addition to murder, Cooke confessed to breaking into more than 250 homes in suburbs around Perth. He also confessed to having stolen dozens of cars and to committing a large number of assaults on women. Andy Hochstetler (2002) observes that even a casual review of the rap sheets of street criminals reveals that it is quite common for them to commit a large number of crimes in a relatively short period of time. Extended episodes of this sort are referred to by police and by offenders themselves as "sprees" or "runs." The former term refers to the situation in which at least two offenses are committed without a break in the action. In contrast, a run involves a situation in which a string of serial crimes is interrupted by sleep, or perhaps by drug-induced inactivity.

A second visual image gives us a somewhat different perspective on the shape and character of waves and is pictured in Figure 1.2. This figure provides an overhead view of the undulation that occurs when, for instance, a stone is dropped into a puddle of water. In many ways, Figure 1.2 comes closer to capturing the colloquial meaning of crime waves—the kind of continual disturbance that comes from some identifiable point of origin and affects the larger body. The description of the crime waves that began this chapter—Black Hand or satanic conspiracies, midwestern gangsterism, and the rest—evoke similar images of criminological pebbles producing consequences that move through the rest of the pond that is society.

Some Uses of Crime Waves

Because we can argue that crime waves are, to a large degree, the product of successful episodic labeling, it might be a good idea to ask in whose interest it is to promote the idea that a crime wave is under way. This question emerges as an important theme in the chapters that follow. Nevertheless, it might be helpful here to give some broad sense of the cast of characters who move the crime wave drama along.

Of course, crime can have a devastating impact on the lives of those who are affected by it. Some people are injured and others die. Some lose their property, and they can suffer emotionally and psychologically. Still others get

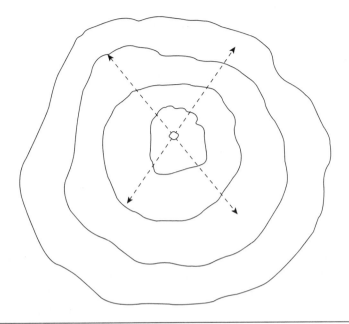

Figure 1.2   Overhead View of Wave

caught up in the mechanisms of a criminal justice system and suffer stigma or the loss of freedom. None of this is in dispute. A more balanced analysis, however, also requires us to be attentive to some of the ways in which public excitement about crime waves produces dividends—sometimes unanticipated—for a variety of groups in society.

POLITICIANS

Politicians can derive considerable benefit from the promotion of a widespread public perception of crisis. In such circumstances, people can often be more easily manipulated toward certain ends if they believe that their interests are under some growing threat. Crime waves are ideal tools for the politician to use in such circumstances. For one thing, they are issues that are pretty unlikely to be controversial, so there is not much risk of alienating voters. With respect to the supposed crime wave against the elderly in the 1970s, politicians took few risks in speaking out loudly and often about the threat to America's seniors. No "pro elderly-victimization" group existed that might be alienated by the fiery rhetoric. Crime waves give politicians an opportunity to talk tough and to promote what are often largely symbolic measures that they claim will combat the problem. Often such measures involve the passage of severe laws meant to control those responsible for the crime wave. The nature of the problem and the proposed solution often make it relatively easy to build broad-based constituencies that even cross party lines. The passage of law is relatively easily achieved and is a moment loaded with photo opportunities. What such laws actually accomplish is another matter entirely. Too often they are redundant with laws that already exist and in many cases they lack the resource infra-structure that might actually make them effective. Effectiveness is sometimes beside the point, however, since it is the demonstrable effort that really matters.

MEDIA PERSONNEL

Clearly, crime waves are great news stories. Throughout the history of popular media, crime has occupied a very prominent position (Sacco, 1995). Daily newspapers are filled with crime stories, and any viewer of local televi-sion news can easily appreciate the journalistic aphorism, "If it bleeds, it leads." Crime waves provide themes around which disparate crime stories, which are the bedrock of local crime news, can be built. In his analysis, for example, of a 1976 New York City crime wave against the elderly, Mark Fishman (1978) found that the crime wave was given prominent coverage by the city's three daily newspapers and five local television stations. "Crime against the elderly" served as a kind of unifying concept that gave coherence to stories that might, on the surface, not be seen to have very much to do with each other.

Joel Best (1999) argues that crime waves seem to be a 19th-century invention. The rapidly developing daily press, intended to attract the readership of the often illiterate or semi-literate urban masses, provided a kind of showcase for melodra-matic and sensationalist crime reporting. Prior to this period, Best argues, crime news tended to focus on the particulars of the case at hand. For example, the mur-der in 1836 of a New York prostitute named Helen Jewittt (Cohen, 1998) became a kind of "crime of the century." Yet Best notes that the coverage of this case was not generalized in the press to stories about a larger problem of violence against prostitutes. In contrast, the tendency in contemporary media to find news themes in crime reporting, to generalize from the particular case to a broader problem, is, as we shall see, one of the defining features of crime wave construction in the media. In the media's reporting of the satanic crime wave of the 1980s, for instance, widely disconnected events as diverse as the assumed desecration of a local graveyard to allegations of abuse in a day care center across the country could be connected through the satanic crime wave theme.

As we will discuss later, crime news is easy to gather and to report, and crime waves provide an opportunity for the detailed exploration of themes that have traditionally proven quite popular with news consumers.

It is not just the news that profits from the emergence of crime waves, however. Movies, "true crime" books, and other popular forms of entertain-ment also ride the wave to ratings success. Particularly important in this respect is the "reality show" genre that came to television prominence in the 1980s (Fishman & Cavender, 1998). All of these products of popular culture tend to reflect the broad-based assumption that crime—especially violent crime—is rampant. Other forms of media, for instance talk shows and made-for-television movies, often are among the first kinds of formats to popularize new problems that, it is typically claimed, affect large numbers of people, even though knowledge of the condition is not widespread (Rapping, 1992).

EXPERTS

Experts, academic and otherwise, often assume a primary role in the popularization of crime waves. They sometimes build quite substantial professional reputations on their purported understanding of the size and dimensions of the crime problem. As experts, they become the authors of best-selling books, stars on the lecture circuit, and the talking heads who are almost permanent fixtures on cable television whenever commentary about a crime wave is judged necessary. Experts are able to lend an air of legitimacy to claims or predictions about crime waves. Their scholarly or other professional credentials suggest objectivity and disinterest to many who hear or read their pronouncements.

> Experts were instrumental in promoting the idea of a crime wave of "super predators," for example. In 1996, then-Princeton sociologist John J. DiIulio, along with two coauthors, published *Body Count*, which warned of a coming tide of violent and predatory juvenile crime. The authors warned that, as high as America's body count is today, a rising tide of youth crime and violence is about to raise it even higher. A new generation of street criminals is upon us—the youngest, biggest and baddest generation any society has ever known. (Bennett, DiIulio, & Walter, 1996, p. 26)

The super-predators would be brutal and "radically impulsive" and would be, in larger numbers than ever, preteen boys, who commit the most serious crimes. For DiIulio and his coauthors this problem had its roots in the inner city where children grow up surrounded by teenagers and adults who are themselves deviant, delinquent, or criminal. By the turn of the century, they warned, the numbers of such super-predators would have increased dramatically. Other experts, along with the mass media and political speechwriters, began to use the term *super-predator* with remarkable ease.

However, the predictions about the coming crime wave never materialized. Rather than increasing, rates of juvenile crime were in decline by the century's end. At best the predictions were merely misguided. At worst, the critics charged they were a covert expression of ultra-conservative politics or, as one critic charged, "utter madness" (Becker, 2001). While DiIulio himself tried to recant, the theory of the super-predators had taken on a life of its own. Increasingly, assumptions about the coming wave of youth violence were used to justify the use of punishment rather than treatment for delinquent youth, and the movement of youth from juvenile to adult courts.

The super-predator episode—in the early stages at least—lent prestige and visibility to those who spoke on the subject with scholarly authority. It is not the only example. Indeed, experts typically form part of any movement that declares a crime wave under way or about to get under way, including those relating to workplace violence, bullying, and crime against the elderly.

While academics are often cited as experts by news stories, a careful analysis of how expertise is used by journalists to report on the crime problem revealed that "intellectuals" were less often cited as experts than were "state managers" (i.e., police officials or political leaders; Welch, Fenwick, & Roberts, 1998). In particular, when specific attention was directed toward the coverage of exaggerated risks of crime, these state managers were much more likely than academics to be relied upon for comment.

POLICING AGENCIES

Policing agencies, like politicians, can gain considerable benefit as public awareness spreads that a crime wave is under way. Typically, the members of the general public are less likely to blame the police for the crime wave than they are to blame the media, liberal social policy, and especially the courts (Sacco, 1998). Crime waves allow policing agencies to plead an effective bureaucratic case of the public servant overwhelmed by the problems at hand but struggling valiantly to "serve and protect." At the same time, requests for new hardware and bigger budgets generally are pressed most effectively when problems reach a crisis stage.

Perhaps the FBI, and its public relations specialists, has shown most clearly how organizational self-presentation can be augmented by a crime wave. In the wave of midwestern bank robberies discussed at the start of the chapter, for instance, the strategy was to create villains of almost mythic proportion who clearly suggested the need for a hero equal to the task (Potter, 1998; Powers, 1983).

The strategy was used again during the serial killer epidemic of the 1980s when the FBI effectively made the case (through its support of books, films, and television shows) that only the kind of scientific law enforcement for which the FBI was famous could deal with the epidemic of serial murder sweeping North America (Jenkins, 1994).

Claims by law enforcement personnel that the threat of crime is escalating of necessity imply the need for an escalation of the response. This often seems to mean the need for helicopters, assault vehicles, and other forms of expensive surveillance technology (Parenti, 1999). This militarization of urban places, which was already a trend in policing in the 1990s, accelerated after the attack on the World Trade Center in 2001.

OFFENDERS

It may seem odd to suggest that offenders might have something to gain directly from the fact that their crimes are seen as part of an escalating crime wave, but there are surely cases in which this is true. For any particular offender, a predatory crime might be more easily accomplished if the victim believes that the offender is one of the frightening new variety to which the media have been paying so much attention lately.

An example of this phenomenon can be found in the Black Hand crime wave that terrorized residents of the Little Italies in New York (and other cities) in the first few years of the 20th century (Lombardo, 2002; Pitkin & Cordasco, 1977; Sacco, 2003). As discussed at the beginning of the chapter, Black Hand extortion was successful largely because victims believed that their offenders were part of a large and powerful criminal conspiracy. It seems pretty clear, however, that this was not the case. Instead, most Black Hand operations were small groups or even sole operators who used the threat of the powerful—if mythical—organization to accomplish their criminal ends. Thus, the snowball effect of newspaper coverage created a kind of momentum that made it much easier to be an extortionist while the crime wave was under way than before it started.

VICTIMS

Victims—or rather the spokespersons of victim organizations—are often among the first and most vocal claimants to argue that a sizeable problem exists and that it is getting worse (Weed, 1990). Of course, it is through such claims that attention is drawn to the plight of crime victims. One consequence might be that steps will be taken to provide victims with support or compensation.

Several victim advocates have become familiar figures in the American popular cultural landscape. John Walsh, for instance, the father of murdered child Adam Walsh, became an early spokesperson in the movement to protect missing and exploited children. Subsequently, he became the host of the very popular Fox television program *America's Most Wanted* and later host of his own daytime television talk show.

Less visible, but perhaps not less influential is Candy Lightener, founder of MADD, Mothers Against Drunk Driving (Reinarman, 1988). In May 1980 her 13-year-old daughter Cari was killed by a hit-and-run driver in a Sacramento suburb. The subsequent discovery that the intoxicated driver was on probation for a previous DUI ("driving under the influence") conviction and the leniency with which the driver was treated by the justice system prompted her to take action. Lightener went on to spearhead an international movement that aims to affect legislation and to educate the general public about the drinking-and-driving problem.

As in the case of MADD, many victims groups have become large and influential national organizations (Weed, 1995). Some critics talk of a "victim industry" and suggest that there are many incentives among the leadership in these movements to exaggerate the size of the victim population (Best, 1999; Fattah, 1986). Some groups have been able to lobby effectively for the rights of victims to be respected by the police, heard in court, and compensated by the state. To a considerable degree this has been accomplished by making the persuasive arguments that what happened to them, or to their family members, could also happen to any one of us. Such claims are obviously made more forcefully when the risks associated with crime are thought to be on the rise.

SECURITY INDUSTRY

Rising rates of crime can mean that many people feel personally threatened. If they come to believe that, in increasing numbers, super-predators walk the streets, satanists are after their children, or those to whom they entrust their savings cannot be trusted, they will take steps to protect themselves. Often these steps involve the private actions of individuals and groups rather than the public actions of governments. In this way, safety from the rising tide of crime comes to be seen as a commodity to be bought and sold in the marketplace.

The kinds of measures people take are many and diverse (Lab, 1992). They buy home burglar alarms, guard dogs, and whistles. They install bars and extra locks on doors and windows. Increasingly, they demand that the places where they work, the schools they attend, and the neighborhoods where they live have levels of security beyond that which they think the police can provide. Those who can afford to do so, move to gated communities or to apartment buildings with elaborate screening systems (Blakely, 1997). More and more use is made in a variety of public settings of video cameras to monitor behavior and presumably control what we believe to be escalating risks.

Of course, when security becomes a commodity, there are fortunes to be made. The growth of private policing and the proliferation of a large number of very sophisticated, very costly security technologies means that private security has become a growth industry. In the United States (as in Canada, South Africa, and Australia) there are more police in the employ of private agencies than there are in the employ of the state. In 1996, while there were 354 police officers for every 100,000 inhabitants, there were 582 private security personnel. Indeed, according to David Bayley and Clifford Shearing (2001), today people on their way to work or to shop are as likely to see private security personnel guarding and patrolling as they are to see public police. Especially since the events of September 11, 2001, the money to be made from the exploitation of citizen anxieties, relating not only to terrorism but also to a host of sometimes ill-defined threats, has increased remarkably.

Conclusion

When asked what pornography is, a famous jurist once said that while he may not have been able to define it, he knew it when he saw it. We can make a parallel statement with respect to crime waves. While we have trouble defining them precisely, we can tell by reading a variety of cues whether or not one is under way. There is more talk about crime, more anxiety, more discussion in the media, more worry about what is to be done.

The suggestion that crime waves are really only about the ways in which crime levels change does not take us as far into the investigation of the crime wave phenomenon as we would like. Indeed, sometimes crime rates do go up during crime waves—but sometimes they do not. Moreover, even when crime rates do go up, it is not entirely clear what the increase means. As we will see in later chapters, crime rates can go up not only because more people are committing more crime but also because we are counting crime better than we used to or because we are policing crime more effectively than we used to. These latter two kinds of pressure on the crime rate suggest that the social climate of the crime wave may be an important source of the escalation.

By now the reader might be asking a simple but important question— what does all of this have to do with me? The easy answer is, "A great deal." This is perhaps most obvious for the student of criminology. As we will see in subsequent chapters, the study of crime waves requires us to investigate a wide range of criminological issues relating to, for instance, crime measurement, crime policy, public perceptions of crime, and crime and the mass media. The critical analysis of crime waves benefits those who might have only a passing interest in academic criminology, however. All of us, in our day-to-day lives as members of society, can find ourselves playing roles in crime wave dramas. Law-and-order political candidates ask for our votes. Broadcasters do their best to get us to watch commercials by telling us that if we miss the news tonight we miss vital information about the newest scourge sweeping the land. E-mails bombard our computers, warning us about increases in the activities of marauding youth gangs and urban terrorists. Through a wide variety of channels we are asked to feel compassion for the victims of crime and hostility for those who commit it. Perhaps we ourselves are victims or offenders and seek to put our own situations in some larger context. In order to address any of these issues, it is necessary that we be able to approach what we are told about crime waves by journalists, politicians, and other "opinion makers" as informed consumers. In the marketplace of crime information, as in any other marketplace, critical skills and healthy skepticism are the first lines of defense.

2

Why Do Crime Rates Go Up and Down?

Dislocation, Diffusion, and Innovation

As discussed in the last chapter, widespread perceptions that a crime wave is under way often develop in the context of rising crime levels. So, in this chapter we discuss a question that is fundamental to the study of crime waves: Why do crime levels go up and down over time? Other related questions about, for instance, whether variations in crime levels reflect changes in our ability to count crime, or changes in levels of media attention to crime, are bracketed for the time being (and discussed in later chapters). Instead, we focus on how criminal events are distributed in time. Why are there suddenly more of them and then suddenly less of them?

Sometimes the changes in crime levels from one year to the next, or one month to the next, really suggest only random patterns. Perhaps there was one robbery in my town last month and two this month; or maybe there were no murders last year and one this year. These kinds of differences might not really mean very much in a statistical sense. In Chapter 3 we will talk about how and why people tend to read more significance than they should into such non-trends. For now, we want to focus on changes that are somewhat more substantial and of some real significance.

The question of why crime levels change over time does not have a simple answer, for several reasons (LaFree, 1998a). First, many of the explanations in which criminologists are most interested tend to focus our attention upon aspects of the human experience that resist sudden change. Biology, for example (about which criminologists have written a great deal), does not take us very far in trying to make sense of why crime levels change suddenly. This is because biology does not. Shifts in our genetic or physical character take place slowly over many generations, and the rhythm of biological change simply does not match the rhythm of rapid crime level changes.

Second, changes in crime rates suggest collective rather than organizational phenomena. In other words, tracking the development of relatively sudden crime level increases (or decreases) is different from tracking the development of a labor union or a new religion. Typically, crime level changes do not involve any conscious effort on anyone's part to coordinate the actions of individuals in the context of some kind of organizational structure. Instead, the changes involve lots of disconnected individuals deciding at about the same time to do things they didn't do before, or doing them in greater numbers than they did previously. Of course, crime rate increases may involve some degree of mutual influence (in the case of copycat crime, for instance), but even in these cases the activities of the individuals involved are not coordinated.

Third, crime rates like elevators have ups *and* downs—booms and busts, crests and crashes (LaFree, 1999). A useful explanation of crime level change has to make sense of both of these dimensions. We need to address not only why crime levels go up but also why they come back down. Interestingly, criminologists have tended to be much more interested in the former kind of question than in the latter. A chronic problem in much criminological thinking has involved a disproportionate emphasis on the reasons why crime "is" rather than the reasons why it "isn't." The major theories of crime and delinquency— for example, anomie, subculture, social learning—all try to explain why people become criminal and almost never, or only incidentally, why most of them eventually become "uncriminal."

Finally, crime rate increases and decreases are not always as obvious to everyone as we might think. Sometimes they can be hidden from public view, even though the trends might be accurately noted by those most directly affected. In the late 1980s, for instance, a relatively small number of young people in the United States were committing murder at a high rate while the homicide rate for other groups in the society was falling (Blumstein, 2002). Any examination of the overall trend in murder rates would not have suggested a major increase, while an examination of the rates for specific age groups would have indeed indicated something else. Sometimes very careful diagnostics are necessary before we speak with confidence that crime level increases are, or are not, under way.

Any investigation of why crime levels go up and down requires us to focus on several different kinds of factors. Over the years, criminologists have developed many explanations intended to make sense of the crime patterns we observe. The general bias in criminological theorizing has been to emphasize stability rather than change. In other words, most theories seek to explain why particular kinds of patterns of crime exist at any one point in time rather than why they change over time. For our purposes, however, arguments about shifts in levels of crime are arguments about (relatively rapid) social change. Three types of change processes are the focus of attention in this chapter: dislocation, diffusion, and innovation. The general point is that crime levels vary along with these social and cultural processes.

Our starting point in this discussion is the nonrandom character of involvement in criminal events.

The Demography of Offending

Demography is a field of study that focuses on the ways in which populations are structured and how they change over time. Demographers attempt to understand how changes in birth rates or death rates or how varying patterns of immigration or migration determine who makes up the population at particular historical moments. Why should any of this matter to us? For a simple reason: We know from a very large amount of research evidence that the risks of committing a crime, and the risks of being a victim of crime, are not randomly distributed in any population. The members of some social categories are much more likely to be involved in criminal events than are the members of other social categories. Of course, this is contrary to what the media often tell us. Dramatic television, reality programs, and the nightly news often encourage us to think about crime as a totally random occurrence (Best, 1999). It isn't.

The recognition that crime is nonrandomly distributed in populations has a very significant implication. If there are sudden shifts in the relative proportions of the population who are more (or less) likely to be involved in crime, there will also likely be shifts in how much (or how little) crime occurs. When crime levels shift up or down, they do so at least in part because of underlying shifts in the size of the groups that make up the population.

The two most relevant demographic dimensions in this respect are the maleness and the youthfulness of the population.

MALENESS

While males and females represent approximately equal groups in the population, the research evidence clearly indicates that crime, in almost all of its manifestations, is a largely male phenomenon. For most categories of crime, men are more likely to be offenders, and for most categories they are more likely to be victims as well (Flowers, 1989).

National arrest data gathered by the FBI and posted at the agency Web site indicate, for instance, that in 2002 about 77% of arrestees were males. Men made up 82.6% of arrests for violent crime and almost 70% of the arrests for property crime. There is nothing unusual about such results.

These patterns are strong and consistent, and the lower offending rates for females cannot be explained away with reference to chivalry or some other benign tendency on the part of justice system officials. When general samples of youth and adults are asked to report to researchers their involvement in criminality (irrespective of whether it ever came to the attention of the police), males once again emerge as the more criminal group (Burton, Cullen, Evans, Alarid, & Dunaway, 1998). In a similar way, surveys that ask crime victims about the characteristics of the people who victimize them find that males are more likely to be named as offenders. An analysis of trends from 20 years of national victimization studies revealed that victims perceived their offenders as males in 85% of all single-offender victimizations, in 95% of rapes, and 92% of robberies (Zawitz et al., 1993).

Males make up not only the significant number of offenders but also a significant number of victims. With respect to homicide, for instance, while males are about eight times more likely than females to kill someone, they are also about three times more likely to be killed (Adams & Reynolds, 2002). Except for rape and various other forms of sexual assault, males have higher rates of violent victimization than females, although these differences have grown smaller in recent years.

Of equal interest is the fact that it is not only criminal misbehavior, narrowly defined, in which males seem to predominate, but a whole range of troublesome conduct. Males, according to a range of data sources, are more likely than females to use alcohol and other drugs, to drive dangerously, to be sexually promiscuous, and to engage in a number of other socially disruptive behaviors (Gottfredson & Hirschi, 1990). Some theorists argue that this is not surprising given that such behaviors share common ground with many forms of offending. Like crime, these related behaviors are risky, thrilling, and promise short-term rewards (Gottfredson & Hirschi, 1990).

Why are males so much more likely than females to engage in the kinds of behaviors that are widely regarded as troublesome? Criminologists provide a helpful short list of answers to this question. Some nominate differences in biology and stress the ways in which testosterone affects action (Courtwright, 1998). Others argue that it has more to do with the exclusion of women from the race for "the American Dream." Women, by implication, have been less likely to experience the strains and frustrations of socially induced failure (Adler, 1975). Still others maintain that the differences have to do with the lower levels of control to which males are typically subjected (Hagan, Simpson, & Gillis, 1988). Lower levels of control mean a greater freedom to act in ways that reflect narrow self-interest (Burton et al., 1998). Much crime (and other forms of socially disruptive behavior) can be said to express such self-interest.

Whatever the reason for the difference, the demographic fact remains. When the number of men is greater or when the number of men in the population shifts dramatically, we might expect levels of crime to change accordingly.

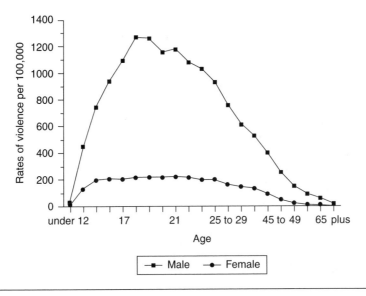

Figure 2.1   The Age–Crime Curve

Source: http://www.fbi.gov/ucr/addpubs.htm

YOUTHFULNESS

We know that in addition to sex, there is a strong association between youthfulness and criminal offending for both males and females (Flowers, 1989). While this relationship has been documented for most of the common types of crimes around which crime wave anxieties swirl, there are exceptions. Corporate crimes, for instance, or elder abuse tend to involve offenders who can be substantially older than average.

As with sex, the relationship between crime and youthfulness seems to be pretty robust in that it holds for a range of societies and a range of historical periods for which relevant information is available. The importance of the relationship between youth and crime is evident in all of the types of data that criminologists typically use in research. In police data, in studies of self-reported criminality, and in surveys in which crime victims are asked to describe their offenders we consistently learn that offenders tend to be young (Adams & Reynolds, 2002; Tittle & Grasmick, 1998; Zawitz et al., 1993). Criminologists often speak of an "age–crime curve" (as pictured in Figure 2.1), which shows how engagement in crime varies over the lifecycle. For most types of crime, there is a relatively early peak in offending with a steady decline thereafter (Tittle & Grasmick, 1998). As in the case of sex, there is no shortage of explanations as to why youthfulness and crime correlate. While criminologists have tended to emphasize the social character of youth rather than its biological character, both kinds of factors seem to matter. Given the importance of the link between youthfulness and crime, it is reasonable to speculate that sharp rises and falls in crime levels might be linked to sharp rises and falls in the size of this youthful "at-risk" population (Philip & Laub, 1998; Steffensmeier & Harar, 1999).

Several researchers have suggested that there has been too great a tendency to emphasize the brute force of such demographic change (Killias & Aebi, 2000; Levitt, 1999). While the overall decline in homicides that began in the 1980s can to some degree be attributed to the baby boom generation having outgrown its crime-prone years, the even bigger crime bust of the 1990s took place when the proportion of young people in the population was increasing (Blumstein, 2002; LaFree, 1999). The general problem is that crime level changes in the population greatly exceeded changes occurring in the structure of the population (Blumstein, 2002). Of course, we need to remember that each of us has a sex as well as an age. While we can separate these factors for analytical purposes, in reality they play themselves out in combination. The problem with crime is really a problem of young men (much more so than old men or young women). Why this should be so is less clear.

While demographic shifts in the population are important, they matter less than we might expect them to, given the male and youthful character of so much crime. Yet this is less paradoxical than it might at first appear. Crime levels are determined not by demographic factors alone but by the combination of demography and historical and social circumstances that make crime more likely.

Social Dislocations

The need to explain relatively sudden increases in crime levels requires us to think about how extreme events might upset social order. There are strong social scientific reasons to do so. The famous French sociologist Emile Durkheim (1897/1951) used the term *anomie* to describe, among other things, the kind of dramatic social episodes that upset regular social patterns and disconnect people from group life. Three types of episodes are of particular interest: war, sudden economic change, and institutional breakdown.

WAR

While it might seem simple at first, the question, "Is war a cause of abrupt crime level changes?" is pretty imprecise. This is because we might reasonably expect war to have more than one kind of effect. It is reasonable to suggest that crime rates will fall during wartime. After all, members of the demographic group at greatest risk of committing crime (i.e., young males) will be removed from the civilian population in very large numbers. In addition, the sociological argument can be made that when the members of society face a common enemy, they tend to be less predatory toward each other (Coser, 1956). As well, the kinds of crimes, like gambling or drug use, that depend on proactive policing policies to ferret out violators will have lower rates of discovery if policing resources are directed toward the war effort.

We might expect other effects in postwar periods, however. Large numbers of young males, trained in violence, detached for long periods of time from neighborhoods and families, might not be expected to make an easy transition back into society. Their sudden and abrupt reentry into civilian life could be related to equally sudden increases in crime levels. This idea has clearly become embedded in popular culture. A large number of feature films in the 1980s and 1990s, for instance, such as *Dead Presidents, Rambo,* and *The Deer Hunter* featured the maladjusted Vietnam veteran. Often the stock characters in such films are violent, homeless, and psychologically maladjusted. Not surprisingly, veterans groups take real exception to such one-dimensional portrayals.

There have been several research attempts to investigate the effects of war on postwar crime level change. Often the investigators make use of homicide data, largely because such data are more reliable and more readily available for the investigation of long-term trends. When taken together, the results of these analyses are less consistent than we would like. Dane Archer and Rosemary Gartner (1984), for instance, undertook a cross-national analysis of the effects of war on rates of murder. They found that most of the combatant nations in their study experienced substantial postwar increases in the rates of homicide. Moreover, these increases occurred in both victorious and defeated nations and involved more murder among those who had served in wars as well as those who did not. In a consistent way, historian Ted Gurr (1981) found that in Germany and Austria, in the aftermath of World War I, the rates of most kinds of crime climbed sharply.

In contrast, a study by Eric Monkkonen (2001) of homicide in New York City found only scant evidence that wars lead to sudden increases in murderousness. An examination of the effects of five wars led Monkkonen to conclude that only after World War I was there a really notable increase in homicide and even that increase was lower than what many might assume it would be. Similarly, historian Roger Lane (1997) notes that the dominant effects of the urban industrial revolution that followed the U.S. Civil War were to push homicide rates down, not only the United States but also in Sweden, Australia, and England.

There is also some inconsistency regarding the behavior of crime rates during wartime. While rates of crime and murder fell during the Civil War and World War I, they did not fall during the war in Vietnam (Gurr, 1981; Lane, 1997). Even more interestingly, Coleman and Moynihan (1996) demonstrate that during the years of World War II there was in London, England, a 69% increase in rates of indictable offences. To some degree, these huge increases could be attributed to the massive influx of young males from other western nations. Coleman and Moynihan note that there were in London at the time as many as 20,000 military deserters. It is likely that to some degree the declines in American crime rates during this period were reflected in the increases in London and elsewhere in the United Kingdom.

Questions about the effects of war on crime levels are complex. Of course, types of crimes differ from each other with respect to their causes and contexts. Do we expect that violence, crimes against property, and crimes against the public order would all be affected by war in the same way? In addition, are there important differences with respect to the care we take in measuring crime at different points in history? It would not be unreasonable to argue that we are more willing to put resources into accurate crime measurement when we are not distracted by war than when we are. There are important questions to ask about war, as well. Wars can be highly variable events and of course can produce highly variable effects. How major was the war? Was it fought in the homeland or on foreign soil? Did it involve a volunteer army or a conscripted army? What was the nature of the economic and social environment to which the soldiers returned at the conclusion of the war? Were various regions of the country engaged in the war effort in different ways? It is likely that the answers to all of these questions matter with respect to the kinds of impacts war has on the rapid transformation of crime rates. In other words, war likely exerts its influence in combination with other kinds of influences.

HOW THE WEST BECAME WILD

In the last several decades of the 19th century, the American West was a rather violent place. *Tombstone, Open Range, Unforgiven,* and hundreds of other Hollywood films have popularized the idea of a crime wave in the Old West to such a degree that it is difficult to separate empirical fact from cultural mythology. However, historians have shown that while the frontier was a dangerous place, it was not consistently so. Some towns in the Old West had very high crime rates and some did not, and those that did have high rates of criminal violence were not violent in general, but violent in particular ways.

In his study of violence on the Trans-Sierra frontier, for instance, McGrath (1984) found that bank robbery, rape, burglary, and serious juvenile crime seem not to have occurred very frequently. In contrast, shootings and shoot-outs among badmen and miners were common events. McGrath contends that contemporary murder and assault rates, despite common assumptions about the dangerousness of American cities, were much higher in many frontier towns of the late 19th century. Other historians have shown that, like the Trans-Sierra mining towns, the so-called cow towns of Kansas also had very high rates of murder and assaultive violence (Marks, 1989).

What explains this pattern? One answer stresses the way in which major historical developments—especially the Civil War—combined to promote rapidly escalating rates of violent crime in places like Tombstone, Arizona, or Dodge City, Kansas (Courtwright, 1998). The Civil War was a bloody conflict, and historians suggest that battlefield casualties and disease resulted in more than 600,000 deaths and thousands of other injuries and infirmities. While many young boys went off to war, many of those fortunate enough to return did so as brutalized, battled-hardened men. Though young in years, they had already seen a lifetime of pain and misery. For veterans of the Confederacy there was, as well, the frustration and anger born of defeat and occupation.

The end of the Civil War coincided with important social changes that occurred largely in the northeast. Industrialization was under way and cities were growing rapidly. Both the urbanization and industrial growth were fed by unprecedented rates of immigration, first from Ireland and later from Russia, Italy, Germany, and elsewhere. The growth in population created a huge demand for food—especially for beef. A popular kind of beef cattle, the longhorn, was native to Texas and could be grown there in numbers sufficient to feed the populations of the growing cities. Meeting this demand posed a logistical problem, however: how to get the beef from Texas to New York and other cities in the northeast. It was in this historical context that the cattle drive and the legend and lore of the American cowboy were born.

Cattle drivers would walk the cattle from Texas northward to small towns in Kansas where the cattle would be sold and shipped by train to Chicago. There the cattle could be slaughtered and the meat processed in assembly-line fashion at the huge rendering plants operated by Swift or Armour. Once prepared for shipping, the meat could move east in the refrigerator train cars built by George Pullman, another Chicago entrepreneur.

Despite the romance and legend of the cowboy and the open trail, the work associated with the cattle drive was dangerous and grueling. Not surprisingly, large numbers of southern Civil War veterans found work on these cattle drives. The towns at the end of the drives, Dodge City, Wichita, or Ellsworth, were developed to address the most immediate and basic desires of the almost exclusively young, male, southern cowhands who arrived with the cattle (Tefertiller, 1997). Saloons, gambling dens, and houses of prostitution could be found in abundance. The chemistry for assaultive and lethal violence was clearly in place (Courtwright, 1998). Single young men were the dominant demographic. Typically, they were fully armed, angry, using alcohol heavily, and, as veterans, accustomed to violence. Famous "shootists" like Wyatt Earp and Bat Masterson were hired by town officials to enforce the law or at least to try to ensure some semblance of social order (Barra, 1998; Marks, 1989). A similar dynamic characterized life in contemporary mining towns such as Deadwood, South Dakota; Tombstone, Arizona; and those on the Trans-Sierra frontier (McGrath, 1984).

Violence in all such towns rapidly escalated in the years after the Civil War, in part because of the war. However, the war's brutalizing effects were indirect rather than direct. These effects became especially problematic in the context of towns populated almost exclusively by young single men (Courtwright, 1998). Such effects, in this view, might be expected to decline as social change corrected the demographic imbalance and as the cohort of angry, young unattached males got married and grew older or died from natural or other causes.

ECONOMIC DISLOCATIONS

The most common explanations of why crime rates might suddenly go up or down tend to focus on economic variables (Allen, 1996). The logic of such explanations is usually rather straightforward: As economic conditions worsen, crime levels can be expected to increase. Conversely, as economic conditions improve, crime levels will decline.

Despite the glibness that often characterizes arguments of this sort, the empirical picture is considerably more complicated for a number of reasons. First, there is no shortage of ways in which "economic conditions" might be operationalized for research purposes (Braithwaite, 1979; Freeman, 1995; Hagan, 1995; Neustrom & Norton, 1995). Some researchers talk about increasing economic inequality; others speak of increases in the number of poor people. Still others are concerned with the effects of inflation or variations in the business cycle. Such diversity makes it difficult to generalize about worsening economic conditions in any meaningful way. Second, because crime is a rather large and heterogeneous event category, there is no reason to think that worsening economic conditions (whatever this might mean) would be related to *all* kinds of crime in the same ways (Conklin, 2003; Freeman, 1995). Finally, research into the effects of various types of worsening (or improving) economic conditions on various types of crime have been undertaken at quite different levels of aggregation. In other words, researchers have tried to understand whether economic conditions of a particular type make crime more likely at the individual level, neighborhood level, the city level, the state level, or even the national level. It does not follow that what one observes at any one level can be generalized to any other level.

One consequence of this state of affairs is that the accumulated body of research evidence seems able to support a variety of positions. At one end of a theoretical continuum, some Marxist scholars, for instance, might see the relationship between crime and the economic engine of society to be almost self-evident (Chambliss, 1994; Reiman, 1998). How could anyone look at the social locations of crime in society and the characteristics of the offenders or victims and not end up concluding that economic conditions are of immense relevance to the generation of crime in society? At the other end of such a continuum are scholars who are critical of what they see as undue attention paid to economic factors (Gottfredson & Hirschi, 1990). They argue that falling rates of many kinds of crime during the Great Depression provide evidence against any simple suggestions regarding the effects of economic conditions (Brantingham & Brantingham, 1984; Monkkonen, 2001).

A most articulate spokesperson of this latter view is Marcus Felson (2002), who has written that "it is a mistake to assume that crime is part of a larger set of social evils such as unemployment, poverty, social injustice or human suffering" (p. 12). Felson is led to this position from a careful consideration of much of the empirical evidence relating to crime and economic conditions. In particular, he is struck by the finding that in the 1960s and 1970s, very large increases across a variety of crime types were statistically associated with large improvements in the domestic economy. Indeed, Felson argues that contrary to what Marxist critiques of American capitalism might have us believe, several European nations with vastly more comprehensive welfare programs experienced similar increases and according to some research, at least, continue to have rates of many kinds of crime that exceed American rates.

In general, it seems clear that the effects of economic change on crime levels are not straightforward but highly contingent. Nowhere is this clearer than in the study of the relationship between crime and one of the most researched economic factors—unemployment. The novice investigator can be forgiven for assuming that there must be a mountain of research to support the conclusion that the crime rate is profoundly affected by the unemployment rate and if that rate should shoot upward, crime will too. After all, so many of the theories of conventional criminology suggest that if people are out of work, they may experience greater motivation to break the law. To be sure, there are several studies that make this argument, but they tell only a small part of the story (Freeman, 1995). Any effects unemployment might have are complicated (Karmen, 2000).

To begin with it is obvious that, at the individual level at least, some kinds of crime require employment. Corporate crimes, embezzlement, or theft in the workplace are all crimes that become more likely if one has a job and less likely if one does not. In a different way, some researchers have suggested that upturns in the rate of unemployment can actually lead to a reduction in the rates of many types of crime. When people are out of work in large numbers, there are fewer consumer goods being produced and therefore fewer to steal. In addition, when people are out of work they spend less time away from home (at work, at play, or on vacation). This means they can more effectively guard their homes against theft or against breaking and entering (Cantor & Land, 1985).

Thus, there does not appear to be any simple relationship between crime rates and unemployment rates. Recent studies of the crime dip of the 1990s, for instance, suggest that while decreases in crime and in unemployment were correlated, improvements in the crime rate may have predated improvements in the rate of unemployment. Though changes in labor markets may have reinforced the crime dip, they were not the initial cause of it (Conklin, 2003).

Another very significant complication relates to the fact that the rate of unemployment describes only one aspect of the relationship between crime and the labor market. In this respect, it is helpful to distinguish between "primary" and "secondary" labor sector jobs (Crutchfield, Glusker, & Bridges, 1999). Primary sector jobs are characterized by a good living wage, healthy benefits, and the potential for long-term, regular employment. By contrast, secondary jobs are characterized by low pay, a lack of security, and limited prospects for future employment. While we might expect primary jobs to be good insulators against crime, we are less confident about the value of secondary jobs in this regard. People who have bad jobs with little financial security or little hope for the future are still employed, but not in a way that might mitigate the effects we traditionally associate with unemployment.

In any case, several writers have argued that the crime rate increases of the 1970s and 1980s may have been related to a restructuring of the U.S. economy that moved many people from primary to secondary labor markets (Grant & Martinez, 1997; Wilson, 1987, 1996). The shift was a profound one, especially for the old rust-belt industrial cities of the Northeast and Midwest. Traditional industrial jobs that had for decades been available to low-skilled urban dwellers disappeared in large numbers. These jobs moved from city to suburb, from the north to the Sunbelt, and in many cases from the United States to countries where American corporations could operate more profitably. In many other cases, they disappeared altogether.

When such jobs did exist in large numbers it was possible for people nearer the bottom of the social structure to earn a good wage. A breadwinner could support a family by building cars or working in a steel mill and could usually expect to hold the job until retirement. As such jobs moved or vanished, they were replaced (if they were replaced) by jobs in the service sector. These jobs are much more typically part of the secondary labor market. While the industrial worker could plan for and provide for a family, the fast food employee or discount superstore "associate" would have much more trouble doing so.

Of course, not all members of society were affected by this transformation to the same degree, and it was young minority men who most acutely experienced these changes (Wilson, 1996). If they sought jobs in the primary sector, they would be the last hired and first fired. Lacking few other skills or experience and unable to follow higher-paying jobs to the suburbs or the Sunbelt, their only legal options involved low-reward employment in the secondary labor market. In many cases, however, such jobs did not provide powerful disincentives to crime.

The effects of this transformation was not only a problem for the individual. Indeed, entire communities were affected. The so-called urban underclass, it has been argued, was largely a product of the economic transformation that greatly reduced inner-city residents' chances of stable and rewarding employment (Conklin, 2003; Marks, 1991; Wilson, 1996). It became more difficult to form families, and neighborhoods became increasingly unstable (Neustrom & Morton, 1995). Over time, the idea of permanent and steady work and all that it implied lost traditional meaning. In such a social context, higher rates of crime became more likely.

An important implication of this position is that the key to reduced crime rates might reside deep within the economic structure of society. Well-paying, stable jobs could provide an effective buffer against surging crime levels. A more cynical approach might involve hiding whatever relationships exist in this respect. In 2004, the annual *Economic Report of the President* asked whether service jobs (like those in the fast food industry) might be recategorized as manufacturing jobs. According to the authors of the report:

> For example, mixing water and concentrate to produce soft drinks is classi-fied as *manufacturing*. However, if that activity is performed at a snack bar, it is considered a service. (www.frwebgate.access.gpo.gov/cgi-bin/multidb.cgi)

Blurring the distinction between manufacturing and service jobs, of course, makes it more difficult to see those job losses and therefore to discern how job losses associated with the primary labor market affect crime level changes.

INSTITUTIONAL BREAKDOWN

One of the more significant attempts to investigate the origin and history of rapid upward shifts in American crime rates was undertaken by Gary LaFree (1998a). His focus was the post–World War II crime rate increase, which, as discussed at the beginning of the previous chapter, was almost unprecedented in its magnitude. In brief, LaFree's thesis is that rapid social and economic change in the postwar period created a crisis of legitimacy that made rapidly escalating crime rates possible. LaFree uses the term *legitimacy* to refer to the relative ease with which major social institutions are able to ensure legal (and social) conformity. He argues that three major social institutions have as a primary function the promotion of conformity and the discouragement of criminal conduct. First, the political institution passes laws and mounts the machinery of criminal justice. Second, the economic institution controls crime, in large part, by providing the means by which people can meet their material needs. In this way, criminal motivation is held in check. Third, and perhaps most basically, the family institution socializes new societal members and thus teaches law-abiding behavior.

For LaFree, it is in the changes in these institutions, in their reduced abil-ity to control crime, that the roots of the crime level increases can be located. In the 1960s, he notes, a number of developments undermined the confidence that people had in the political institution. Perhaps most notable in this respect was the recognition of widespread discrimination involving African Americans. The legitimacy of the economic institution was threatened by high rates of inflation and economic inequality. At the same time, rising rates of divorce, higher rates of out-of-wedlock birth, and related changes called into question the legitimacy of the traditional patriarchal nuclear family. Of course, these changes did not occur in isolation. Instead, what happens in each institutional sphere affects what happens in the others.

These changes in legitimacy within the political, economic, and family institutions were most profoundly experienced by African Americans, and the particular problems with crime experienced by this group can be understood as a logical outcome. LaFree is able to marshal considerable evidence in support of his thesis. The relevant data indicate rather clearly that the kinds of crime in which he is interested—traditional street crime—rose rapidly during the postwar period. As well, a variety of attitudinal measures and other social indicators support his claims about the decline in the legitimacy of the major social institutions. As LaFree points out, the specific timing of the postwar increase rules out competing explanations and thereby lends additional support to the argument about the decline of institutional legitimacy.

Diffusion

A second set of social processes that help us to understand why crime rates might suddenly escalate (or de-escalate) involve social and cultural diffusion (Brantingham & Brantingham, 1984). *Diffusion* refers to the various ways in which a form of behavior (or an attitude or other cultural artifact) travels through a population. In the older language of the sociology of collective behavior, researchers would have used the word *contagion* to describe this process. This older term makes us think that the process by which behavior spreads is unthinking and almost automatic. While this idea might make sense in a description of stampeding cattle, it seems to have little to do with the transmission of relatively complex behaviors (like crimes). While the term contagion is still sometimes used as a synonym for diffusion, it is generally recognized to have more metaphoric than literal value (Locher, 2002, p. 11).

For most writers, the spread of behavior through a population is understood as a far more rational process. Individuals observe (directly or vicariously) and evaluate the consequences of others' behavior and then make a decision whether or not to adopt the behavior themselves (Myers, 2000). From the perspective of contemporary social science, this usually involves four elements: (a) the people or person with whom diffusion originates, variously called sources or emitters or transmitters; (b) something—a fashion, a fad, a way of acting or dressing, and so on—that is diffused; (c) people who adopt the thing that is being diffused, variously called adopters or recipients; and (d) the means by which the diffusion occurs, often called a channel or linkage (Best, 2001b). There is a large body of research that documents the way in which various aspects of the culture, news, ideas, new products, and other items diffuse both within and across populations (DeFleur, 1988). While most of these studies focus on routine aspects of social life, some researchers have shown that diffusion models are useful in understanding other kinds of behavior, such as strikes (Conell & Cohn, 1995) or riots (Myers, 2000).

We can ask whether crime rate changes are explicable in terms of these same kinds of diffusion processes. Claude Fischer (1995), an influential urban sociologist, has argued that increases (and subsequent decreases) in violent crime tend to diffuse from cities to less urban places. Fischer maintains that violent acts—just like clothing styles or musical forms—are loaded with cultural content. This means that violent acts "behave" the way other aspects of the culture behave. Most new fashions, dances, or musical styles, Fischer points out, emerge in cities and move outward to the hinterland. While city-dwellers might take the innovation and diversity of urban life for granted, those who live their lives in smaller communities or rural areas often describe a visit to the city as exciting precisely because it has these qualities. Violence, for Fischer, is like a fad. It starts out in bigger cities and somehow diffuses to smaller ones. He was able to demonstrate this through an analysis of violent crime rates in California counties between 1955 and 1975 (Fischer, 1980). Fischer found that the wave-like violence patterns reached their peaks and valleys first in more urban places.

The elements of diffusion often appear to be evident during crime wave episodes. A particularly interesting example involved the Black Hand crime wave that was described at the beginning of Chapter 1. It will be recalled that this particular crime wave occurred in the Italian neighborhoods of many large American cities during the first couple of decades of the 20th century. At its core, Black Hand crime involved a crude kind of extortion in which more prosperous members of these neighborhoods were told that if they wished to avoid harm, they would need to pay a specified sum of money to the authors of the threatening extortion note.

It appears that as time went on, and as knowledge of the Black Hand methodology began to diffuse widely, it was taken up by all categories of offenders who sought to acquire some quick cash, or to frighten or get revenge against their enemies (Sacco, 2003). The Black Hand letter became a readily available technique that greatly simplified criminal intimidation for those for whom it might otherwise have been a very difficult thing to accomplish. To make some quick money, anyone who wished to do so could spread terror to enemies or victims by claiming an affiliation with the powerful criminal organization the Black Hand symbol was claimed to represent. The Black Hand method could be put to a wide variety of uses by offenders who wished to achieve a wide variety of criminal goals. A sampling of cases from the *New York Times* for the period in question gives some indication of the degree to which the Black Hand method had diffused:

- March 16, 1908—The musical director of the Metropolitan Opera is warned via a Black Hand note to eliminate Nessler's "God Keep You" solo from a concert program
- February 7, 1909—A grocer sends a competitor a Black Hand note to try to drive him out of business
- May 24, 1911—A Black Hand letter is received by the Women's Political Union; it made no specific demands, but was intended to intimidate
- June 20, 1915—A discharged nurse is accused of writing a Black Hand letter to scare a former employer who had fired her
- August 1, 1915—A group of boarding school girls send Black Hand letters to some prominent citizens of Santa Monica, California, because they "thought it would be a lark to scare the fashionable community"

Central to any discussion of the diffusion of crime is a consideration of the channels through which diffusion takes place. Obviously, potential adopters need access to the behavior of others if they are going to evaluate and imitate it (Myers, 2000). While some diffusion of criminal behavior occurs in the context of intimate interpersonal groups, it is of course the mass media that have tended to occupy the attention of researchers. So-called copycat crimes provide perhaps the clearest example of crime diffusion.

COPYCAT COPYCAT

Because of their very apparent newsworthiness, copycat crimes often receive extensive treatment in the news media. One such case occurred in January of 2003. It involved two brothers in Riverside, California, who were arrested for the murder of their mother. According to the police, the accused had tried to evade capture by decapitating their mother and cutting off her hands. More to the point, however, the police also reported that one of the sons had said that they got the idea for the grisly mutilations by watching an episode of the extremely popular HBO program, *The Sopranos* (http://edition.cnn.com/2003/US/West/01/27/decapitated.body.ap/)

That copycat crimes happen is not in dispute (Surette, 2002). On some occasions some members of the mass audiences of movies, television, or video games will engage in imitative behavior. Most of us have heard of a situation in which one incident of school violence or of terrorism was followed closely in time by a remarkably similar act. What is in dispute in such cases is the extensiveness of the phenomenon (Surette, 2002). If such reports are merely anecdotal, they do not take us very close to an explanation of why crime levels might suddenly rise or fall.

A number of studies, especially those undertaken by sociologist Derek Phillips (1979, 1980, 1983), present evidence that suggests that the effects of media on the occurrence of copycat crimes are quite substantial. In some of his studies, Phillips looked at how high visibility suicides, as reported in the news, seem to have led to significant increases in rates of suicide. In other studies, he examined how prizefights may have exerted an impact on levels of interpersonal violence, specifically homicide. Critics, however, suggest that the studies are problematic (Surette, 1998). For instance, it can be argued that events like prize-fights, suicides, and homicides do not occur randomly and that observed patterns of association might reflect coincidental timing. At a basic level, it is also important to ask why the overwhelming majority of audience members who regularly attend to murders, muggings, and mutilation on television and in the movies never engage in copycat behavior.

On the other hand, it is not difficult to see how copycat crime might stimulate dramatic crime level increases. Several distinct stages can be identified:

Stage 1: a criminal event with unusual (and newsworthy) characteristics occurs

Stage 2: the incident is reported in the news media

Stage 3: some members of the audience assess the act as one that can help them meet some objective they seek (fast cash, revenge, etc.)

Stage 4: these audience members commit acts with similar features

Stage 5: the news media find the copycat character of the crimes even more newsworthy and report on these incidents

Stage 6: return to Stage 3

Eventually, of course, the rates would wind down for a number of reasons. For one thing, in the short term at least, the media will over time come to find these incidents less and less newsworthy and will cut back on reporting them. For another, the crimes might become the object of intensive criminal justice intervention.

In reality, it is difficult to demonstrate that the process of copycat crime really does happen in this way. This very simple process involves some very complicated research questions. As Dennis Howitt (1998) has noted, while copycat crime may occur, "the evidence in its favor is more than occasionally flawed" (p. 90). A comprehensive review of much of the literature by Surette (1998) concludes that while copycat crime might be common enough to influence the overall crime picture, the effect might have more to do with influencing offenders' choices of methods than with influencing their decisions to commit crimes at all. In other words, we are really likely to see copycat effects only among that portion of an audience that is already predisposed to behave in a criminal fashion. What diffuses through the population is not a motivation to offend but some options about how they might offend. The case of the sons who were charged with killing and decapitating their mother is probably consistent with this conclusion.

There are of course more general ways in which crime might be said to diffuse from media and through audiences (Ferrell, 1998). These processes don't involve the imitation of a particular way of committing specific crimes. Instead they involve the diffusion of values and lifestyles that are thought to increase the risks of offending. In this respect, suspicion is often cast upon various elements of youth culture, especially music (Gray, 1989). In the early days of rock and roll, for instance, the music was blamed for the spread of delinquency and for the riotous behavior that was often reported to have occurred at live rock and roll shows (Nasaw, 1993). In one case, for instance, the 1956 appearance of Bill Haley and the Comets at the National Guard Armory in Washington, D.C., resulted in a number of fights that started in the armory building and spread to the street. The manager of the armory placed the blame squarely on the music and stated, "It's the jungle strain that gets 'em all worked up'" (Martin & Segrave, 1988, p. 30). Thus, as the music diffuses throughout society, it was argued, delinquency and disrespect for law can be expected to follow.

While many other forms of music such as heavy metal and punk have been subject to similar critiques, it is perhaps rap music and other forms of hip-hop culture that have excited the greatest concern (Rome, 2004; Russell-Brown, 2004). In its earliest forms, rap music was intended as an antidote to the influence exerted upon youth by gangs, violence, and drugs in poor, inner-city neighborhoods. The music was often political and very upbeat. In time, however, the development of "gangsta rap"—especially on the West Coast—tended to celebrate some of those aspects of inner-city experience that are typically defined as social problems. To some degree, the change reflected the desire of some record producers to consciously market their music to the west coast gangs (Marriott, 1999). Much, but certainly not all, rap music came to focus on violent and misogynist themes (Armstrong, 2001). Viewed from another perspective, the music grew angrier as guns, homicide, and crack became increasingly obvious aspects of urban life. The gangsta style, as reflected not only in the music, but in the styles of dress, use of language, and worldview diffused from big cities (particularly Los Angeles) to small towns in America and elsewhere. Many people have argued that conformity to the focal concerns of hip-hop culture encourages gang formation and involvement and makes offending and victimization more likely life experiences. As rap journalist Ronin Ro (1996) has eloquently stated:

> While mainstream media haggled over censorship issues surrounding the music, the gangsta rappers began translating their on-wax fantasies into full-scale reality. Many were soon entangled in legal problems and shootouts and their listeners grew further entranced. Soon the listener—young, lacking role models or authority figures, and somewhat bored with life—would accept the gangsta rapper's lyrics as gospel. (p. 8)

Many in society find explanations that blame youth culture for increases in youthful misbehavior reassuring in a fundamental way. They suggest that the problem with youth is the result of bad choices youth make. In this way, the adult world and social institutions escape any careful scrutiny. But there are several problems with this kind of account. First, there is a consistency in this style of argument that should make us suspicious. Whatever the historical period, adults always seem able to identify the criminogenic character of youth culture (Ravitch & Viteritti, 2003). As suggested, jazz, swing music, rock and roll, folk music, heavy metal, punk, and rap have all been likely suspects when reasons for the criminal conduct of young people have been sought (Grey, 1989). Second, the focus, for instance, on the violent or misogynist character of rap music discourages an appreciation of the ways in which these themes permeate all aspects of popular culture. Violence against women, the celebration of murder, and a dislike for and anger toward legal authority are not inventions of hip-hop culture. They are merely given unique expression there. When Eric Clapton sang the Bob Marley lyric, "I shot the sheriff" during the 1970s, no one really seemed to think that he had. In contrast, when rapper Ice-T's metal song "Cop Killer" was released several years later, the media firestorm suggested that a line had been crossed that had never been crossed before. Violence is not a creative theme that is by any means restricted to rap music. As hip-hop artist Beanie Sigel has stated, "The terminator is the governor of California—nobody talks about that. He makes movies about killing people with guns all day and he is the governor" (Golianopoulos, 2004, p. 121).

Third, it is important to point out that there is a sense in which the content of much rap music (or other forms of youth culture) draws upon the experiences of the artists and is resonant with the interests and experiences of the listeners. Thus, the music is more a reflection of lives lived than a cause of how they are lived. Finally, there is a tendency on the part of those who make arguments of this type to assume that young people are unable to exercise any critical judgment or to think about or reflect on what they hear and see. There is certainly reason to question this assumption. Research by Mahiri and Conner (2003) found that among a sample of students drawn from middle school, there was indeed a critical posture toward and a nuanced view of the lyrical content of rap music. To be sure, there will always be a large segment of any mass audience that will not appreciate intended irony or understand the provocative character of any art form. It would, however, be unfair and misleading to characterize most audience members in this way. In short, arguments about the diffusion of powerful youth culture to explain crime rate increases are probably overstated.

Innovation

A third kind of social process that requires attention is innovation. Dictionaries typically define innovation as the introduction of something new, and that is really all that is intended by the use of the term in this context. Three types of innovations are considered: social, market, and technological. The introduction of significant new elements into social life can have profound implications for the rates at which established or new kinds of crime occur.

SOCIAL INNOVATIONS: SHIFTS IN ROUTINE ACTIVITIES

In the late 1970s two sociologists, Lawrence Cohen and Marcus Felson (1979), attempted to explain why rates of predatory crime climbed as dramatically as they did during the post–World War II period. Unlike many other writers, they rejected the logic that said the increase in crime could be explained narrowly in terms of an increased tendency on the part of offenders to offend. Instead, Cohen and Felson argued that the successful commission of direct-contact predatory victimizations (like homicides, rapes, burglaries, or vandalism) does not depend just on the presence of an offender who is ready and willing to commit the crime. Two other elements are equally essential. First, there must be a suitable target against which the offender can act. This might be a person to rob, a home to break into, or a wall to vandalize. Second, it is important that the offender encounter the target in the absence of anybody or anything that might stop the crime from happening. Predatory crimes can occur only when these three elements—the motivated offender, the suitable target, and the absence of capable guardianship—come together in time in space. The greater the frequency with which these elements encounter each other, the higher we can expect rates of crime to be.

In their explanation of the crime rate increases of the 1960s and 1970s, Cohen and Felson focused on the ways in which new organizational patterns of everyday life affected the rate at which these elements combined. In general, they argued, the period witnessed a broad shift in the locus of "routine activities" away from the home. Several key indictors of this trend can be noted:

- In greater and greater numbers, women whose lives had been largely organized around the household returned to school or entered the workforce
- Vacations became longer and travel became cheaper and as a result, vacations were more likely to be spent away from home
- The frequency with which people dined away from home increased giving birth to, among other things, the fast food industry
- Divorce rates were increasing and people were waiting longer and longer to get married

As a result of these and other changes, the number of smaller and single-person households proliferated.

The sum total of these changes was that people were becoming more mobile. Increasingly, those social spaces beyond the home, rather than the home itself, became the site for work and leisure. Not coincidentally, the period also witnessed a kind of revolution in the design of lightweight, durable consumer goods. Televisions, tape recorders, radios, microwaves, and all of the other products that flooded the consumer market were getting smaller, lighter, and easier to move from one location to another.

The implication of all this change for rates of predatory crime is obvious and can be easily demonstrated with reference to a crime like household theft or burglary. On the one hand, people were stocking their homes with greater and greater numbers of household goods (increasing target suitability). At the same time, they were spending more and more time away from home (thereby lowering the level of guardianship they were able to exert over their homes). In short, given the increased levels of target suitability and the decreased levels of guardianship, we need not argue that there had to have been more offenders in the population for the crime rate to go up. Even a stable number of offenders could produce more crimes since the rate at which they would encounter suitable targets in the absence of capable guardianship can be expected to increase.

There is a sense in which we can think about these crime increases as a kind of deskilling of crime that makes offending a more accessible choice to a wider range of potential crime event participants (Felson, 2002). In the "old days," burglary was much more of a high-skill crime. One had to know how to case a residence and how to get in the house without being detected. Once inside, the offender needed to know what to steal. Where was the money likely to be hidden? Which jewels in the jewel box were real and which were fakes? Then the offender needed to know how to escape with whatever merchandise was stolen. What was the best route out of the neighborhood? Next the offender needed to find a fence willing to buy the stolen merchandise: Who would be able to unload this jewelry? What was a good price?

Of course, in the wake of the social organizational innovations described above, the commission of breaking and entering was greatly simplified. How much skill is really required to break into an empty house in a neighborhood full of empty houses? Once inside, there is no need to search for jewelry or to know anything about jewelry. One can easily locate the DVD player or personal computer or videocassette recorder (VCR). After all, such items are very compact and easy to carry (often with handles conveniently placed by the manufacturer). Once out on the street, the offender can probably walk around without attracting any suspicion. Even if the owner were to drive by and see the thief with the owner's VCR, suspicion would probably not be aroused. All VCRs, after all, look pretty much the same. Unlike in earlier times, one need not worry about finding a specialized fence. The market for "cheap" DVD players or other electronic goods is rather large if the price is right. Or perhaps the offender chooses to keep the items for personal use. This can be done with considerably less risk and somewhat greater versatility than might have been the case if the item stolen was a pearl necklace.

We learn a valuable lesson from routine activities theory. Specifically, we learn that changes in the ways in which we organize the daily business of living can have profound implications for the rate at which crimes occur. Accordingly, we might think about how more recent shifts in the organization of everyday life might be related to crime level decreases. Several questions suggest themselves. What role do all of the new home entertainment technologies play in keeping people home? How does the diffusion of cell phone technology facilitate the mobilization of social control in ways that were previously unknown? How do "flex" work schedules, "work at home," and home schooling contribute to increases in home guardianship?

MARKET INNOVATIONS

When the law is used to try to control public appetites, the results can often be other than what is intended. The creation of illegal markets, almost by definition, means the creation of new categories of offending. In some cases, illicit commodities can be redesigned to allow for the exploitation of new market sectors. Prohibition provides us with an example of the first kind of innovation, and the "crack epidemic" of the 1980s provides an example of the second.

The story of the manufacture, sale, and use of alcohol is, without much exaggeration, the story of America. As one historian of alcohol in America has noted,

> For colonists, it served to assert independence; for warring states, to affirm local diversity or national unity; for democrats, equality; for immigrants, identity; for women, emancipation; for the wealthy, status; for the country as a whole, civilization. (Barr, 1999, p. xi)

The history of alcohol in America, however, has often been punctuated by efforts to restrict its use. The best-known and most significant episode of this sort was the enactment of national prohibition in 1920 (Behr, 1997).

The movement toward prohibition was multifaceted. In part, it reflected some central concerns of early feminist politics regarding the destructive effects of alcohol on family life. Also of great importance were the efforts of early industrialists to try to minimize the losses in productivity that they attributed to the use of alcohol by members of the working classes. These lessons about the need for discipline were dramatically reinforced by the American experience with loss and sacrifice during World War I.

To a considerable degree, the movement to ban the sale and manufacture of alcohol also reflected what sociologist Joseph Gusfield (1963) has called "status politics." Alcohol use was a social practice most typically associated with the urban immigrant and Catholic working classes in the early decades of the 20th century. In contrast, more established Protestant, Anglo-Saxon majorities tended to abstain from alcohol use. Gusfield argues that the battle over the legality of alcohol was at least in part a battle over whose lifestyle would dominate and be enshrined in law.

National prohibition was created by the Eighteenth Amendment to the Constitution, which was passed in 1919 and became law one year later (Root & De Rochemont, 1994). While the law was intended to control supply, it really had no appreciable effect on demand. One outcome was the creation of a sizeable illegal market in alcohol. The mythic elements of the Roaring Twenties—the hot jazz music, the gangsters, and the speakeasies—are all rooted in this illegal market.

However, the market realities of prohibition had a much darker and less glamorous side. As with all illegal markets, when commodities are outlawed, state agencies are unable to regulate manufacturing and sales. In the context of an illegal marketplace, business disputes can't be settled in court. As a result, violence and intimidation often provide the means by which business partners or competitors resolve their differences.

As discussed in the beginning of Chapter 1, the City of Chicago probably gained the most notorious reputation in this regard. It is estimated that between 1920 and 1933 there may have been as many as 400 gang-related killings in that city (Lane, 1997). Much of this violence was related to disputes over territorial markets in the city. Gangs "owned" the businesses in particular neighborhoods, and while efforts were made to achieve some kinds of peaceful coexistence, the relationships were often fragile and the potential for danger ever-present. A key fault line in the city involved the long-term conflict between the "Southside" gang led by Al Capone and the "Northside" gang that was controlled by a succession of much less famous rulers. Indeed, virtually every leader of the Northside gang between 1924 and 1929 either died in a violent shootout or narrowly escaped such a violent death (Hoffman, 1993; Schoenberg, 1992).

The operation of these large illegal markets had a number of effects other than those relating to the violence of dispute resolution. Of particular importance in this respect was the large-scale political corruption that the huge profits of prohibition made possible. The gangs involved in the sale of alcohol sought to operate in as stable an environment as possible. The buying of corrupt judges, police, and prosecutors helped ensure such stability. At the same time, though, such corruption no doubt undermined general respect for legal institutions.

The development of the crack markets of the 1980s provides an interesting point of comparison with prohibition. The market for crack developed not as a result of the passage of a new law but as a result of a change in the way in which an already illegal product could be marketed and used. Cocaine, of which crack is a derivative, had long been a popular drug among the relatively more affluent sectors of society. In contrast to powder cocaine, however, crack emerged as an inexpensive alternative that could be smoked to achieve a very rapid high (Johnson, Golub, & Dunlap, 2000). Because it could be produced with relatively low technology, and relatively little expertise, it was marketed as a rather cheap drug. It had particular appeal among the poorest and most marginalized segments of the population, particularly within large urban centers (Karmen, 2000).

Most analysts have concluded that the escalation of the crack market in the late 1980s was responsible for the dramatic increases in violence among young African American men during this period (Blumstein, 2002). In particular, between 1984 and 1991 participants in the crack market were responsible for a large number of the murders that occurred in major American cities. Typically these murders involved other market participants rather than "innocent bystanders" and usually had much more to do with the instabilities of the market than the pharmacological effects of the drug itself (Brownstein, 1996; Conklin, 2003).

There were several characteristics of the crack market that were particularly conducive to violence, particularly to lethal violence. First, as Brownstein (1996) notes, the crack market operated according to a "freelance model." This means that while participants in the market might cooperate for mutual gain, they did not do so in the context of conventional employer-employee relationships. Authority was not centralized and market activities were not regulated. Instead the market was open and populated by a large number of merchants, each with a relatively small amount of product to sell. Battles over shares of the market or particularly profitable areas were common and often fatal (Karmen, 2000).

Second, the crack trade tended to recruit juveniles who, as we have seen, are at high risk of behaving criminally across a variety of situations (Blumstein, 2002). Not only were young people usually willing to work more cheaply, they also tended, because of their ages, to be somewhat less vulnerable to the harshest sanctions of the criminal justice system. As well, the rapid growth of the crack market created a sizeable demand for dealers—particularly as older drug merchants were being given longer prison sentences in greater and greater numbers. The willingness of young people to engage in risky behavior and the lack of other, legitimate options available to minority males also contributed to their high level of involvement.

Third, crack sales tended to operate in the context of open-air markets. While street corner sales made it easy for buyers and sellers to find each other, they faced considerable risk of robbery or arrest. Even the "normal" business transaction could easily escalate to violence. The typical crack user would seek out a seller several times each day (Johnson et al., 2000). Often the customer might be seriously agitated as a result of the drug, a lack of sleep, or for a variety of other reasons. The potential for something to go wrong in such a transaction was considerable. Largely to deter competitors or criminal predators, many sellers carried firearms (Blumstein, 2002). The development of weapon technology and the profits derived from crack sales made possible an arms race (Karmen, 2000). Increasingly, crack dealers moved from cheap handguns (known as Saturday night specials) to AK-47s, Glocks, and Uzis.

It goes without saying that the destructive effects of escalating violence were in no sense restricted to the crack market. The need for money to buy crack led to the commission of other crimes such as robberies or burglaries. The tendency for crack sellers to arm themselves led others to do the same for the sake of self-defense. Further, high arrest rates contributed to problems of family formation, and the resulting lack of visible male role models further exacerbated problems with violence.

In the 1990s the crack market and the high levels of violence associated with it began to decline for several reasons (Blumstein, 2002). The generation that came of age during the worst years of the crack problem, and that had lost friends and family members to the violence, experienced market disincentives not experienced by those who had gone before them. As the market shrank, it consolidated with fewer customers and more organized forms of distribution. Such factors helped stabilize the marketplace (Brownstein, 1996). In addition, aggressive police crackdowns moved much of the remaining crack business indoors and away from street corners (Blumstein, 2002; Johnson et al., 2000). These changes afforded the typical drug transaction greater security and reduced the need for lethal firepower.

TECHNOLOGICAL INNOVATIONS

We can generally understand technology as the body of knowledge or the tools that are used to transform available resources into some usable form. New technologies are generally intended to simplify tasks or to allow them to be accomplished more efficiently. At the same time, new technologies often have very profound impacts on the amount, character, and distribution of crime in society.

From the point of view of the consumer and business, for instance, credit cards (along with bank cards) have simplified consumerism in many ways. It is no longer necessary to carry large amounts of cash; nor do storeowners need to endure the same risks that were likely when they found it more necessary to take checks or to keep large amounts of cash on the premises. Importantly, the wide availability of such cards also helps to ensure that consumers' spending habits are not be restricted to whatever amounts of cash they might have on hand.

Yet the wide availability of credit cards has created a large number of new criminal opportunities and changed the ways in which more traditional crimes (like theft or fraud) might be committed (Mativat & Tremblay, 1997; Ritzer, 1995). Most simply, credit cards (or credit card numbers) can be stolen and used by someone other than the legitimate owner of the card. In addition, cards can be counterfeited or acquired through processes of fraudulent application. Unscrupulous telemarketers can use deceptive tactics to place charges on a "customer's" credit card. At the same time, credit card companies can take advantage of their customers by charging excessive or hidden fees for the issuance or the use of a card.

The car presents an even more complicated case. Indeed, it can be argued that automobility has been one of the major (if not the major) technological transformations of the last century (Kay, 1998). The personalization of transportation, the very high levels of car ownership, the building of automobile-dependent suburbs, and of 43,000 miles of high-speed interstate highway changed just about every aspect of life in America (Jackson, 1985; Lewis, 1997). The car's relationship to crime is very complex. Automobile thefts, carjackings, impaired or reckless driving, "road rage," and a host of other car-related crimes occupy a great deal of the time and attention of the police and other criminal justice agencies (Corbett, 2003). The building of low-density automobile suburbs has greatly reduced the density of communities and dramatically lowered the levels of guardianship that people are able to exert over their property (Felson, 2002). As well, the widespread use of cars made possible "motorized patrol," the major means by which cities were policed for decades.

In a similar way, as our discussion of the crack market suggested, changes in weapons technology have affected how and with what consequences violent conflicts occur. Geoffrey Canada's (1995) aptly titled *Fist Stick Knife Gun* describes how increasingly lethal weaponry has changed the risks and the nature of disputes, especially among urban minority youth. It is, of course, too simple to suggest that that levels of violence are somehow merely a function of available weaponry. In his historical account of murder in New York City, Eric Monkkonen (2001) was able to demonstrate that while guns and knives made it easier to express murderous rage, they were not the primary cause of such rage. According to Monkkonen, even without guns and knives, murder rates in New York would still have climbed dramatically in the 1970s and 1980s. Such rates would not have been as high as they were, but they would still have been higher than in many European cities.

An understanding of the ways in which technologies affect the levels and distribution of crime is complicated by the fact that new technologies often make their appearances together. The effect of each is therefore often compounded by the effects of the other. Consider the combined influence of new weaponry and the automobile during the crime wave of gangsterism that occurred in American cities (and in the rural Midwest) during the Roaring Twenties and into the Dirty Thirties.

Prior to the mid 1920s, gangsters who were at war or who were seeking to settle a score or enforce discipline with deadly force almost always did so with pistols or knives. Gangland assassinations, for instance, were intimate and therefore messy affairs. Marksmanship could determine success, and considerable risks were involved in any effort to get close enough to ensure successful assassination.

The situation was dramatically altered by the introduction of the submachine gun. Developed for military use by Brigadier-General John Taliaferro Thompson, the "tommy gun," as it came to be known, altered the ecology and the dynamics of gangland violence (Helmer & Bilek, 2004). The weapon was able to fire 800 45-caliber rounds per minute and weighed only about 10 pounds (Helmer & Mattix, 1998). Each round could penetrate a quarter-inch steel plate and the gun could be used to stop a car in its tracks (Schoenberg, 1992). Owners of submachine guns were not required to have licenses, and at about $200.00 the price was right. With the introduction of the submachine gun, gangsters had at their disposal a far more intimidating and dangerous weapon. The gangland shooter no longer needed to get close to a victim (and therefore risk being shot or identified). Nor was it any longer necessary for the user of such a weapon to fire with accuracy. As long as one pointed the gun in the general direction of the target, the rapid-fire spray would probably mean that at least some of the bullets would find their mark.

The new weapon technology along with the automobile made drive-by shooting possible. We might tend to think of such crimes as an invention of Los Angeles gangs in the 1980s but of course their roots are much older, as widely reported shootouts involving gangsters such as Al Capone and many of his contemporaries demonstrate.

The increase in bank robberies by Depression-era bandits also made effective use of the new technologies. Bank robberies are more easily accomplished if one can brandish a frightening and wildly destructive weapon. As well, as the historian Claire Bond Potter (1998) says of the bandits of the Depression,

> At least one bank raid occurred every week in the tristate area in 1930. They almost always provoked a police chase, often joined by state troopers, vigilantes or deputized citizens. A combination of new paved highways and intricate back roads made it a land of opportunity for daring criminals who drove fast and knew the country well enough to elude pursuers. State lines were a short drive in any direction and several cities provided a full array of criminal services. (p. 67)

These examples suggest further ways in which crime is deskilled. As crimes become easier to commit they become more accessible to a wider group of potential offenders. In this way, technology can be seen to contribute rather directly to the contexts within which crime waves develop.

A more comprehensive attempt to explore the relationship between technology and crime level changes is provided by McQuade (1998). He begins by distinguishing between physical and social technologies. The former refers to the actual tools that are used to accomplish some task, while the latter refers to social practices. At any point in time, each type of technology can be either simple or very complex, and over time both forms of technology become more complex. The tendency toward technological innovation renders existing technologies obsolete as new technologies develop.

Crime, like all areas of human endeavor, has important technological dimensions. Indeed, criminal patterns themselves can be thought of as social technologies that are often accomplished through the use of physical technologies. To use a simple example, the practice of extortion is a kind of social technology in which particular forms of knowledge regarding victim behavior, risk, and potential gain are employed to accomplish a particular objective. The gun that might be used to efficiently threaten the extortion victim who is undecided about whether to cooperate is of course a kind of physical technology that facilitates the achievement of the offender's objectives.

Policing can also be understood to have important technological dimensions. Rapid response, law enforcement, or problem solving are all social technologies, facilitated through the use of computers, motor vehicles, radio communications, and other physical technologies. To a considerable degree the problem of crime and justice is a problem of technological struggle between offenders and policing agencies. Each attempts to use technology to gain an advantage over the other. In this way, particular methods of committing crimes become obsolete as policing becomes more effective. As well, particular styles of policing become obsolete as offenders develop adaptive technologies.

McQuade (1998) argues that because crime is technologically dynamic, it is useful to distinguish three categories of crime. The first category, Ordinary Crime, is most familiar. These are crimes that occur in a variety of places, are already prohibited by well-defined legal proscriptions, and are routinely documented by policing agencies. Burglary and robbery are Ordinary Crimes in this sense. In contrast, Adaptive Crimes are technological variations on Ordinary Crimes. To a considerable degree, Adaptive Crimes can be prosecuted with existing legal tools. Finally, what McQuade calls New Crimes involve radically innovative uses of novel or existing technologies. Such crimes occur rarely, and their occurrence may not be recognized as a pattern at first. The discovery of New Crimes may be of considerable interest to media outlets eager for novel stories, and public reaction may involve shock and amazement. At the same time, the technological uniqueness of new crimes means that the legal and prosecutorial tools to address the problems that New Crimes present may not be in place. In its early stages, "computer crime" exemplified this category in all significant respects. Over time, New Crimes become Adaptive Crimes and Adaptive Crimes become Ordinary Crimes.

McQuade (1998) argues that an understanding of the technological character of crime and policing helps us to make sense of the process by which crime rates rise and fall. When a number of New Crimes with similar content occur, a new "technology crime wave" is said to develop. For McQuade, such waves decline as countervailing police technologies develop to meet the challenge of these New Crimes. They gather steam in that lag time between their initial occurrences and the mobilization of a technologically adequate police response.

Conclusion

This chapter has considered a number of explanations as to why we might observe relatively sudden crime level variations. Obviously, theories about rapid crime changes need to take into account other elements of the social, cultural, and economic systems to which these changes can be meaningfully related.

Three types of change have been discussed in this chapter, each of which implies a rather distinct set of social processes. Processes of dislocation focus our attention on how ruptures in the social fabric might disconnect people from each other and create the circumstances conducive to crime rate increases. Arguments about diffusion encourage us to think about how particular kinds of criminal behaviors might roll through populations in ways that suggest a crime wave is under way. Finally, processes of innovation promote crime by introducing new elements into social life that upset the delicate balance between crime and conformity.

It is important to add that there is not necessarily any one explanation here that makes more sense than the others. All are important processes that might become more or less influential in particular circumstances at particular historical periods. As well, it is important to recognize that within real-life social contexts, these processes need not be as separable as this discussion has suggested. For example, innovations of a social or technological nature can of course be seen to diffuse throughout society. In a related way, wars not only cause social dislocations but also spur various sorts of technological development. The analyst of any specific crime level increase needs to be sensitive not only to the individual but also to the combined effects of the processes discussed in this chapter.

3

Crime Waves by the Numbers

This chapter is concerned with the statistical meaning of crime waves. Of course, one of the major ways in which we "know" a crime wave is under way is when crime statistics tell us so. Crime statistics, like many forms of social (and other) statistics, appear to us as objective facts. We contrast them in our minds with opinions or beliefs. Statistics, after all, are rich in scientific meaning (Pfuhl & Henry, 1993).

Most of us, however, have an uneasy relationship with social statistics. While we recognize numbers as facts, we also seem quite willing to dismiss statistics out of hand. "Figures don't lie," we sometimes say. But we also like to recall British statesman Benjamin Disraeli's observation that there are "lies, damned lies, and statistics." How this ambivalence is expressed with respect to crime statistics is an important issue and part of what concerns us in this chapter.

Our discussion of crime statistics parallels themes that are explored in other chapters. The most important of these themes concerns the issue of social constructionism. In contrast to the view that emphasizes statistics as objective reflections of the empirical world, we need to appreciate crime statistics as social constructions. Like other cultural products, they are outcomes of social processes. What do we count? Who counts? When do we count? How do we count? None of these questions has a preordained answer. Instead, our answers reflect social decisions. This is crucial. Crime statistics that reveal to us that a crime wave is under way are social constructions in precisely the same way that a nightly newscast about rising crime is a social construction.

Thus, crime statistics matter, as crime stories in the newspaper matter, because they encourage perceptions about the levels of crime in our society. There is an important difference, however. Most studies of crime news proceed from the assumption that to some degree public estimates of the amount and type of crime in society reflect the amount and type of crime we encounter in the news. The implication of such arguments is that we are all our own accountants. We make crude calculations about high or rising crime levels based on the amount of raw material the media present to us. By implication, the more crime we find in the news and other media, the more likely we are to think that crime is rising. But as Dennis Howitt (1982) argues, maybe we don't "do the math" ourselves. Rather, we need to recognize that one of the more common kinds of news story involves the routine reporting of crime statistics. In the most direct way, statistical news—about a "new threat" or "rising crime levels"—provides the members of the public with the most immediate evidence that crime is on the rise.

In general, then, it is essential that we understand where crime statistics come from. Moreover, since most of us who do encounter crime statistics do so in the mass media, it is important as well for us to appreciate how crime statistics become news and what kinds of news they become.

Numerate and Innumerate Consumers

Our starting point in this discussion, though, is the end point of the process— the "average" consumers of crime statistics. For many observers, the love-hate relationship with social statistics of all kinds is rooted in the high levels of innumeracy among members of the general public. The term *innumeracy* connotes a condition comparable in many ways to the more familiar concept of illiteracy (Paulos, 1988). Most of us pride ourselves on being literate and understand the serious problems likely to befall anyone who is not literate. Innumeracy, however, is less well understood as a problem. Still, many (if not most) people lack even a rudimentary understanding of how social statistics are generated, how they need to be interpreted, or what we can or cannot learn from them. As mathematician John Allen Paulos (1988) has written, "The same people who can understand the subtlest emotional nuances in conversation, the most convoluted plots in literature and the most intricate aspects of a legal case can't seem to grasp the most basic elements of a mathematical demonstration" (p. 118).

Innumeracy can take many forms. One of the most problematic is what some analysts have referred to as "number numbness" (Dewdney, 1993). This can be defined as a widespread inability to make sense of numbers that are very large or very small. Number numbness can create problems when we attempt to make sense of crime levels without a proper context. For instance, according to Bureau of Justice Statistics data, in the year 2000 there were 1,949 homicides in the United States involving victims 50 years of age or over (Bureau of Justice Statistics, 2002). On its own the number is huge. Indeed, it is about 50% of the homicide figure we find for the group for whom we might naturally expect murder to be a much more serious problem—those aged between 18 and 24. For this group, the number of homicides in 2000 was 3,933.

In the case of older Americans, the figure represents untold amounts of pain, suffering, and grief on the part of family members left behind. It describes almost 2,000 lives cut short, plans uncompleted, and dreams unfulfilled. The tragedy implicit in such a number is not in question. However, tragedy is relative, and when we contextualize this number with reference to the size of the population involved, we get a somewhat different perspective. If we ask how many homicides this represents in a relative sense, the number is, as these things go, a relatively small one. One thousand nine hundred forty-nine homicides of people 50 years of age or over represents a rate of 2.5 homicides for every 100,000 people in this age group. Those aged between 18 and 24 have a murder rate that is six times higher: 14.9 per 100,000. To focus only on the size of these (large) numbers without a sense of their context is to lose any understanding of relative risk. Even when numbers are carefully compiled (as homicide statistics usually are), they rarely tell the whole story (Best, 2001a).

Our innumeracy creates confusion in many different ways. On the one hand, we are suspicious when arguments are made to us without statistics (Crossen, 1994). At the same time, we tend to lack the tools that might allow us to react with appropriate skepticism. As Paulos (1988) notes, mathematical certainty (even if unfounded) can be invoked to "bludgeon the innumerate into a dumb acquiescence" (p. 67). Minimally, our innumeracy makes it difficult for us to appreciate the complexity or nuances of arguments about how much crime there is or about how much the levels are changing.

Several factors can be used to explain contemporary levels of innumeracy. Critics point, for instance, to the lack of rigorous mathematical education in schools (Paulos, 1988). Many people have never taken even a basic statistics course, which would teach the skills necessary to evaluate statistical information (Crossen, 1994). In addition, while most people would feel extreme embarrassment about being illiterate, no such stigma seems to adhere to innumeracy. Indeed, people (even many professors) often speak with pride about their inability to use or understand statistics. In fact, it is not the innumerate, but the highly numerate who are often stigmatized in our society when we speak, for instance, of the "math nerd" (Dewdney, 1993). As well, many people have trouble with the impersonality of mathematics. In the mass media, we are encouraged to think about the personal and the emotional. In our news and in our public rhetoric, we often seem much more comfortable with drama and emotion than with statistics (Cohl, 1997). In part, this reflects a widespread sense that there is something fundamentally impersonal, or even dehumanizing, about social statistics (Paulos, 1998). As a consequence, we are free to interpret an inability to come to terms with statistical arguments as a healthy indicator of the depth of our humanity.

The Statistics of Crime Waves

Arguments about crime waves are, in one sense, arguments about how crime waves change over time. Can we say with some degree of statistical certainty that crime has gotten worse? Of course, "gotten worse" is a highly problematic phrase. It might mean that crime is becoming more violent or that the violence is becoming more vicious. It might mean that crime, however violent or vicious, has begun to victimize more vulnerable victims. Usually, though, the claim that crime is getting worse is a claim about how crime levels are increasing. But this too is problematic. Whether we think about crime rates as higher (or lower) depends on the comparison point. During the 1990s, for instance, overall crime rates were falling but they were still higher than they had been at the midpoint of the 20th century (Mosher, Miethe, & Phillips, 2002). Although the data are somewhat unreliable, the best estimates of long-term trends suggest that, at least since the 17th century, American crime patterns have been cyclical, with a major peak in the middle of the 19th century (Brantingham & Brantingham, 1984). Resolving arguments about crime level changes over time turns out to be a rather complicated business. It is not a surprise, then, that the average consumer of crime statistics as found in mass media or in political speeches (or shoddy pop scholarship) is often confused.

Statistics in the Raw

We have already seen how dangerous it is to make casual interpretations of raw numbers. It follows logically that efforts to determine whether a crime wave is under way will be undermined if we rely unduly on such numbers, yet errors in this respect are easy to make. A relatively small number of very high visibility crimes can occur within a rather short period of time. If our observations are not grounded in some broader perspective, it may appear that some problem is indeed rapidly deteriorating.

Consider, for instance, the celebrated cases of road rage that occurred during the 1980s and again in the 1990s (Best, 1991; Fumento, 1998; Glassner, 1999). While the "epidemic" nature of the problem was taken as a given in many quarters, researchers were hard pressed to find careful and systematic evidence of more aggressive driving on the nation's roads, especially when account was taken of the numbers of drivers on the road and the number of miles driven. It might even be argued that the celebrity crimes of corporate offenders in the early years of the 21st century suggest similar phenomena. The rapid discovery of crimes involving Enron, Global Crossing, "domestic maven" Martha Stewart, and others within a very short period of time, led many to argue that a "corporate crime wave" was under way. While the designation had a certain rhetorical flair, its substantive meaning remains uncertain. We might ask, after all, about the rate of such crimes relative to the number of corporations and about whether such a rate had changed during the period in question. As we will see in our discussion of crime news in the next chapter, it is easy to come to such conclusions. It is, after all, the rarity of events that makes them noteworthy and newsworthy. While a school shooting, for instance, might attract widespread attention, two school shootings (an even rarer event) will attract even more attention and become the subject of even greater public discussion.

There is a further ironic twist to the use of raw numbers as indicators of crime wave trends. It can be argued that even if the actual rate at which some phenomenon occurs is in decline, some will read the data as indicating a worsening problem. "Worse" in this sense might mean that the problem continues (even though it does so at reduced levels). It is not therefore the relative rate at which incidents occur but the fact that cases continue to occur at all that can promote the conclusion that a crime problem is deteriorating, even while it might be improving. So, for example, we might learn that 10 murders occurred in our city last year and 5 occurred this year. While the reduction might indicate a shrinking problem, some will be less struck by the relative rate of occurrence and more struck by the observation that five more of their fellow residents died this year.

Some psychologists have noted our tendency to discern clear patterns in randomly occurring events. When we flip a coin, for instance, we expect heads and tails to alternate more often than they actually do. What we observe are clumps of heads or clumps of tails. While these clumps, or runs, of head or tails are perfectly consistent with a notion of randomness, the fluctuations appear more patterned than they are. In the same way, the chance or purely random fluctuations in the stock market, for instance, can look to uninformed observers like a disturbing or promising trend. The occurrence of a small number of unusual or particularly aberrant crimes might not indicate any real statistical trends, no matter how much we talk about these crimes or how confidently or how loudly journalists declare the existence of such a trend. As Gilovich (1991) notes, this tendency to recognize patterns in empirical phenomena is a very important skill. It is, after all, the way in which great scientific advances are made. However, the discovery of patterns when none exist can easily lead us astray (Paulos, 1988).

Small, raw numbers can also create serious problems when they are converted to percentages. This is because percentages can hide unimportant or random differences. So, for example, if one attack on a tourist in a resort town occurred last year and two occurred this year, we have two ways of expressing what we have observed. On the one hand, we might say that one additional person was attacked (and that the differences between the two years can be attributed to chance). On the other hand, we might state boldly that attacks to the resort town increased by 100%. The second statement is much more ominous than the first.

Barry Glassner (1999) demonstrates the problem with reference to an American Automobile Association study of road rage. According to Glassner, the study concluded that during the 1990s, road rage incidents were increasing at a rate of 7% per year such that by 1997, the rate had increased almost 50%. The problem, however, is that the study actually compares two relatively modest absolute numbers. The number of such events was 1,129 in 1990 and 1,800 by 1996–1997. The difference is a grand total of 671 incidents, and these incidents are spread over millions of drivers in 50 states over a 7-year period.

Jacobs and Henry (1996) have provided a similar critique of data offered in support of claims about a "hate crime wave." The authors analyzed New York City police department data that purported to show that for the first 4 months of 1990 there was a 12% increase in hate crimes when compared to the same period of 1989. Of perhaps greatest concern, it was argued, was that the number of hate crimes directed toward Asians almost doubled between 1989 and 1990. The authors maintain that a closer examination of the data tells a more complicated story. According to Jacobs and Henry, there were 11 bias crimes against Asians in the first 4 months of 1990 as compared to 22 reports for all of 1989. The question posed by Jacobs and Henry is a provocative one: Is an increase of 11 incidents really all that alarming in a city that for 1990 was home to 512,719 Asian residents and the setting for 710,222 index crimes?

Another questionable use of raw numbers in the tracking of crime waves involves the presentation of such numbers in ways that suggest they have somehow been standardized when in reality they have not. One of the major devices used in the creation of this misimpression is the *crime clock*. The crime clock is a method of data presentation that purports to show the frequency of crime in a way that takes the timing of the offences into account. While crime clocks are widely used by the FBI and many other policing organizations, they have a rather deceptive character.

The crime clock described in Figure 3.1, for instance, indicates that in the United States in 2002 there was a violent crime committed every 22.1 seconds. How is this figure arrived at? The estimate involves two quantities. One is an estimate of the police-reported violent crimes. For the United States in 2002 that number is 1,426,325. The second figure we require is a count of the number of seconds in a year. This figure is easily calculated (365 days × 24 hours × 60 minutes × 60 seconds) as 31,536,000. Dividing the former figure into the latter yields the estimate of one violent crime every 22.1 seconds.

While this number looks suspiciously like a "crime rate," it really is not. A crime rate counts the number of crimes relative to the variable size of some at-risk population. Rates are usually expressed per 1,000 or per 100,000 members of the population. In the present case, the rate of violent crime in the United States would be calculated as

$$\frac{1,426,325 \text{ violent crimes}}{288,368,698 \text{ people in the population}} \times 100,000 \text{ (constant)}$$

2002

Every 2.7 seconds: One Crime Index Offense

Every 22.1 seconds: One Violent Crime

Every 35.3 seconds: One Aggravated Assault

Every 1.2 minutes: One Robbery

Every 5.5 minutes: One Forcible Rape

Every 32.4 minutes: One Murder

Every 3.0 seconds: One Property Crime

Every 4.5 seconds: One Larceny-Theft

Every 14.7 seconds: One Burglary

Every 25.3 seconds: One Motor Vehicle Theft

Figure 3.1   Crime Clock

The rate of violent crime for the year 2002 is 494.6 crimes per 100,000 members of the population.

It may appear that crime rates and crime clocks are telling us the same things but they are not. The reason is simple. The size of the population is a variable, and as we calculate changes in the crime rate from year to year we are taking into account not only how the number of crimes changes, but also how the size of the population changes. In contrast, the number of seconds in a year is not a variable but a fixed quantity. To see what difference this makes, compare the data from the year 1983 with the data from the year 2002.

In 1983, there were fewer violent crimes measured in an absolute sense (1,258,087) and a smaller population (233,791,994), but of course the same number of seconds in the year (31,536,000). The rate of violent crime per 100,000 members of the population is quite a bit higher (538.1). The crime clock, however, would suggest that we can expect a slightly longer gap between violent crimes, at every 25 rather than every 22 seconds. Clearly, the crime clock misleads us into thinking that we are seeing the data in some way that standardizes these numbers, when in reality all we are seeing are raw numbers presented in a more rhetorically impressive manner. Clearly, we can think of circumstances in which the crime rate might remain the same from year to year (because the number of crimes and the size of the population grow in proportionate ways) while the crime clocks suggest that a major crime wave might be under way.

Emergent Problems

Sometimes it is useful to make a distinction between established and emergent crime problems. The differences have to do with the relative newness of the category in question. Crime problems like homicide or vandalism or white-collar crime have relatively long cultural and legal histories. In contrast, crime categories like "home invasion," "carjacking," "cyberstalking," or "road rage" are relatively recent inventions. Of course, many of the behaviors to which these labels apply might predate the labels themselves by many years. What is new is the socially constructed character of the category to which the label applies. As Best (1999) has shown, the last couple of decades of the 20th century saw the creation of a number of categories of new crimes and new victims. When we speak of these categories in ways that assign them a kind of taken-for-granted reality, we often lose sight of their socially constructed character. It is important for us to recognize that these crime categories exist as ways of classifying experiences, assessing moral worth, and as objects of public discussion only because claims about the need to recognize these problems have been effectively made.

As argued in the Chapter 1, the successful construction of a new social problem depends upon the ability of claims-makers to impress upon audiences of lawmakers, journalists, and the members of the general public that the problem is serious and deserving of attention. One of the ways this is accomplished is through statistical arguments that provide dramatic and compelling evidence that the problem is a sizeable and growing one.

Such arguments might provide the first occasion on which most of us ever hear about the problem or about its dimensions. Often we are asked to draw an implicit kind of contrast between the present and some sort of idealized past in which the problem was less serious or did not exist at all. Of course, such implicit comparisons require critical scrutiny. Jacobs and Potter (1997), for instance, argue that in the case of hate crime we are asked to believe that rates are at an all-time high. This is difficult to accept, however, given the history of near genocide of native peoples and racist violence against African Americans.

One problem facing those who attempt to make the statistical case for new crime problems is that these compelling statistical data often do not exist. Indeed, a lack of statistical information can be interpreted as a kind of proof that no one is bothering to take the problem seriously. In other words, we tend to document problems that concern us and ignore those that do not. Yet even in the absence of trend data, claims-makers still need to be able to argue that this problem is either as bad as it has ever been or that it is getting worse.

Where will such numbers come from? In some cases, they are simply "guesstimates" provided by those who seek to establish the problem's legitimacy (Best, 2001). As Neil Gilbert (1997) notes, in the early stages of social problems construction it might be only those who are most deeply interested in the problem who bother to think about and try to convince others regarding the frequency or growth of a crime problem. Victims groups and victim advocates of various sorts may be those who are expected to speak to the statistical dimensions of the problem to which they seek to direct our attention. This sort of vested interest in a problem's development can be accompanied by a real interest in the production of numbers that are big and growing and very little interest in the production of numbers that might be correct (Reuter, 1984).

In the case of the missing children crime wave of the 1980s, an early estimate by Jay Howell, executive director of the National Center for Missing and Exploited Children, estimated that between 4,000 and 20,000 children were abducted by strangers each year (Forst & Blomquist, 1991). Other estimates placed the number of missing children at between 1.8 and 2 million (Best & Thibodeau, 1998). Many individuals involved in law enforcement critiqued these estimates and suggested that the number of children abducted by strangers might be much closer to 100. Indeed, they argued that the very large numbers simply did not make sense in terms of personal experience. Over fifty thousand Americans died in Vietnam, and most people knew someone whose family was affected by the war in this way. But how many of us know someone whose child was abducted by a stranger? Despite such objections, these large estimates of the number of missing children were widely accepted as correct (Forst & Blomquist, 1991).

While guesses sometimes serve to give emergent problems statistical form, another approach is to reconfigure existing data in ways that provide the needed numbers. Perhaps the best example of this phenomenon in recent years was provided by Philip Jenkins's (1994) discussion of the serial killer crime wave in the 1980s. Early estimates of the size (and hence the seriousness) of the serial killer problem estimated that as many as 20% of all American homicides in any given year might be the work of serial killers. But where did this number come from? Unlike some early social problem estimates, it was not just made up. Rather, it came from a skillful if curious reinterpretation of official homicide data.

Using police-reported crime data, some justice officials estimated that between 1976 and 1985 about 17% of all homicide circumstances were listed as "unknown." During the same period, 29% of all homicides indicated that the relationship between the victim and the offender was "unknown." In a further 16% of cases, it was revealed that the offender was a stranger to the victim. For the year 1983, then, these officials made the unwarranted assumption that most of the unknown and stranger homicides were the work of serial killers. As Jenkins argues, the essential problem here is the implicit assumption that an unknown homicide circumstance is the same as "no apparent motive," and that no apparent motive is the same as "motiveless." Such statistical sleight of hand meant that missing information could be imaginatively transformed into information of a particular kind, and the result was an estimate of the number of serial killer victims in the 4,000 to 5,000 range.

Why are large and increasing numbers so important to those who seek to establish a beachhead with respect to an emergent crime problem? Most obviously, they show that a problem is important *because* it is widespread. When the numbers are large, those who have been personally affected by the problem can believe that they are part of a larger social dynamic. Those who are not personally affected (and have no basis for judgment) are likely to be impressed by estimates of the widespread and worsening problem (Best & Thibodeau, 1998). Often the impact of large numbers can be personalized through rhetorical forms that indicate that "1 in 10," or "1 in 4," or even "1 in 2" people will experience the problem.

There is a further ideological benefit that derives from large and increasing numbers. They tend to move the search for the causes of crime waves away from individuals and toward broader social, economic, or historical factors (Gilbert, 1994). Often those who seek to formulate new problem definitions also seek to promote social change and to avoid victim-blaming. Of course, large numbers are useful in this respect in that they encourage the search for depersonalized explanations of crime waves.

Big numbers are important not only for putting an issue on the agenda for public debate and discussion but also for keeping it there (Gilbert, 1997; Nelson, 1984). The inability to show that a problem is getting worse, or at least as bad as it has always been, can cause relevant parties such as journalists or lawmakers to lose interest. According to Cook and Skogan (1990), this is exactly what happened in the case of the elderly victimization crime wave of the 1970s. Early research, which employed very inadequate sampling and measurement techniques, suggested that the elderly were the most frequently victimized group in society. Starting in 1972, however, data from the methodologically rigorous National Crime Survey began to show with remarkable consistency that this was not the case. In fact, these data showed year after year that the elderly were the least—not the most—likely to become victims of crime. In the presence of such a statistical onslaught, arguments for a crime wave against the elderly began to collapse.

Of course, sometimes the opposite happens. Initial problem estimates can be quite resistant to challenges from more carefully conducted, state-sponsored research. This process is an interesting one. Claims-makers who have a direct interest in the development of a new social problem tend to promote large estimates of the problem. In the absence of other estimates, these numbers become the only game in town (Best, 2001). Moreover, such numbers are typically understood by their advocates and by audiences as underestimates. Because it is always easy to show that there exist cases that we don't learn about, these often inflated numbers gain additional credibility. As these numbers gain legitimacy (and are the only numbers available for a period) they can become resistant to challenge. When later, more carefully conducted, and often more disinterested research is undertaken it may provide considerably lower estimates. These revised estimates are sometimes read by critics as an attempt on the part of government officials to deny the gravity of the problem.

More generally, as Gillespie and Leffler (1987) argue, data collection methods always have political overtones and the burden of proof will always rest with those whose research challenges the status quo. Their methodologies will be subject to greater scrutiny by those who are proponents of the definitions of the problem the new results challenge.

Statistical Record Keeping as a Social Process

The collection of any kind of crime data can be understood as a social constructionist process. What ends up in any kind of crime tally is a product of a large number of interlocking decisions made by a wide variety of actors involved in the process.

This is true with respect to both of the two major data sources used by criminological researchers: the Uniform Crime Reports and the victimization survey (MacKenzie, Baunach, & Roberg, 1990; Mosher et al., 2002; O'Brien, 1985). The Uniform Crime Reports (UCR) are often referred to as "police data." UCR data are gathered and collated by individual policing agencies according to a standardized set of reporting rules. The data are submitted to the FBI and made available to criminal justice agencies and other interested users nationally on an annual basis. The crime clock (discussed earlier) represents one of the most famous outputs of the UCR system.

The other major data source is what is known as the victimization survey. Such studies attempt to generate counts of crime by asking people directly about their experiences during some specified period of crime (e.g., during the previous 6 months). Many researchers claim that since the counts are generated directly from the members of the general public (rather than by the police), they are more accurate measures. This is because they are unaffected by the vagaries of criminal justice system processing. The best-known example of the victimization survey is the National Crime Victimization Survey, which has been an important data source since its inception in 1972 (Bureau of Justice Statistics, 2002).

The point we need to appreciate is a more general one—in either case, the production of crime data must be understood as a social activity. Rather than passively reflecting some objective world of crime, they actively construct a subjective world of crime. It is of course in the nature of social constructions that we often end up thinking of the worlds we have constructed as having an independent existence (Brownstein, 1996). In other words, we reify these statistics and relate to them as though they have a much more rigorous existence than they actually have.

What does it really mean to say that social statistics are social constructions? There is really nothing mystical or mysterious about this process, although it is complicated and involves many different elements (Coleman & Moynihan, 1996). Consider, for instance, the UCR counts of assault. If a woman is struck by her husband, does she, in the first instance, think of the incident as a legal infraction that should be reported to the law? Perhaps not. Certainly there have been strong cultural pressures that have encouraged women and men to think about assaults of this sort as somehow "different" or more normal than other kinds of assault. If she does think of it as an assault, does she phone the police? Maybe, but maybe not. Perhaps she might be worried that the police won't really protect her and that her actions might put her at greater risk in the future. Or maybe she is too ashamed or blames herself for what has happened. If she phones the police, do they send a squad car? If they do send a squad car, do they decide a "crime" has been committed? If they decide a crime has been committed, do they decide to treat it officially? If they do treat it officially, can we be confident that this piece of data won't get lost in the police information system?

All of this is to say that crime levels end up being what they are as a result of a very large number of interlocking decisions of this type. This does not imply that these decisions are simply made in some random fashion, since this is clearly not the case. Citizen reporting, police deployment, and police discretion, for instance, are themselves socially patterned and predictable (Gottfedson & Gottfredson, 1988). Nor is it to say that there is never any sort of relationship between the number of crimes objectively occurring and the number of crimes that end up in our statistical tallies. In the case of legally defined homicides, for example, the counts in UCR records quite closely approximate the number of murder victims in society. But even in this case, our decision to treat some kinds of killing (but not other kinds) as murder or the judgments made by coroners in mysterious circumstances point to a social constructionist process (Box, 1981; Douglas, 1967). It is important to add, as well, that these processes are largely organizational in nature. How police, victim interest groups, statistical agencies, or other criminal justice bodies construct crime depends on the cultures and the structures of these organizations. The implication is important. Statistical crime waves come and go at least in part because of the manner in which these organizational process change over time. There are several interesting complications in this respect.

REDEFINITION

If our legal definitions of crime can be thought of as categories, then statistical record keeping, at a very fundamental level, involves sorting experiences into such categories. If the categories change over time, then of course so will the number and the kinds of experiences that get sorted into them (Maxfield & Babbie, 1995). Several authors, for instance, have pointed to the highly variable ways in which important concepts like "gang" and "gang behavior" are defined over time or across jurisdictions for policy and therefore for statistical purposes (Katz, 2003; McCorkle & Miethe, 2002; Peterson, 2000).

Such a situation helps explain, in some cases, why measured levels of crime shoot upward rapidly. Barry Glassner (1999) argues, for instance, that as time went on, the conceptual category of "road rage" became wider and wider. Eventually, it included incidents that did not even involve violence or happen on highways. At one extreme, he points out, is labeling as road rage an incident in which one individual engaged in tailgating before being involved in an accident. Joel Best (2001) makes a similar point with respect to the growth of child abuse during the 1960s. The deterioration of the problem, advocates said, was evident from the fact that the number of reported cases grew from 150,000 in 1963 to 3 million in 1995. Importantly, Best points out, over that period the definition of child abuse broadened to include not only physical violence but also emotional abuse and neglect. In a similar way, Chasteen (2001) notes, feminist redefinitions of rape have encouraged an understanding of the crime as involving an increasingly wider range of behaviors that share as a common element the violation of a woman's nonconsent.

TOLERANCE

How much crime we end up counting depends to some degree on the level of tolerance for crime. In this regard, we can think about tolerance as an individual as well as a community-level phenomenon (Horowitz, 1987). Thus, individuals might differ from each other with respect to how severe an offense must be before they are willing to call the police, and communities might have very different standards regarding what does and what does not offend local standards of conduct.

In this respect it is useful to distinguish between reactive and proactive policing (Black, 1970). In simple terms, the former refers to those instances in which police get involved in the lives of citizens as a reaction to a request from a member of the public that they do so. Proactive policing, on the other hand, refers to the kind of citizen contact that police personnel themselves initiate. Most kinds of crime come to the attention of the police as a result of the former type of mobilization. In other words, at least with most standard forms of victimization, the police become involved because someone—usually a victim, a victim's relative, or a witness—phones the police or flags down a squad car (Gottfredson & Gottfedson, 1988).

Research suggests that victims often don't call the police because they assume (quite correctly) that there is really very little the police can do in particular situations. Often as well, they tell victimization researchers, they do not call the police because the crime was a relatively minor one. In addition, people may be less interested in calling the police if they have other options available to them for dealing with the situation. In the case of wife assault and sexual assault, women often do not call the police for other kinds of reasons. They fear the offender or the misogynist stigma traditionally associated with these crimes.

Clearly, the willingness to report crimes to the police can vary over time. For instance, greater public discussion of various kinds of victimization might encourage more victims to come forward. To the degree that the police take special care to encourage reporting, through public relations efforts or through the development of special programs, reports to the police could escalate (Sacco & Silverman, 1982). In this sense, we can imagine how a rising crime rate could fuel further reporting (Loseke, 1999). Calling the police is in a sense a form of censure and as the willingness to tolerate crime at an individual level decreases, our crime statistics may increase.

Proactive policing suggests a parallel set of issues at the community level. In this case, we need to recognize that crime counts can reflect the eagerness or the aggressiveness with which policing agencies pursue particular kinds of tasks. Crimes involving drug sales, for instance, are unlikely to be reported by the buyer or the seller. It is really up to the police to discover such crimes, and how many they discover will depend on the way in which they utilize available human and financial resources.

Programs of so-called zero tolerance in schools, for instance, demonstrate easily the point being made here. Such policies are characterized by the corporate decision to treat troublesome behavior officially. In other words, in the school system, the policy of dealing with school violence informally is replaced by a policy stating that the police will be called in ALL cases. It seems pretty obvious that one immediate consequence of such a policy would be a rapid increase in the number of cases entering the official record.

BOOKKEEPING QUALITY

Any systematic attempt to collect large amounts of data will be plagued by errors. This will happen despite the best intentions of all concerned. Cases will be overlooked or recorded incorrectly. In complex data systems, there are problems of "case attrition." Simply put, cases that enter the system get lost somewhere along the way. We can expect more problems to occur the larger the amount of data that needs to be processed. It has also been argued that the errors might be most acute with respect to the cases that occur least frequently. In other words, a few serious cases buried in the midst of large numbers of nonserious cases might more easily be lost.

Of course, improvements in data collection can reduce dramatically the number of errors that occur. A hallmark of highly professionalized policing agencies is the tendency to take collection and record maintenance very seriously. Again, a consequence of better and more faithful record keeping could be an increase in the rate at which crimes are recorded.

THE MANIPULATION OF STATISTICAL RECORDS

There are all kinds of reasons why state (and other) agencies in society might seek to manipulate crime statistics in a deliberate fashion. As some scholars have argued, it is helpful to think about the statistics maintained by social agencies as a kind of bureaucratic propaganda (Altheide & Johnson, 1980). Accordingly, such statistics serve to convince others of the legitimacy of the organization in question.

For instance, the police might wish to create a public impression that they are doing a good job, or that particular policies that are intended to control crime are working effectively. It has been argued that in the 1970s, crime rates in many major American cities fell as a result of deliberate efforts to make the statistical case that the crime control policies of the Nixon administration were working well (Mosher et al., 2002). Alternatively, there may be strong bureaucratic pressure to keep the numbers high or even to show them increasing. In such circumstances, statistics can be used to make a powerful argument about the need for new resources to combat a problem that appears to be spiraling out of control.

Of course, crime statistics also reflect on the prestige and reputation of the area or organization for which reports are made. In this respect, Maier (1991) reports that some New York City police precincts used to deliberately suppress their crime statistics to protect the reputation of particular neighborhoods. In a somewhat different way, Mosher and colleagues (2002) describe how statistical reports of university and college crime have been manipulated in order to protect the reputation of particular educational institutions. Although state and federal governments mandate the collection of such data, it is obvious that high university or college crime rates will worry the parents of potential freshman and embarrass the alumni. One very obvious case of such manipulation is evident in the actions of University of Pennsylvania officials in 1996. In its federally mandated report, the university indicated that 18 robberies had occurred, whereas the police reported 181. The university was able to keep the numbers down by not reporting incidents that had taken place on streets that crossed the campus or in buildings that it did not own.

The notion that "numbers speak for themselves" is true only to the extent that we fail to exercise critical judgment. Often, the graphs and charts that are supposed to unambiguously show particular kinds of trends are themselves forms of manipulation. Consider Figure 3.2, which shows a dramatic upward shift in a hypothetical rate of homicide over a 5-year period. The visual image is striking but its meaning is unclear for obvious reasons. While the graph shows the period over which the change occurs, it does not show the units of measurement of the homicide rate (Huff, 1954). Are Points A and B 10 and 25 incidents per 100,000?; or 10 and 10.2 respectively? There is no way to tell.

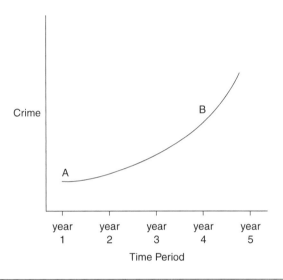

Figure 3.2   Hypothetical Crime Levels Over Time

James D. Orcutt and J. Blake Turner (1993) show how drug use data were presented in *Newsweek* magazine in ways that lent statistical credence to the magazine's claim that a "coke plague" was under way in America. While the authors did not dispute the reality of a drug problem, they did question the relationship between the data with which the graphic artists were working and artwork they produced for the magazine.

Statistics in the Media

The media have the ability to take claims that are issued elsewhere in the society and diffuse them widely. In the process, however, the media turn those claims into various forms of news and entertainment.

One consistent feature of this transformation is the detachment of statistics from the research methods that produce them. An interesting non-criminological example of this problem is the "one rat for every person" statistic (Sullivan, 2004). In short, it is widely believed and frequently reported that in large cities the rat population is approximately equal to the human population, yet few people know the source of this statistical estimate. It origins are to be found in a study of the rat population in England conducted in 1909 by an investigator named W. R. Boelter. He surveyed the English countryside (leaving out towns and cities) and concluded that there was roughly one rat for each acre of cultivated land. At the time, there were about 40,000,000 acres of cultivated land in England, thereby yielding an estimate of about 40,000,000 rats. As well, by historical coincidence, the population of England at the time also happened to be about 40,000,000. Thus while in England in 1909 it made a certain amount of sense to talk about the parity of the rat and human populations, there is nothing generalizable about this statistic. While numbers can assume lives of their own, the methodology that generates them is less well known. Of course, it is difficult to critique a statistic when its origins are unknown.

In a related way, we learn from watching television or reading the newspaper that crime problems are big and getting bigger. We tend to find out relatively little, by contrast, about how we know what we know about the statistical dimensions of crime problems. The claims-making that surrounded the emergence of the problem of elder abuse in the 1980s is a good case in point. As the problem was being established, many advocates argued that "one million elderly people are abused in America every year." As Best (1999) has noted, there is something magical about the one million figure, and it is surprising how many social problems seem to reach this benchmark. But where did the figure of one million abused elders come from? According to Steven Crystal (1988), the estimate came from a survey mailed out to 433 elderly residents of the Washington, D.C., area. Respondents to the survey were asked about several types of abuse including physical, psychological, material, and medical abuse as well as neglect. Seventy-three people or about 17% of the total sample responded. Of that number only 3 people (or 4%) reported abuse. Advocates argued that if that 4% figure were extrapolated to all elderly Americans it would represent one million victims. The problem, of course, is that the estimate is too unreliable to allow such an inference to be made with any degree of confidence: Each victim in the sample would have to represent 333,333 people.

Two broad questions need to be addressed in an analysis of media treatments of crime statistics. First, how do such statistics enter the news flow? Second, how are statistical reports packaged so that they are consistent with our understanding of what news is? Each of these questions is addressed below.

WHERE DOES STATISTICAL NEWS COME FROM?

The origin of statistical crime news is potentially quite diverse. In practice, however, most news of this type seems to emerge out of the pronouncements issued in one form or another by state agencies (Sacco, 2000b). It is sometime argued that any kind of unsubstantiated statistical claim can find its way into news. While this is true, journalistic practices tend to favor "official statistics" for the same reasons that journalistic sources tend to favor official news of all sorts (Ericson, Baranek, & Chan, 1989; Gans, 1979). Like other kinds of "official news," official statistics are widely perceived as authoritative and objective, and they can be easily accessed by journalists (Brownstein, 1996). Those involved in news production, however, like most members of society, lack the training and background that allow them to dissect the methods that produce crime statistics (Cohl, 1997). Not surprisingly, therefore, they prefer numbers that many members of their audiences will perceive as being above any type of partisan fray. Journalists feel little inclination to look elsewhere for alternative statistics—especially when the resolution of any such debate might necessitate a side trip into arcane methodological topics that journalists aren't qualified to address and in which audience members are not really interested (Crossen, 1994). Federal and state agencies, policing services, and university researchers, for instance, have well-articulated relationships with media agencies and are important sources of "official numbers" (Fishman, 1978).

One of the reasons official statistics dominate the news has to do with the more general nature of crime coverage. By and large, the kinds of crime problems to which news media attend are those that are already on the public agenda. Thus, the media tend to be more involved in problem maintenance than in problem construction (Nelson, 1984). The official (and quasi-official) agencies assigned the responsibility to collect routine crime information become the major source of statistical news.

Of course, in those circumstances for which no other data are available, journalists must turn elsewhere for statistical estimates. Their sources in such cases are likely to include members of victim advocate groups. Alternatively, journalists might access frontline workers whose estimates of the size of the problem are are drawn from experience with, for instance, victims in shelters for battered women or abuse hotlines (Gilbert, 1994).

STATISTICS AND THE NEWS FLOW

On its own merits, a statistical report might not be the most newsworthy of items. How, then, do crime statistics become news? Like other kinds of claims about social problems, statistics need to be hung on some kind of news hook. Research suggests that crime statistics enter the news flow in three distinct ways (Sacco, 2000b).The first involves the data release. On an annual or other regular basis, federal, state, or municipal agencies release data that describe crime trends or data on new crime problems. Typically, the agency will make available a press release with key findings and user-friendly charts and graphs. Such new stories often concern trends, shifting crime patterns, or emerging problems.

A second major news hook involves articles or news items that question existing beliefs about rates of crime (Gilbert, 1994). For instance, a researcher might release the results of a study that causes us to ask whether rates of rape or sexual assault or abuse are as low as they have sometimes been made out to be. Best (1988) showed, for instance, how the *Denver Post* and other newspapers covered the "missing child" issue in the early days of problem construction in ways that seriously questioned the estimates put forth by advocates. In a similar way, Anthony Doob (1995) discussed how Canadian media critiqued the high estimates of violence against women yielded by a national survey by calling into question the motives and the methods of the researchers.

A third type of news hook involves the use of statistics as "background" information with respect to some more substantive theme. A feature magazine or newspaper article about rising rates of road rage, for instance, might include, as a sidebar, a graph showing recent increases in the size of the problem. Typically, these data might be presented with little comment regarding either the sources of the data or the variety of interpretations that might be made of them.

STATISTICAL NEWS AND NEWS VALUES

Like other kinds of news, stories about statistics need to polished and molded in order to fit the demands and the conventions of the medium in question. This can be accomplished in a variety of ways.

Statistical News Can Be Entertaining

As stated, there is a widespread view among both journalists and members of the general public that statistics are not all that interesting. It is necessary, therefore, to dress such stories up in ways that increase their entertainment value. In this respect, journalists might, for instance, make use of irony and humor. News articles dealing with a national study on car theft, for instance, might talk about which city will be awarded the "car theft crown." Graphics can also be used to intensify the dramatic feel of a news presentation. In the study of drug use trends described by Orcutt and Turner (1993), the data described patterns of use but the graphic purported to describe a "coke plague."

One major strategy is to turn statistical stories into human interest stories. This is accomplished by putting a "human face on the figures." A report of a study of child abuse, for instance, might begin with a narrative about the abuse of one particular child. The focus of the story is then on the ways in which the case is typical of a larger problem that is described by the study.

Statistical News Is Important

Statistical claims become important news when journalists emphasize the significance of the findings. A study of violence against women, we are told, is a "landmark study" with wide-ranging implications. Research pointing to "a national shame," as it was claimed the early studies of elder abuse did, or that "confirms our worst fears," as studies of gang violence are sometimes claimed to do, are packaged as more than mere social science.

Statistical News Is Objective News

If statistical news tends to consist largely of government pronouncements, how are media able to construct themselves as objective? One way this is accomplished is through efforts on the part of journalists to promote a self-critical style. In a way that seems to suggest real disinterestedness, news articles often speak of the "hype" (which they themselves generate) that exaggerates the threat that crime poses. In this respect, journalists often call upon academic and other experts to provide "perspective." Objectivity can also be manifested though the routine coverage of party politics by which "administration" studies can be critiqued by interest groups or by a competing political factions. In this way, journalists are seen as not committed to a particular version of the story but as engaged in the same kind of detached and objective reporting that is involved in the reporting of other kinds of stories.

Conclusion

The investigation of crime waves necessitates an understanding of how crime statistics are shaped, formed, and made available to consumers. The words we use to describe the phenomena in which we are interested—epidemic, flood, torrent—and of course *crime wave* itself, are terms that clearly lend themselves to statistical expression (Jacobs & Henry, 1996).

Crimes statistics must therefore be seen as one of the central means by which crime waves are constructed. It is when we learn that crime statistics are rising that we come to understand that a crime wave is under way. As we have seen, however, our observations in this respect might be less straightforward than at first appears.

Crime statistics, like all forms of statistics, are subject to considerable potential distortion. Some of this distortion results from the vagaries of any form of data collection. The counting of crime is a complex undertaking. There are always unresolved questions about how crime is to be measured and how populations are to be sampled for research purposes.

There are also intentional sources of distortion. Statistics are often a site of social conflict in our society. Arguments about escalating rates of crime can easily be turned into arguments about how resources are to be employed and about who is most deserving of our attention or even our sympathy. Claims-makers, in order to draw attention to what they see as a problem condition, provide extreme estimates of the size of the problem and the rate at which it is growing. In a related way, policing agencies (and other bureaucratic organizations) have sometimes played fast and loose with the statistical facts in order to gain bureaucratic advantage.

All of these problems are compounded by the high level of innumeracy in the general population. Many—or perhaps most—people in the population lack the skills to think critically about statistical evidence. The consequences of this state of affairs are not always uniform. On the one hand, we are made vulnerable to statistical arguments because we possess no natural defenses. On the other hand, we are often suspicious of numbers and believe that they cannot be trusted. The problem, of course, is that these positions do not correlate with the quality of statistical evidence in any consistent way. We are, it seems, as likely to be impressed by faulty statistical logic as we are to be dismissive of robust statistical evidence.

Crime statistics are themselves social constructions. Whether we end up seeing a crime wave in our tables, charts, and graphs depends not only on what is going on in the world that we intend to represent numerically, but also on how we do the counting. The parallels between statistical work and news work need to be carefully considered. The latter process is discussed more fully in the following chapter.

4

Mass Media and Crime Waves

An understanding of mass media structures and processes is central to any effort to make sense of how crime waves unfold. That crime waves might find their origins in the ways in which journalists construct the world for their audiences is not a new insight. More than a century ago, legendary American reporter Lincoln Steffens recognized the power of media managers to shape the collective view that crime is spiraling out of control. In his autobiography, Steffens (1931) wrote, "There's always a crime wave." Perhaps somewhat more specifically, there is, in Steffens's view, always the potential for a crime wave. What varies over time, for Steffens, is not the raw material (or actual crimes) out of which crime waves are constructed but the amount of press attention that is paid to crime. He tells the reader how he personally made a crime wave during the 1890s. One slow news day, according to Steffens, he wrote a rather lurid account of a crime. The next day, editors of rival papers demanded of their own journalists that they not be bested by Steffens, and other stories about other crimes also received prominent treatment. Very soon, a spiral was underway and Steffens was forced to respond with more sensationalist reporting of his own. Soon all of the New York dailies were full of screaming headlines about crime and violence. News items that might have received little or no attention from journalists, that might have been tucked away in the back pages of the tabloid press, were given prominent treatment.

This chapter explores the issues to which Steffens's analysis draws our attention. It is important to point out that the situation in our time is more complicated than it was in the period in which he was writing. Journalists are both more blatant and more subtle; media outlets are more plentiful and more varied. Audiences are more literate and yet more susceptible to the power of images.

The emphasis in this chapter is on the news and information media since they provide the central forum, in the contemporary period, in which claims-makers construct crime waves. The focus, while perhaps clear in the abstract, creates two practical problems for us. The first concerns the fact that news media differ from each other in terms of their emphases, their reliance on the written or spoken word or on the visual, their invasiveness, and a wide range of other dimensions. While we need to keep such differences in mind and to note them from time to time, it is perfectly appropriate to seek some larger truths about the content and influence of crime media.

A second problem concerns the assumed uniqueness of the media category called "news and information." The contrast implied by this designation is most typically with media entertainment. Indeed, traditional media scholars drew a rather sharp distinction between news and entertainment. As will become clear, this distinction—if it ever was clear—has become very blurred. Television programs like *Cops* or *20/20* or *Dateline NBC* combine elements of news and entertainment. These hybrids are often referred to by names like "reality television" or "infotainment." More broadly, it can be argued that, in the context of commercial media, there really is no practical difference between news and entertainment. As cultural critic Neal Gabler (1998) forcefully argues, entertainment has become the central paradigm of contemporary media. Indeed, he suggests, entertainment has conquered reality.

More useful for our purposes than the distinction between "news" and "entertainment" is a distinction between media forms that purport to describe aspects of the real world and those that do not. In other words, we are most interested in how journalists, interviewers, talk-show hosts, and the makers of "fact-based" dramas "cover" the crime story. It is through this type of content that crime waves are constructed. The newscast, the episodic drama "ripped from today's headlines," and the made-for-television movie (which, it is claimed, is "based on an actual incident") are our central concerns.

Importance of Crime to Mass Media

That crime and policing are key themes in all forms of media—news and entertainment—seems beyond dispute (Stark, 1987). Irrespective of the historical period or the type of medium, crime and crime control provide central forms of narrative. Even a casual observer of contemporary media must be struck by the near cultural obsession with crime. The commercial television schedule, in any given season, includes numerous dramatic programs that focus on the cop and the criminal. *Law & Order* and *CSI* are recent examples of a genre that has roots in the very earliest days of the medium. Most typically these programs focus on and ask us to identify with agents of crime control rather than offenders. A program like *The Sopranos* is the exception in this regard. Daytime talk-show hosts (like Maury Povich) sometimes seem to focus in almost single-minded fashion on "out-of-control teens" and on the use of lie detectors to trap them in their falsehoods.

What is true of television is true of other media. As of early 2004, the Internet Movie Database (http://www.imdb.com) listed almost 13,000 films as belonging to the crime genre. A major Internet bookseller (www.amazon.com) offers its customers more than 10,000 true crime books from which to choose. Hip-hop musicians commonly rap about homicides, gang life, and drug dealing. *Grand Theft Auto, True Crime: Streets of LA,* and *Dynamite Cops* are popular video game titles.

With respect to news, several systematic analyses of newspaper and newscast content show quite clearly that crime is a major news category. For newspapers, depending on audience, market, style, and several other variables, crime news accounts for anywhere from 4% to 28% of all news, averaging around 7% (Surette, 1998). This makes it the third largest news category found in newspapers. In the case of television news, analysts have found that about 13% of total network news is devoted to crime. For local newscasts, the proportion is considerably higher. As many critics have commented, crime, along with accidents and fires, forms the substance of local newscasts.

THE INCREASE IN CRIME COVERAGE

While crime has always figured very prominently in the media culture landscape, most observers agree that the amount of crime news and information available to us has increased dramatically over the past several years. There are many reasons for this.

AN INCREASE IN CARRYING CAPACITY

Americans have never had so much access to so many forms of mass media at any point in history. There are in the United States about 1,500 daily newspapers; 11,000 magazines; 12,000 radio stations; 1,500 television stations; and 25,000 theater screens. There are as well about 40,000 book titles published each year (Biagi, 1998). Through personal computers, at home or increasingly in public settings, one's ability to access newsmagazines, newspapers, and online video and audio is almost limitless. To a degree, of course, the proliferation of media sources is misleading. While the number of media outlets has grown geometrically, the tendency toward media concentration intensified in parallel fashion. In short, more and more newspapers, radio and television stations, and other forms of mass media are owned and controlled by fewer and fewer corporations (McChesney, 2004). According to a leading authority on media ownership concentration, Ben H. Bagdikian (2000),

> As the United States enters the twenty-first century, power over the American mass media is flowing to the top with such devouring speed that it exceeds even the accelerated consolidations of the last twenty years. For the first time in U.S. history, the country's most widespread news, commentary and daily

entertainment are controlled by six firms that are among the world's largest corporations, two of them foreign. (p. viii)

The simultaneous diffusion of media and concentration of ownership has led some to question whether our situation is best described as one characterized by "many more voices" but really only "one ventriloquist" (http://www .fortune.com/fortune/brainstorm/0,15704,483495,00.html).

Of course, all of these media technologies require content, and some kinds of news and information will serve as better fodder than others. Crime news like celebrity news and sports news is readily available and adaptable to diverse media technologies. The flow of crime news seems limitless, as does the appetite for such news on the part of many segments of the media audience.

DIFFUSION OF NEWSGATHERING TECHNOLOGY

In earlier periods, the capture of an ongoing crime on film or videotape would have been an extremely rare occurrence. Video and film production involved the use of cameras that were heavy and obtrusive. The technologies have changed dramatically, however, over the past several years. Cameras have become smaller, lighter, and by implication much more portable. The consequence is very apparent to any viewer of television news (Fishman & Cavender, 1998). The widespread use of security cameras and the number of cameras in the hands of journalists and ordinary Americans has produced a flood of videotaped assaults, car chases, and convenience store robberies that find their way onto newscasts. Quite obviously much of this video has no general news value. A violent grocery store robbery caught on tape in Topeka, Kansas, would not be of interest to a national audience in the absence of dramatic images. Indeed, entire programs have been developed around the availability of video of "the world's scariest car chases," employees being "busted on the job," or even America's "funniest" private moments.

CHANGES IN JOURNALISTIC MORES

In earlier, perhaps more innocent times, journalistic ethics dictated that some kinds of stories should not be covered. "All the news that's fit to print" might not include a large number of sex crimes, for instance, or would at least suggest a need for caution and restraint with respect to the ways in which such crimes should be covered. In this respect, Curtis (2001) shows how the coverage of the Jack the Ripper murders in 19th-century London pushed journalists beyond the customary mores of the time. Curtis argues that while the police reporters of the day were quite accustomed to bullets and mortal stab wounds, pelvic mutilations or the removal of a victim's uterus involved the exploration of new journalistic territory.

More contemporary coverage has shown little restraint, whether the topic is Lorena Bobbit's castration of her husband or President Clinton's sexual escapades in the Oval Office. In general, there are fewer prohibitions about the kinds of stories that can be covered or the kinds of details that should be made available to audiences. To some degree, this change reflects the tabloidization of mainstream media (Glynn, 2000). With respect to broadcasting specifically, Kooistra and Mahoney (1999) argue that early debates about who owned the airwaves and what broadcasting model should dominate have been resolved in the direction of corporate control. Over the past several couple of decades, regulatory philosophies have emphasized noninterference by government. These policies of nonregulation reflect a view that television (or any other electronic medium) is just another appliance that imposes on policy makers no additional burden of responsibility. This view was best expressed by President Ronald Reagan's choice to head the Federal Communications Commission, who described television as "just a toaster with pictures" (Leanza & Feld, 2003). If television news coverage of crime seems more lurid and sensationalist than it used to be, this is probably because it is.

POLITICIZATION OF CRIME

The growth of crime coverage is also to an extent attributable to the increasingly complex political meanings with which crime has come to be associated. "Rising crime" and the victims movement, for example, are legitimate news stories even for media outlets that tend to pay less attention to crime. In a similar way, crimes like wife assault, rape, or incest have been considered emblematic of the victimization of women and thus have figured centrally in any discussion of feminist political concerns (Johnson, 1996).

PROGRAMMATIC CHANGES

Commercial media are profit-making enterprises. Whatever else they strive to achieve, a primary intention is to generate revenue for owners and stockholders. A primary means by which this is accomplished is keeping costs low. Many of the forms of media content that maximize crime narratives are remarkably inexpensive. Local newscasts, newsmagazine shows, reality programs like *Cops* and various forms of "trash TV" (Keller, 1993) such as daytime talk shows, and tabloid news shows have relatively low production costs and yet generate considerable profit (Killingbeck, 2001).

Typically, programs of this sort do not require filming in expensive locales or high-priced acting talent, which can threaten the profit margin of corporate broadcasting (Beckett & Sasson, 2000). While the audience for many reality programs is perhaps smaller than some think, there are still millions and millions of viewers and when combined with the relatively low production costs, considerable profit can be generated (Fishman, 1998). In contrast, while a show like *Friends* might draw much bigger audiences, it is worth remembering that each member of the cast of that situation comedy was paid one million dollars per episode during the final years of the program's run (http://edition.cnn.com/2002/BUSINESS/02/12/friends/index.html).

It is not surprising that news and information programs that rely so heavily on crime content have proliferated to the degree they have.

How Do the News Media Cover Crime?

As stated, there are important differences in the ways in which various types of media "cover" the crime story. Despite these differences, however, it is possible to see "the big picture" through an assessment of key thematic elements that characterize coverage. These elements most importantly include atypicality, simplicity, personification, and status-quo orientation. Each is considered in turn.

ATYPICALITY

Implicit in our definition of news is the notion of the unusual or nonroutine occurrence. As journalism professors tell their first-year students, if 1,000 planes take off and one crashes, we are unlikely to read the headline, "999 PLANES LAND SAFELY." From one perspective it is the failure of events to meet our expectations of what is supposed to be or what is supposed to happen that leads such events to be categorized as "news." Thus, accidents, fires, floods, the deaths of celebrities and, importantly, crime fill our newspapers and newscasts.

Of course, not all crimes are treated equally in this respect. Consistent with a principle of atypicality, crimes that are more unusual are more likely to attract the attention of journalists and others in the media who speak to us about the problem of crime. All of the major data sources criminologists use to measure crime indicate rather clearly that crimes against property, for instance, occur at a much higher rate than do crimes of violence. National Uniform Crime Report data posted on the FBI Web site for the year 2002 indicate that about 60% of so-called index crimes that come to the attention of the police involve larceny and theft, 10.5% involve motor vehicle theft, and a further 18% involve burglary. In contrast, 7.5% of the crimes were aggravated assaults and 3.5% were robberies. Less than 1% involved rapes (0.6%) or homicide (0.1%) (http://www.fbi.gov/ucr/cius_02/pdf/2sectiontwo.pdf). To be sure, our counts of violent crime are plagued by serious problems of underreporting. Still, even other kinds of studies that, for instance, ask members of the population directly about their experiences with crime also lead irrevocably to the conclusion that crimes that victimize our property are considerably more common than crimes that victimize our persons.

Not surprisingly, crimes of violence are given much more attention than other crime categories (Ohlemacher, 1999; Spitzberg & Cadiz, 2002). Moreover, within the category of violence, it is murder, the least frequently occurring violent crime, to which the greatest amount of attention is directed (Paulsen, 2003). One need think only of the biggest crime news stories of the past several years (O. J. Simpson, the Menendez Brothers, Scott Peterson, and Robert Blake) to recognize that with few exceptions they tend to be murder stories. In a similar way, the hybrid programs like *Cops* focus our attention on the problem of violence. As Schlesinger, Tumber, and Murdock (1991) note, such shows emphasize murder, armed robbery, and sexual violence and in so doing select crimes from the "popular end of the market." Most broadly, crime coverage is largely synonymous with the actions of the predatory criminal—"the dark menacing figure who leaps from the shadows to rape, rob and murder" (McCorkle & Miethe, 2002, p. 81).

The attention to atypical crimes and atypical offenders, however, produces an ironic outcome. As newscasters and journalists focus on murder and other acts of violent predation, such events come to be seen as normal and commonplace (Kappeler, Blumberg, & Potter, 2000). The more serious a crime is, in general, the smaller the number of people who will have direct experiences with the crime. By implication, the more serious the crime (like murder), the more people tend to be reliant on second-hand information, such as that made available by the media (Ohlemacher, 1999). This routinization of violent crime coverage suggests an important part of the puzzle regarding the manner in which media construct crime waves.

SIMPLICITY

Media accounts of crime, like media accounts of other news categories, often tend to strip complex social realities to their least complicated forms. As Spitzberg and Cadiz (2002) note, "Media consumers may increasingly rely on the media to structure and simplify reality into more manageable forms" (p. 131). Simplicity has almost become a kind of mantra among many in the media. Conservative radio talk-show hosts routinely tell their audiences that issues like crime aren't complicated at all and that simple solutions are available to those who are not tricked by intellectual elites.

This tendency toward simplification is implicit in the way in which most news stories are written or presented. We tend to think about news as the reporting of discrete events that occur in the period between the publication of subsequent editions of a newspaper or subsequent television broadcasts. Such events are presented in ways that allow narrative elements to dominate. The stories we are told—about murders, about robberies, or about rapes or corporate wrongdoing—rarely are placed in larger contexts (McChesney, 2004). We learn little about broader crime trends or about the ways in which social structural or historical factors relate to the occurrence of such events (Krajicek, 1998). Rarely does crime reporting mean reporting about criminal justice policies and the politics of crime control.

In some ways, the demands of particular media forms encourage the simplification of social problems like crime. Some commentators have argued, for instance, that the visual character of television promotes a triumph of image over substance. In part, we can recognize the greater attention paid to violent crime as reflective of the greater visual possibilities that predatory interpersonal acts make available. Crime scenes, "perp walks," bloody sidewalks, or crowds of onlookers provide convenient, often jarring pictures that accompany the telling of simple stories (Spitzberg & Cadiz, 2002).

In contrast, it has been argued that corporate crimes receive considerably less media attention because they generally suggest much more complicated narratives. Like many forms of political crime, corporate crime lacks visual intensity and certainly in the context of corporate owned media, might on occasion suggest a topic of some sensitivity. It is worth noting, however, that while corporate crime is discussed less frequently than acts of personal violence, it is not as invisible as some crude versions of conflict theory would have us believe. One study, for instance, found that in the period from the mid-1970s to the mid-1980s, 40% of television evening newscasts had at least one story about corporate crime (Randall, 1985). Moreover, the "corporate crime wave" of the early 21st century showed that under some kinds of circumstances, such coverage can be quite extensive.

Organized crime provides a particularly vivid example of the broader implications of the tendency to simplify. Throughout American history, there have been several periods in which news media strongly suggested that society was in the grip of a rampant wave of gangsterism. The concern about organized crime in reportage has always been characterized by what Michael Woodiwiss (2001) has called a "dumbing of American discourse." The standard organized crime narrative as revealed in news reports of government hearings, interviews with "ex-mobsters," television documentaries, or book-length treatments of the topics usually provides some variation on a single theme. That theme emphasizes organized crime as a product of alien predatory conspirators who brought organized crime to America.

The legend of the Mafia is perhaps the clearest example of this argument. In short, mafia theories contend that organized crime in America exists only because foreign criminals from the south of Italy brought their criminal lifeways to these shores. Moreover, organized crime grew to achieve immense influence only because powerful individual gangsters with Italian surnames like Capone or Luciano or Costello were able to work their will despite the best efforts of law enforcement and decent society.

The problem with this dumbing down is that it prevents any sophisticated understanding of why organized crime exists and how it relates to the rest of the social order. The simplifications of mafia theory do not encourage us to ask how the character of American social structure provides fertile ground on which such criminality can flourish. The attention paid to ethnicity in such a model discourages a discussion of socioeconomic inequality. As a result, we really are not prompted to think too much about the ways in which a wide variety of groups, who share in common nothing more than the historically specific character of their subordinate status, have found organized crime an available channel of upward mobility (O'Kane, 1992). It is also important to note how the dumbing of discourse on organized crime encourages us to consider only some members of organized crime networks to be actual organized criminals. The corporations that made use of gangsters to control labor strife, the politicians who gained and granted favors to ethnic gangsters, or the law enforcement agents who are involved in relationships of corruption could all be called "organized crime." The former problems are much more historic, while the latter one continues to have currency. However, we tend to reserve that label for the ethnic outsider and then argue that these outsiders "infiltrated" legitimate business and corrupted the political or legal system. While theories like "the Mafia" offer us the convenience of simplicity, they fail to speak to what are surely some of the more vexing empirical examples of this phenomenon.

In a similar way, the media discourse on terrorism in the period after the terrorist attacks on the World Trade Center and the Pentagon on September 11, 2001, sought simplicity (Reynolds & Barnett, 2003). As the media widely reported President George W. Bush's dichotomous declaration that "you are either with us or you are with the terrorists," a small number of commentators and journalists sought to introduce some complexity into the discussion. They argued that, despite the horror of the attacks, there was a need to initiate a dialogue about American foreign policy and why others in the world might hate America enough to do what they had done. Such debates did not take root in mainstream conventional media, however, and were quickly relegated to the margins of public discussion.

PERSONIFICATION

Closely related to the simplicity problem is the issue of personification. This refers to the consistent tendency to translate questions about crime and crime control into questions about individuals. We see this perhaps most evidently in the case of celebrity crime (Parnaby & Sacco, 2004). The near obsession in our culture with the lifestyles of the rich and famous (or infamous) promotes a wide appetite for all kinds of celebrity news, including news about crime and victimization (Gabler, 1998). The murder cases involving O. J. Simpson or Robert Blake, the child molestation case involving Michael Jackson, or even the shoplifting trial of Winona Ryder are not noteworthy because of the character or the circumstances of the crimes themselves. Rather, they became points of media focus because of the fame of the principals. The reciprocal situation, of course, involves the manner in which high visibility criminal cases create celebrities whose cachet extends beyond the circumstances in which the media first find them. Scott Peterson, convicted of the murder of his wife and unborn child in California, began to develop a kind of following among "fans" who followed the case. The process involves victims as well as offenders. Earlier reference was made to John Walsh, whose son Adam was brutally murdered, and who became a leader in the threatened child movement and a popular television host.

Of course, most crime reporting has nothing to do with questions of fame or infamy. Nevertheless, the focus remains very much upon the individual. In this sense, crime news suggests a kind of "human interest" story. As defined by Fine and White (2002), human interest stories emphasize "the predicaments and circumstances of particular, but previously unknown, individuals in which the events are presented as irrelevant to public policy." In other words, crime stories are people stories that are marked by personal and often emotional content. Tunnell (1998) notes that the obsession with celebrity and the individual suggests an additional reason why newsmagazine programs, for instance, pay comparatively little attention to various forms of white-collar and corporate crime. Unlike the violent acts of interpersonal predators, stories about white-collar offenders are often less easily personalized. The elements of human drama that we expect in crime reporting seem somewhat more elusive. A very important exception in this respect, of course, was the case involving Martha Stewart, whose corporate offending was of interest largely because of the familiarity of her celebrity persona.

One way in which we can appreciate the role that personification plays in the presentation of crime news is through reference to the narrative style known as melodrama. Melodramatic presentations are those that rely on stereotyped characters and situations and that make heavy use of emotional imagery. Critics often describe soap operas as melodramatic or poorly written screenplays that feature maudlin dialogue and broadly drawn portrayals of good and evil. Shan Nelson-Rowe (1995) argues that the way in which news and other forms of information media encourage us to think about a variety of social problems, including crime, draws substantially on the repertoire of melodrama. Social problems involve scenarios populated by evil villains, innocent and virtuous victims, and heroes who fight the former and champion the causes of the latter (Lule, 1993; Weed, 1990).

Gray Cavender's (1998) analysis of "real-life" crime programs like *America's Most Wanted* shows how such programs promote a melodramatic understanding of crime. These shows largely deal in stereotypes—of gang members, serial killers, satanists, and child molesters. Often viewers are told that the offenders are depraved, amoral, and physically unattractive. Victims, by contrast, are described as attractive and likeable. The host or narrator describes to us the feelings and emotions of the victim and invites an intimacy with the victim through the use of first names. The victims, after all, are people like us, the viewers, and it is easy to identify with their fears and their pain.

Melodramatic imagery often finds its way into press coverage as a result of the active efforts of politicians to define their positions clearly in opposition to their rivals. A particularly infamous episode occurred during the 1988 presidential race when the Republican candidate, George Herbert Walker Bush, undertook to portray his Democratic opponent, Michael Dukakis, as "soft on crime." The episode involved an offender named Willie Horton, a convicted murderer serving a life sentence in Massachusetts where Dukakis was governor. While taking part in a furlough program, Horton escaped to Maryland where he assaulted a man, raped the man's fiancée, and burglarized a house. At the hands of the Republican political strategists, Horton, an African American, quickly became the "poster child" for wanton random violence directed by black men against the white middle class. Publicity portrayed Horton as a wild-eyed and out-of-control villain. The white middle class to whom the publicity was directed could clearly identify with Horton's victims. Of course, the conservative politics of Bush and the Republicans, and their willingness to get "tough on crime," cast them in the role of heroes. The racial politics of the case were lost on no one. Prior to the episode, Horton was known as William and not Willie. The name change was made by Republican strategists to increase the degree of conformity to prevailing African American stereotypes.

According to Anderson (1995), subsequent news coverage of crime was profoundly influenced by the Willie Horton story. In the New York area, for instance, a particular kind of crime story began to dominate coverage of local crime. Such stories had five elements in common:

1. They typically involved lurid and violent crimes like homicide, rape, or robbery

2. The victims were white and middle class, and their offenders often were not

3. Victims were completely innocent, and crimes occurred while people were going about the daily business of their lives

4. The criminals appear to have chosen their victims entirely at random

5. Offenders usually had experience with the criminal justice system and it was implicitly suggested that if the system had been more efficient, the offenders would never have been free

Why does the emphasis on personification matter? There are several answers to this question. First, our attention to crime stories as celebrity news or human interest news obscures the bigger picture. As the old proverb warns, our attention on the trees can cause us to lose sight of the forest. While this problem has increased substantially in recent years with our celebrity dominated media, it is nothing new. Dennis Hoffman (1993) has argued that during the Roaring

Twenties gang rule in Chicago came to be synonymous with the larger-than-life figure, Al Capone. As a result, a group of powerful business leaders swore to get Capone in order to correct what they saw as wrong with their city. Hoffman, however, argues that by focusing on the pursuit of Capone, these civic leaders overlooked the bigger problem—the prohibition of alcohol and the climate of lawlessness it helped foster. The personification of crime problems encourages us to blame individuals for the presence of crime and to seek individual solutions to the problem (Fabianic, 1997; Sotirovic, 2003; Tunnell, 1992). The emphasis is consequently placed, implicitly or explicitly, on the moral inadequacy of individual offenders or the poor choices made by individual victims. What we lose with such a focus is a useful assessment of the relationship between crime and larger structural and historical trends.

In addition, the personification of crime news represents one of the principal sources of the confusion in media culture between news and entertainment. The narrative forms of melodrama, the clear delineation of villainy, innocence, and heroism represent forms of storytelling that seem more like fiction than news. As Jenkins (1994) has noted, the typical serial killer story resembles in many key aspects traditional monster narratives—an evil force walks the land killing victims at will. As well, the serial killer in fiction and in the news has seemed at times interchangeable. Real serial killers are described as "true-life" versions of fictional characters (like Hannibal Lector) and fictional serial killers are described as "inspired by" real-life cases. Is it any wonder that we are often so confused about what is and what it not the news?

Finally, personification provides a significant means by which journalists and other "nonfiction" media producers are able to translate abstract stories into terms that become personally relevant to their audience. In other words, it makes the storytelling of news personally relevant (Best, 1991). Crime stories become life stories (Gabler, 1998). Programs that feature reenactments of criminal events often use tip lines and other forms of viewer involvement to actively engage the audience members and to invite them to become part of the story. All of us, we are told, can form part of a video posse. Some writers have noted the tendency in media to provide practical advice with which viewers and readers can compare their own experiences with those of the victims, and even the offender they meet in crime news. Ogle, Eckman, and Leslie (2003), for instance, discuss how in the aftermath of the shootings at Columbine School in Littleton, Colorado, media coverage taught audience members how to look for violent tendencies in their own children. Watch out, the public was warned, if your child begins wearing black clothing or seems to enjoy Marilyn Manson music.

The broad tendency to personification, like other elements of news presentation, was very evident in the September 11, 2001, attacks. Larger questions about the sources or historical character of international terrorism were overlooked in favor of the very emotional personal stories of victims and their families. Even the response by the Bush administration was portrayed in these terms. The media treated the story, to a considerable degree, as a personal struggle between President Bush and Osama Bin Laden. President George W. Bush himself contributed to the melodramatic representation when he drew on the store of folklore familiar to fans of Western movies. At one point, he told journalists and the nation, "The Taliban must take this statement seriously. I want him [Bin Laden]. There's an old poster in the west, as I recall, that said 'Wanted, Dead or Alive'" (http://www.cnn.com/2001/US/09/17/gen.bush.transcript/index.html).

STATUS QUO ORIENTATION

Critics of contemporary media often claim that the media are "too liberal." In a related way, supporters of the media often claim that they are a "force for change." These statements share in common the belief that media challenge the societal status quo. However, there is more of a tendency for news media to reaffirm than to question existing sets of power relationships (Alterman, 2003; McChesney, 2004).

Many aspects of media coverage of crime are consistent with this view. As we have seen, the news media tend to be more attentive to the crimes of those at the bottom of the social order than those at the top (Welch, Price, & Yankey, 2002). In reality-based crime shows, we typically encounter minority offenders and rarely (or never) encounter corporate or political criminals. As well, the nature of the newsgathering process, as we shall see, tends to provide us with a somewhat distorted view of the success of crime control agents in solving crime (Oliver & Armstrong, 1998). As mentioned, the emphasis on individuals and the lack of attention to structure mitigate against any kind of profound questioning of how crime is exacerbated by social and economic inequalities. Crime is rarely conceptualized as a symptom of deeper societal problems, but is more usually understood as a problem in its own right. There seems to be nothing particularly liberal or progressive in a view of crime as the product of poor and disenfranchised individuals whose crimes reflect innate villainy or in a view of the police as efficient and effective.

The reasons for this are complex. As we will discuss below, one powerful influence on the status quo orientation of crime news is the routine nature of its sources. As Stuart Hall and his colleagues (Hall, Critcher, Jefferson, Clark, & Roberts, 1978) observed, the media tend to reproduce the views of the authoritative sources from which news is collected. A more controversial argument links the conservative status quo orientation of the media to the nature of the media themselves. Corporate ownership of media, critics contend, and the high degrees of ownership concentration, conspire to prevent any truly progressive message from emerging. Jeffrey Scheuer (1999) argues that the proclivity of television to simplify, to deal with pictures rather than words, and to promote superficiality as a virtue creates a sound-bite society. Conservative views and the simple answers they promote to complex questions dominate because they are really just more consistent with the televisual conventions.

Why Do Media Cover Crime as They Do?

There is a simple answer to this question, which we have already anticipated. Most forms of mass media—newspapers, reality programming, television news, "true crime" books—are commercial enterprises (Bagdikian, 2000). The intention is to generate profit and, as discussed, this is accomplished by keeping audiences as large as possible and production costs as low as possible. As Tunnell has observed, crime programs are a commodity (Tunnell, 1992). They are privately produced and sold, and profits are expropriated. The economics of the mass media provide the context for making sense of production and consumption (Bogart, 1995). The relevant issues are perhaps most clearly understood, and most significant, with respect to the study of crime news.

MAKING NEWS

Traditionally, scholarly attention to the news production process has taken one of two perspectives (Killingbeck, 2001; Surette, 1998). Central to both perspectives is the concept of "newsworthiness." On the one hand, scholars have used a "market model" in which the newsworthiness of an event is determined by public choices in the marketplace. It is a demand-side model, which suggests that journalists decide what is or what is not news based on how people vote with their newspaper subscriptions or television remote controls. Such a model suggests to us that the reading, listening, and viewing public gets what it wants (and presumably what it deserves). The media are obsessed with crime and celebrity, we are told, because we are.

In direct contrast is a manipulation model, which emphasizes the supply-side of the equation (Hall et al., 1978). In this view, newsworthiness is determined by powerful groups in society that make self-serving judgments about what will be and what will not be treated as news. From this perspective, the role of news media is to promote the dominant ideology, which serves the interests of those with the power to control media (Schlesinger, Tumber, & Murdock, 1991). Mass media content is not seen to reflect public opinion and public choices but to shape them. Thus, the media are obsessed with crime and celebrity in large part because such content distracts and mollifies us. If we are consumed with a crime panic, like "celebrity stalking," we are less likely to be interested in or thinking about the structured inequality or power differentials that characterize social life.

It can be argued, however, that neither model really captures that complexity of the daily processes by which news is produced. Part of the problem in this respect is that these models encourage us to think about the world as somehow being objectively reported on. In contrast, it is perhaps much more useful to think about the world as being constructed by newsgathering processes (Tuchman, 1978). In this perspective, newsworthiness is really a kind of professional judgment that newsworkers make based on their experience and the demands of the task environments in which they find themselves. Journalists develop routines for making the news work within these routines (Best, 1991; Ericson, Baranek, & Chan, 1989).

The parameters of the newsmaking process are economic and organizational (Bogart, 1995). There is a need to produce news as cheaply and efficiently as possible within the constraints imposed by technology, resources, and production schedules. Given such parameters, some kinds of stories are more likely to be told than others and they are more likely to be told in particular ways. Central to this entire process is the issue of the news source.

CRIME SOURCES

Where do journalists "find" the news? A popular myth emphasizes the proactive role played by the intrepid reporter who prowls the mean streets of the city to get the big story. Indeed, the tireless hard-driving journalist is as much a cultural icon as the hardboiled private detective or the incorruptible cop (Ehrlich, 2004). The empirical reality, however, is much more prosaic. Crime news (like most other kinds of news) is not generally gathered as a result of the investigative efforts of the reporter. Instead, it is a product of the well-articulated relationship between journalists and their news sources (Ericson et al., 1989).

Most commonly, it is the police or other criminal justice officials or state managers who make available to journalists the raw material out of which news about crime is fashioned (Beckett, 1997; Tunnell, 1998). Press conferences and news releases, routinized and carefully ordered, feed the continuous stream of crime news from which journalists draw. In some cases, the police have become even more proactive and have created positions for "Public Information Officers" whose job it is to disclose information selectively to the media. The role of such officers in police organizations, as in any organization, is to cultivate a favorable image of the organization and when things are going badly, to engage in active and aggressive damage control.

It is important to ask what it is about the police and other criminal justice agencies that make them so valuable as sources of crime news. There are several answers to the question. The most general one recognizes that the relationship between justice system agencies and media organizations is symbiotic. Each is able to exploit the relationship in order to accrue organizational advantages.

Journalists seek to tell a compelling story about important aspects of the world as they understand it. Moreover, they seek to do this in the most efficient way possible. The news is supposed to be objective and it is supposed to be authoritative. Clearly, sources that are widely seen to have such qualities greatly simplify the task of newsgathering (Gans, 1979; Tuchman, 1978). The police, for example, are generally understood to be "experts" on crime. In addition, many people see the police as impartial and disinterested and with no particular axe to grind. In sociological parlance, the police (and other agents of the justice system) occupy high positions in a "hierarchy of credibility" (Becker, 1963). By virtue of their professional activity, the police have ready access to an almost limitless number of episodes of crime and disorder and they can greatly facilitate news media access to such incidents. As well, they are able to imbue information about any such incidents with considerable authority (Beckett & Sasson, 2000).

In the typical crime news story, we might read about or hear about the police officer on the scene, or hear a police "spokesperson" discuss how the crime happened and what leads are being followed. Of course, we often encounter other sources in crime news stories (Welch, Fenwick, & Roberts, 1998). Journalists sometimes quote or are seen interviewing experts (academic or otherwise) and politicians. Increasingly, it seems that television journalists spend more and more time interviewing each other about major news stories. Like the police, fellow journalists lend credibility, authority, and objectivity to their pronouncements. As well, their knowledge of media conventions and requirements ensure that their commentary is journalistically useful.

Remarkably, though, the parameters of the discourse tend to be rather narrowly defined. We rarely hear, for example, from offenders or even from victims (Chermak, 1995). In part, this is because such individuals are not as easily accessed as more routine sources, and even if they can be contacted, they may be less media-savvy, less able to speak in the convenient sound-bite terms that expeditious news production requires. Crime news stories often suggest to us a consensus about the character of an issue or that there are (at its most complicated) "two sides to every story." Rarely can commercial news media entertain more complex understandings of social reality. With respect to wife assault, for example, Bullock and Cubert (2002) contend that because journalists (and many in their audiences) see the police as objective, they feel no need to balance their observations with interviews with other people. Thus, the police views of wife assault as something that emerges from the dynamic between men and women is rarely challenged by feminist views that see such violence as more deeply rooted in the fabric of misogynist social relations. In the end, wife assault ends up being understood as a law enforcement problem only.

A similar issue arises in the context of reporting about terrorism. Jenkins (2003) shows that when journalists covering terrorism speak of "informed sources," this usually means representatives from a very small group of organizations, including the FBI, the CIA, the Defense Department, Homeland Security, or conservative think tanks. All such spokespersons offer commentary within an already established media framework regarding what terrorism is and what it isn't. Opportunities for more critical thinking are minimal. For instance, Jenkins notes, the wave of antiabortion clinic violence in the 1990s is never discussed by journalists or their experts as a form of terrorism. The reason, though, is not clear. It is politically motivated violence intended to achieve social change and it is in this sense directly comparable to the other forms of violence that we call terrorism. Even more essentially, presidential critic David Corn (2003) argues that the term *terrorism* itself obscures larger social conflicts. Terrorism, he points out, is a tactic, not an ideology or philosophy. The media (and state) focus on terrorism rather than the much more complicated ideology and interests of the terrorists really makes no sense. It as though, in the aftermath of the attack on Pearl Harbor, the media had focused on "sneak attackism" as the real problem.

While journalists make frequent use of quotes from a variety of politicians and law enforcement officials, they often offer little more than tough talk and simplistic analyses of the crime problem. Overall, they neglect a consideration of the causal connection between crime and social conditions, and reinforce the view that the problem of crime is "owned" by the criminal justice system (Welch et al., 1998). Crouch and Damphousse (1992) have shown, for instance, that press coverage of the satanic crime wave of the 1980s drew on the expertise of a relatively small network of "authorities." As a result, one was hard pressed to find much variation in the way in which events are interpreted. More generally, of course, the reliance on the police in crime reporting reinforces widespread perceptions that they are indeed the experts on crime, and thus the agency that "owns" the problem and crafts its solutions (Fishman, 1978). Routine crime news reporting, and most other types of programs for that matter, present the police in a heroic and unambiguous light and promote the view that something is being done about the problem of crime.

There are, in some cases, even more practical benefits to be derived. Profiling an at-large suspect can result in an arrest and thus another success for law enforcement (Schlesinger & Tumber, 1993). Some analysts have shown how skillful control of media images by policing agencies can facilitate the achievement of organizational objectives. The FBI, for instance, through much of its history quite actively and quite expertly promoted the idea that it was uniquely able to deal with several quite distinct crime threats to the nation, including the road bandits of the 1930s and the organized crime threat of the 1980s and 1990s (Potter, 1998). In his comprehensive analysis of the serial killer crime wave of the 1980s, Jenkins (1994) was able to show how the FBI was able to position itself in media depictions as the only solution to the problem of the roaming, bloodthirsty, and diabolical serial killer. The public image of the agency became a justification for the new center for the study of violent crime in Quantico,

Virginia. In so doing, the FBI overcame opposition to the commitment of human and financial resources to such a project and countered liberal objections regarding new and more intrusive investigation techniques.

In some cases, police and other news sources seem less interested in talking to some undifferentiated mass audience than in seeking to influence other powerful groups in society (Schlesinger, Tumber, & Murdock, 1991). The police chief, for instance, may make pronouncements about crime spiraling out of control not to scare the audience but to force the mayor or the police appropriations board to act. As one media scholar noted, it sometimes seems as though those major institutions are speaking to each other through the mass media and the rest us are just eavesdropping (Tuchman, 1978).

In the terms of social constructionist theory, we can think of the relationship between news sources and mass media as the relationship between the primary and secondary definers of social problems (Hall et al., 1978). Sources get to construct the world for media audiences if they can lend some authority and legitimacy to their views and if they have an ability to speak in the terms the conventions of mass media can accommodate (Best, 1991). While many groups may seek to influence how we think about the seriousness of established or emerging crime problems, this practice of structured access means that some will be able to accomplish this while others will not. Clearly, the arrangement favors the powerful and privileges viewpoints that reflect dominant ideologies (Beckett, 1994; Hall et al., 1978; Spitzberg & Cadiz, 2002).

In some cases the news media appear to do little more than simply widely diffuse the views, opinions, and understandings of their sources. It is for this reason that news articles often bear a striking resemblance to press releases. This is well illustrated by the press coverage of a 1991 fire at the Imperial Food Products factory in Hamlet, North Carolina (Wright, Cullen, & Blankenship, 1995). The fire began when a hydraulic line above a large vat of grease burst and sprayed flammable liquid into the vat. Of 90 workers in the plant, 25 died and 56 were injured. Newspapers that covered the fire showed little awareness that corporate violence could be seen as a criminal act and did not describe the deaths as homicides. As is typically the case, the media were more reactive than proactive. It was not until state managers announced the handing down of manslaughter indictments that the violence was described in media reporting as criminal.

Yet as Joel Best (1991) has shown, the media often transform claims in the process of making them available to their audiences. Aspects of a story may be highlighted or neglected depending on whether the story is judged sufficiently interesting, entertaining, or visual. Ogle et al. (2003), for instance, argued that media writers in the Columbine school shooting case played a key role in spreading the claim that the gunmen had used ethnicity as a criterion in the selection of their victims, despite the fact that this charge had been made by only one primary claims-maker.

How Do Media Generate Crime Waves?

The development of media crime waves draws upon all of the elements of crime media production that have been considered thus far. These include the emphasis on personification, simplicity, atypicality, and status quo orientation. In addition, the use of melodramatic presentation, the increased attention to crime in the media in recent years, and the reliance on official sources for crime news all importantly affect the frequency and the nature of media crime waves.

There is, however, an important additional ingredient that requires discussion. We can describe this ingredient as the "news theme." A news theme is a kind of rhetorical device that makes orderly and coherent the sometimes disparate and disconnected narratives with which the news (especially broadcast news) typically deal. We can think of news themes as motifs or elements that are common to a kind of story. "The worsening economy" is a news theme. Several different stories about a variety of substantive issues (people losing their jobs, companies moving overseas, consumers incurring credit card debt, increase in robberies or drug use) could all be woven into the theme of economic decline. Often, in television newscasts, these themes are explicitly identified with graphics that appear behind the newscaster and that make clear the theme to which the story is linked. News themes not only give any given news report order, but they help organize how news stories will be selected for inclusion in future news reports.

The role played by news themes in structuring crime waves is made very evident by a study of a 1970 media crime wave of crime against the elderly in New York City (Fishman, 1978). The author of the study, Mark Fishman, was able to observe the day-to-day activities of working journalists in a New York City television newsroom and to analyze the crime news found in the city's newspapers. The crime wave against the elderly, Fishman argued, emerged as a way of linking together individual stories about specific acts of criminal victimization. Importantly, Fishman was able to show that crime waves are given real impetus as news agency personnel watch what each other are doing and borrow liberally from each other (Kappeler et al., 2000). Thus, the coverage of crime against the elderly in one news outlet was watched closely by other news organizations, which also began to develop and exploit the theme. This pattern is familiar to most of us. In some cases the tendency of media to rely on each other is more blatant than others. Some stories dominate news and entertainment to such a degree that they seem to assume the form of media obsessions. The O. J. Simpson story, for instance, or the Monica Lewinsky scandal, each in its own time dominated all forms of media, mainstream and tabloid, print and electronic, information and entertainment.

Of course, to sustain a media crime wave, it is necessary for journalists to have access to a continuous flow of incidents that can be reported as part of the broader theme. Fishman notes that in the New York situation, the police saw the coverage of crime against the elderly as indicative of the kinds of stories in which journalists were becoming increasingly interested. As a result, they made more such stories available than would otherwise have been the case. This suggests, obviously, that since crime waves are rooted in the relationship between the police and the media, structural parameters are established regarding what kind of media crimes waves a society will and will not experience. Local policing agencies tend not to be as involved in corporate as in interpersonal predatory crimes and therefore crime waves involving the former are less likely than those involving the latter. According to Joel Best, there is a journalistic rule that suggests that once something happens a third time, "you have a trend." Killingbeck (2001) shows, for example, that during the late 1990s a rather small number (in relative terms) of highly unusual school shootings came to be labeled a trend. A wave of school crime was underway in the minds of many journalists, and each subsequent event could be introduced to media audiences as an instance of an "all too familiar story."

These practices have a long history, as suggested by the anecdote about Steffens at the beginning of the chapter. Adler (1996) cites an even earlier case in his discussion of the "garroting" epidemic in Boston in 1865. As mentioned, garroting, a specific form of violent robbery that involved an attack by teams of offenders, attracted considerable newspaper attention at the time. Press coverage was intended to respect the sensibilities and vulnerabilities of the middle class and at the same time provide sufficient drama to appeal to the large urban working class readership. As a result, garroting began to receive more coverage than other kinds of crime. While other kinds of crime might be seen as isolated events, acts of garroting were understood by press and by readers as instances of a bigger problem. At the start of the wave, journalists wrote specific accounts of specific cases; as the wave progressed, however, newspapers established columns that offered readers a "garroting record" or a "garrotiana."

Thus, as media crime waves develop, they begin to require attention in their own right. In a sense, the story shifts from the individual incidents that comprise the theme to the theme itself. The crime wave, rather than the crimes that comprise the crime wave, forms the story. This is evident as journalists start to talk about "sprees," "trends," "alarming increases," "epidemics," and "spreading cancers" (Beckett & Sasson, 2000; Best, 1991; McCorkle & Miethe, 2002).

As the wave grows, it is fed in a variety of ways. First, the theme itself offers a new definition of newsworthiness, and events are more likely to be selected to the degree that they conform to this theme. News stories that might have been otherwise neglected are now given prominent treatment. The degree to which events fit existing news themes is sometimes called "consonance" (Cohen & Young, 1981).

At the same time, the dynamic of the crime wave may lead to large numbers of new cases being made available for press exploitation. The panic that surrounds a crime wave can promote more rigorous enforcement of laws against the offending behavior. As new cases are "discovered," more cases can be reported upon. In the case of school violence, for instance, in the aftermath of the Columbine shootings, and the emergence of the "bullying" wave, many schools developed zero-tolerance policies that resulted in the policing of acts that would previously have been ignored or at most dealt with unofficially (Killingbeck, 2001).

Another aspect of the development of crime waves themes is through the diffusion of media imagery and themes. In short, what is understood as a growing problem in one place comes to be understood as a growing problem in other places in a short period of time as a result of the news story spread (Jenkins, 1992). Several writers have shown, for instance, that the satanic crime wave of the 1980s diffused in this way from not only within the United States but also to a number of other nations (Best, 2001; Victor, 1993). More generally, Sacco and Ismaili (2001) argue that Canadians attend so closely to American media that they often readily accept American problem definitions. The serial killer crime wave quickly spread to Canada in the 1980s because Canadians were already so familiar with American media images of the problem. In a similar way, a shooting at an Alberta, Canada, high school in 1999 took on added and ominous significance in the aftermath of widespread reporting in the Canadian media of a school crime wave in the United States.

Conclusion

Of course, media crime waves dissipate over time for many reasons. Perhaps most important, news themes are exhausted. Novelty is in many ways the lifeblood of news, and audiences come to see themes as tiresome after a while. In this sense, media crime waves resemble many other kinds of media fads—Oscar fever, *Who Wants to Be a Millionaire?*, television variety shows—were all characterized by rapidly growing media attention and subsequent declines in public interest.

The transitory and ephemeral character of media crime waves, however, should not obscure the larger significance of crime news coverage in general. Two issues in particular require comment. First, as Fishman and Cavender (1998) argue, shows like *Cops* and *America's Most Wanted* seem to put aside the traditional and potentially valuable "watchdog role of the press." The idea that the press should keep an eye on the state, in a critical and independent way, is replaced by a posture that is much more cozy and collaborative. The media come to depend on the police for news and for expertise and as a consequence the tendency to identify with the police seems unavoidable.

Second, how media report crime—and especially crime increases—seems to have important implications for how members of media audiences think about the problem of crime (Oliver & Armstrong, 1998). There is evidence to suggest that media crime news is a dominant source of information for many people (Lowry, Nio, & Leitner, 2003). Important effects, in this respect, relate to what media analysts call "agenda setting" (Shaw & McCombs, 1977). This means that while the media may not be very effective at telling us what to think, they are perhaps much more effective at telling us what to think about. Crime news attention to violent interpersonal crimes and to an assumed increase in such behavior set the parameters of political discourse. Audiences may reach somewhat different conclusions from those reached by media commentators, but they end up focusing on the same issues. Of course, when we are busy talking about the spiraling rates of satanic crime or school massacres or child abduction we are *not* busy talking about corporate malfeasance, political corruption, or other kinds of crimes that don't fit the crime wave paradigm as easily. In a related way, the almost exclusive attention to crime as an individual phenomenon does not draw our attention to more complex structural forces. The conclusions we end up drawing relate to the value of punitiveness and other conservative solutions to the problem of crime (Sotirovic, 2003).

5

That's the Rumor

If you are like many people, you are already familiar with the stories (or variations on the themes) depicted in Box 5.1. Perhaps someone passed you a photocopy or, more probably, you received a cautionary e-mail (usually with a very long circulation list) like one of those on the page opposite. We read such messages, take them to heart, and sometimes with the best of intentions send them along to everyone we know who also need to be warned about assaults in parking lots, reckless youth, and the risks of random HIV infection. Because these tales have a ring of authenticity to them (they are rich, for instance, in specific detail), we rarely pause to question their credibility.

The skeptical consumer of Net lore who investigates these warnings will learn quickly that all of them are without foundation (www.snopes2.com). These messages are not warnings about real-world situations but "urban legends" with no basis in reality. As such, they merely represent the most recent manifestation of the age-old processes of gossip and rumor transmission that in the period before the computer took place primarily over coffee, across the back fence, or around a campfire.

This chapter is concerned with the ways in which our talk about crime, of all kinds, constructs our understanding of emerging and worsening crime problems. As the examples in Box 5.1 illustrate, the kinds of talk about crime that we have with each other often direct our attention to previously unrecognized but burgeoning threats. *When we hear from and tell each other stories about crime, we actively engage in the process of socially constructing crime waves.*

One reason, perhaps, is because the study of mass media, unlike the study of much interpersonal communication, allows an opportunity to critique structures of power in society. In addition, the subject matter of mass communications, traditionally at least, has been much more available than the more ephemeral subject matter of everyday talk. Libraries maintain collections of daily newspapers, magazines, and film and television programs to which the interested researcher has ready access. Finally, as Jack Levin and Arnold Arluke (1987) argue, much talk about crime and other topics is viewed as a trivial issue in part because people exchange gossip and spread rumors when they are in informal and apparently inconsequential circumstances. In other words, when people are idly chatting about matters that may or may not be true, it does not really appear that anything of significance is really occurring.

In contrast, this chapter argues that any effort to make sense of the constructed character of crime waves must take these very often banal and apparently unimportant conversations, e-mails, rumors, and tidbits of gossip very seriously. We will see that much of what we talk about when we talk about crime (whether it is "true" or "untrue") provides a kind of window on the fear and insecurities of members of society. There is nothing particularly mysterious about any of this, however. Quite simply, we are interested in hearing about and we pass on stories regarding matters that concern us and about people and conditions we feel threaten us.

Talking About Crime

The folklorist Eleanor Wachs (1988) has shown that stories about crime and victimization comprise an important part of contemporary urban folklore. Almost every resident of every city has a story to tell about a crime that happened or almost happened. Sometimes these stories are very personal and other times they are about friends or somebody at work or at school or a neighbor. Wachs argues that, from one perspective, these stories can be understood as cautionary tales intended to alert those who hear them. In this sense, these stories that we tell are coded warnings about the people, places, and situations that one needs to avoid as one negotiates the public spaces of the city. An analysis of "storytelling" sessions among New Yorkers allowed Wachs to derive a number of such warnings, including the following:

- Have a good mental map of New York City
- Be inconspicuous
- Learn some self-defense tactics
- Avoid enclosed areas
- Cooperate with your assailant

Viewed another way, these stories, especially when told by victims, have therapeutic or cathartic value. Telling others about one's victimization or about one's close call might help the individual in question to work through the incident, to deal with questions of self-blame, or to understand better why "bad things happen to good people" (Lejeune & Alex, 1973). Others might relate similar stories or offer reassurance. Almost certainly, they will be interested in hearing the dramatic and the human interest content the typical crime victim story contains.

By all accounts, talk about crime is very common. Just as it seems to dominate so many forms of mass media, so it also seems to dominate many of the conversations we have with each other. This was nicely illustrated by an early study of public reactions to crime in three major American cities. The authors of the study, criminologists Wesley Skogan and Michael Maxfield (1981), found that when residents of these cities were asked about their best sources of information regarding local crime, they named not the mass media but friends and family members. The crime stories neighborhood residents told and heard from each other tended to concentrate on violent as opposed to other kinds of crime. As well, stories about atypical victims (female or elderly victims of street crime, for instance) had much greater currency than stories with more run-of-the-mill narrative elements. In a sense, interpersonal communication channels seem to function much like mass media channels. They are dominated by and diffuse most widely stories that are novel (involving less common victim categories) and high in dramatic (often violent) content.

The 1981 study by Skogan and Maxfield showed, however, that there is a key difference between the stories that flow through mass and interpersonal channels. Specifically, local networks focus on and diffuse local stories. In other words, interpersonal rumor and gossip about crime are likely to be about people we known personally or people we surely could know. It is much more difficult to dismiss such stories by telling ourselves that they happen to distant others. Talk thus magnifies the importance of local events and spreads them far and wide. Of course, in high crime neighborhoods, there are more such stories to tell, but talk magnifies the impact of these stories to an even greater degree. As stories spread through local networks, perceptions of the prevalence or of the rapidity of increase of local crime can be affected dramatically.

Conversations about local crime focus not only on its manifestations but also on its causes. In order to understand better how people think about the causes of crime, Theodore Sasson (1995b) undertook an analysis of the discussions of a large number of local community groups in the Boston area. Of the various types of explanations discussed by residents, one is particularly relevant to any attempt to make sense of why local crime rates might rapidly shift upward. This perspective emphasizes the idea of "social breakdown" as a cause of crime. Ideas grouped under such an explanation typically contrast contemporary behavior and behavioral standards with those of the past in ways that clearly favor the latter. In earlier times, it is argued, parents disciplined their children and neighbors watched out for each other. Today, by contrast, children run wild and neighbors no longer are interested in each other's well-being. Crime rates have risen because "things in general have gotten worse." Order and authority have broken down. Rates of divorce and of out-of-wedlock births are skyrocketing. Of course, there is no shortage of anecdotal and impressionistic evidence that can be marshaled in support of this interpretation of why crime waves develop.

Sasson notes that this idea of social breakdown has both conservative and liberal dimensions. The more conservative version attributes increases in crime and disorder to the breakdown of family and community that was fostered by years of permissiveness and government sponsored antipoverty policies. In the more liberal versions, the sources of breakdown are to be found in high rates of unemployment, systemic racism, and the flight of capital from cities.

Rumors and Legends

What are rumors? According to Fine and Turner (2001), rumors are brief unsubstantiated bits of information that get passed through social networks. It is in fact the unconfirmed or unsubstantiated character of rumor that is its defining characteristic (Locher, 2002). While it is often rather easy to verify a rumor, most commonly those who hear and who pass the rumor along don't bother to do so. Indeed, rumors are repeated precisely because they are viewed as credible. Of course, for our purposes, the ultimate truth or falsity of given rumors is not really a central concern. Consistent with the constructionist perspective, it is useful for us to think of rumors as "truth claims."

Rumors come in many different forms (Miller, 2000). Some concern particular products. For example, the story has been widely circulated that the soft drink *Mountain Dew* will shrink testicles and lower sperm count, or that McDonald's hamburgers contain worm meat. Disaster rumors circulate during earthquakes, floods, wars, famines, and other natural or human disasters. For instance, in the aftermath of the 1994 Northridge earthquake in Los Angeles, the story spread that government agencies deliberately underestimated the size of the quake in order to avoid paying emergency relief funds (http://www .snopes.com/legal/fema.htm). A third kind, termed the "conspiracy rumor," gained very wide currency at the turn of the 21st century. Widely available folk narratives described a range of conspiratorial views of the social and political order. One of the most fanciful tales described how government agencies had cooperated to cover up news about the crash of a UFO in the New Mexico desert in 1947 (Shermer, 1997). An equally imaginative set of rumors revolved around claims that the moon landing had been a hoax (Plait, 2002). A final kind of rumor, which is of considerable interest to criminologists, is the atrocity rumor. Such rumors attribute acts of violence, usually horrendous violence, to groups that are socially marginalized or that occupy outsider status. Rumors that blame the spread of violence on wild minority youth or the homicidal tendencies of AIDS sufferers exemplify this category.

According to Jeffrey Victor (1993), it is important to understand the nature of the relationship between those highly specific rumors that others tell us or that show up in our e-mail inboxes and "urban legends." In contrast to rumors, urban legends are stories that continuously circulate in society—they disappear from view at some points in time and reappear at others. These legends, which are broadly drawn, assume a much more specific form in the context of rumors about specific people and specific places.

For instance, anti-Semitic legends about Jewish atrocities against non-Jewish youth have circulated since ancient times. Even in the contemporary period, the racist claim circulates that the preparation of certain foods for Jewish holiday celebrations requires that the blood of non-Jewish youth be added to the recipe (Victor, 1993). From time to time, however, such legends fuel highly specific rumors.

In Orleans, France, in May of 1969, stories spread that Jewish clothing store merchants were kidnapping teenage girls in their stores and selling them into forced prostitution (Morin, 1971). It was also rumored that the Jewish storeowners were able to get away with these crimes because they had been able to bribe local police and political officials. Although the incident had no basis whatsoever in reality, it provoked a social panic. Stores owned (or thought to be owned) by Jewish shopkeepers were boycotted and in some cases vandalized. One immediate antecedent of the rumor could be found in reports of "white slavery gangs" that had been given prominent treatment in the French tabloid media. While these reports made no specific reference to Jewish involvement in these crimes, the rumor in Orleans built upon traditional European anti-Semitic ideas about the role of Jewish slavers. Different communities were characterized by rumors of this type because of the wide cultural availability of the resources (anti-Semitic legends, tabloid reports of white slavery) out of which these rumors could be constructed. For these reasons, similar stories reappeared in 1974 and in again in the mid-1980s (Victor, 1993). In these later cases, those who believed these stories used the early reports from places like Orleans as a kind of "where there's smoke, there's fire" evidence to support the belief. That the earlier stories were shown to be without foundation was largely irrelevant.

Such relationships, Victor (1993) argues, help explain the well-researched rumor panic about satanic crime that swept through so many rural communities and small towns in the 1980s. The widespread but illogical and erroneous belief that thousands of satanists were kidnapping and mutilating children, desecrating graveyards, and engaging in ritual abuse and ritual sacrifice resulted in large numbers of innocent people being fired from their jobs, arrested, and sentenced to prison (Crouch & Damphousse, 1992; DeYoung, 1997; Hicks, 1991; Richardson, Best, & Bromley, 1991). While in particular towns these rumors identified perhaps specific teachers in specific day care centers, the rumors find their origins in long-standing legends about satanic conspiracies.

The Rumor Process

Why do rumors begin? One popular answer to this question locates their origins in the psychological processes of individuals (Fine & Turner, 2001). In other words, it is argued that rumors develop as individuals endeavor to solve personal problems or as they err in some attempt to make sense of information to which they have access. Rumors about the wrongdoing of others might result from one's desire to get revenge against those who are claimed to be misbehaving. Alternatively, a rumor about the misdeeds of others might originate in misheard or misremembered information. A fictional story about a serial killer who strikes on a college campus on some noteworthy date (like Halloween) is recalled at a later point as something that actually happened and is repeated to others with that suggestion.

Also, it should be remembered that passing on a rumor puts the teller of the story at the center of attention, however briefly. Like other forms of folklore— telling a joke, asking a riddle, quoting traditional wisdom—the passing on of a rumor involves performance elements that, for many people, have their rewards. Rumor transmission can also confer status on the one who tells the story. After all, to be first with the rumor, especially with the warning of dangers that lie just around the corner, is to be in the know while others in the group are not.

While rumor dissemination can be understood in terms of such individual dimensions, it is perhaps even more important to recognize the extent to which this is a social process. Thus, the emergence of rumors can be linked to the character of the social contexts. As several writers have noted, rumors seem most likely to emerge in settings where people lack access to more authoritative forms of information. Stated differently, rumors seem to spread most widely and most quickly when other forms of information are unavailable or untrustworthy. During wars, riots, or natural disasters, for instance, when established channels have broken down, rumors often run rampant. In a related way, when people feel that established forms of communication cannot be trusted, rumors serve as a form of "improvised news" (Shibutani, 1966). It is for this reason, for instance, that alienated and disenfranchised groups may depend on their rumor networks for information about the machinations of more powerful groups. This also helps to explain why there are always so many rumors in circulation about topics like Bigfoot, alien abductions, or crop circles. Until relatively recently, these topics tended to be ignored or not taken seriously by conventional media (Goode, 1999). This meant that rumor networks provided the only source of information for those interested in or worried about phenomena of this type.

Social context also importantly determines how stories will be shaped and interpreted. For instance, long-term group conflicts or suspicions influence the content of rumors. One important implication of this fact is that, in the rumor process, crimes might be attributed to an "out group" long before any evidence is available to support such a claim. In the immediate aftermath of the bombing of the Alfred P. Murrah federal building in Oklahoma City in 1995, several stories circulated (fuelled largely by irresponsible media reporting) that the bombing was the work of foreign—most likely Middle Eastern—terrorists (Miller, 2000). One British tabloid featured on its front page a photograph of a firefighter cradling a baby with the accompanying headline, THE NAME OF ALLAH (Ronson, 2002, p. 189).

The "Mexican organ theft rumor" provides a more recent and perhaps more gruesome example (Radford, 2003). During the 1990s a string of unsolved killings of mainly young women occurred near Ciudad Juarez, and El Paso, Texas. Very little progress had been made in the investigations when on April 30, 2003, a Mexican assistant attorney general announced that 14 of the nearly 90 victims were killed so that their organs could be harvested. The implication was clearly that the organs were being sold to wealthy Americans. In this way, the rumors both reflected and fuelled powerful anti-American sentiments. Neither the statement issued by the assistant attorney general, nor any subsequent retellings of the rumor, could explain why only women would be killed or how it was even determined that organs had been removed (since almost all of the bodies were badly decomposed). In spite of the absences of any physical evidence, such rumors have been prevalent in much of Latin America and in parts of Africa and Russia where negative views of Americans (especially rich Americans) are widely shared.

The story also borrows imagery from earlier organ theft legends that circulated during the early 1990s (Donovan, 2004). In the typical telling of these earlier versions of the story (which many college and university undergraduate have heard), a group of young men go to a big city for a weekend of fun. One of the young men tells his friends that he has met a young woman and plans on spending the night with her. When his friends have not heard from him by late the next morning, they go to his room. What they discover shocks them. Their friend is asleep in a bathtub filled with ice water; there is a fresh surgical closure on his back and a note next to the tub that tells the reader to "call 911." The surprise ending of the story is that the individual's kidneys have been removed—presumably to be sold. As the story traveled around in the decade of the 1990s, it tended to be told about specific people or specific cities or specific hotels. The story suggested to many a wave of organ thefts that represented a dangerous threat to the unwise—and presumably promiscuous—traveler.

Studies of the social process of rumor transmission have attempted to understand how rumors change, grow, or diminish as they are passed from one person to another. In a very early study, psychologists Gordon Allport and Leo Postman (1947) tried to demonstrate that as rumors spread they are modified in three distinct ways. First, they are *leveled*. This means that as they move along through social networks, they grow shorter. Words and the details they provide become fewer. Second, rumors become *sharpened* and in a sense this is the reciprocal of leveling. Thus as some details fall by the wayside, those that remain come into much sharper focus. Finally, with respect to *assimilation,* the details of the rumor become absorbed by the content of the cultural context. In the original experiment performed by Allport and Postman, study participants were shown a picture that portrayed (among other things) a white man holding a razor and speaking in what appeared to be an agitated manner to a black man. As the rumor was passed from one participant to another, however, subsequent versions moved the razor from the hand of the white man to the hand of the black man. In this case, assimilation occurred such that the raw empirical observation of who had the razor was made to conform to the pre-existing cultural stereotypes regarding who is and who is not more likely to be a violent and dangerous person.

The kind of experiment done by Allport and Postman (1947) resembles the popular game of telephone in which one person passes information on to another person in serial fashion. Anyone who has played this game has some sense of how the original message can be distorted and how processes like leveling, sharpening, and assimilation might work. Despite its apparent value, the serial transmission model underestimates the complexity of the rumor transmission process. For one thing, in the real world, it is often the case that we hear rumors, such as those about new criminal threats, from more than one source. This is because more than one version of any particular rumor is in circulation at any given time. As a result, we may hear variations of the same rumor from a number of sources and mistakenly come to believe that we are being told about several different incidents differing from each other in the specific details of who and where and when. Not surprisingly, we might easily come to believe that a problem (of roving gangs, organ thieves, or perfume robbers) is spiraling out of control.

In addition, in the real world, rumor diffusion involves a more complex division of labor than a model of serial transmission would suggest. Shibutani (1966), for instance, identified a number of complementary social roles that group members might play. The *messenger,* for instance, is the person who brings the rumor to the group. The *interpreter* puts the information contained in the rumor in some kind of context and evaluates it in terms of past experiences. The *skeptic* doubts the account and demands proof that the rumor is true. The *protagonist* emerges when someone advocates for one particular interpretation over another. The *auditor* forms part of the audience whose allegiance protagonists may attempt to win. Finally, the *decision maker* takes the lead in deciding what needs to be done. Although some of these roles might match our personalities better than others, it is typically the case that each of us plays different roles in different rumor episodes depending on, for instance, how much we care about the rumor in question or what positions, more generally, we occupy within the groups to which we belong.

RUMORS AND NETWORKS

Although the spreading of rumors is a public process, it is to a considerable degree bounded by the social networks to which people belong. Rumors about a rash of serial killers on campus or about new strains of date rape drugs may have great currency among college students but may be completely unknown to the residents of nursing homes.

The network- or group-specific character of the rumor transmission process has been nicely illustrated by studies of rumors regarding drugs and related forms of inner-city crime. Researchers have shown that a large number of rumors circulate within African American networks that explain the crack epidemic of the 1980s and the associated decline in the quality of urban life for minority residents with reference to conspiracies involving whites. While such rumors have great currency and are widely known within inner-city communities, they are often all but unknown beyond these communities.

In the early 1990s, the folklorist Patricia Turner (1993) collected from African American respondents more than 200 rumors linking the urban drugs crisis to some kind of conspiracy involving powerful whites. Depending on the substance of the rumor, those others might be said to be "the government," "higher-ups," "powers that be" "the Reagan administration," "the CIA," or "the FBI." According to Turner, these rumors fell into one of two categories. Many reflected a theme of "benign neglect" in that they maintained that those with power simply allowed inner cities to be overrun by crime and drugs. In this sense, problems of drug and crime were just part of an overall assault on black communities that also included substandard education, police brutality, and a general lack of social services. In contrast, rumors that fall under the category of "malicious intent" suggest that it may have been a government agency (such as the CIA) that quite deliberately introduced crack cocaine into inner-city neighborhoods as part of a larger program of genocide.

Sasson's (1995b) study of rumors about crime and drugs among African American residents found similar patterns. Such "theories" of urban crime have flourished, Sasson argues, because unlike more traditional "liberal" or "conservative" views of crime they resonate with the real-life experiences of those who spread them. Many residents of the inner city have experienced racism and are sensitive to its systemic manifestations.

With few exceptions these conspiratorial understandings of the problems of urban crime and violence are rarely given any time or attention by mainstream media. The exception, of course, might be the journalist who is interested in debunking such rumors. As in the cases of Bigfoot and alien abductions, the lack of attention that mainstream media pays to these rumors underwrites rather than threatens their credibility. Such inattentiveness is, after all, consistent with a conspiratorial understanding of the problem. In a very general way, these rumors can be thought of as "counter hegemonic" in that they challenge traditional orthodoxies regarding urban crime.

INTERPERSONAL AND MASS COMMUNICATIONS

While it is important to distinguish processes and structures of mass communications from processes and structures of interpersonal communications, we need to note some important points of intersection. It is true that when we talk about increasing crime, we tend to talk about local people and local conditions, but we also talk a lot to each other about the news and information that the mass media make available to us. Because of what we see on television, for example, we often find ourselves in conversations about so-called celebrity crimes. Sometimes our concern with local developing crime problems originates in particularly notorious episodes to which the media widely attend. For example, talk about local gang problems can be fuelled by extensive media coverage of gang issues (McCorkle & Miethe, 2002). Similarly, public discussions about crime in local schools can increase dramatically following a very high profile case like the Columbine school shootings in 1999.

Rumors and urban legends about crime often move between mass and interpersonal channels in a multistage process. On some occasions, those involved in news production might pick up and transmit a rumor because it is believed to be an authentic new story. In this way, a rumor becomes a "fact." Each Halloween, well-intentioned journalists file stories warning parents about the rash of treat tamperings that are believed to have occurred in other places in previous years (Best & Horiuchi, 1985; Rogers, 2002). Careful analyses of the Halloween sadism story, however, suggest that there is really no evidence to indicate that serious problems of candy tampering have ever occurred in American neighborhoods (Best & Horiuchi, 1985). Journalistic objectivity does not require that "proof" of such claims be presented, only that someone be referenced or presented as saying that the incidents occurred. Thus, equally well-intentioned police chiefs or community crime prevention or public health officers might be interviewed in such a story, lending credibility to claims about what *could* happen if parents did not exercise due prudence. In a similar way, journalists have often legitimated political rumors as facts by attributing them to, for instance, a "highly placed administration source."

As Brunvand (1989, 1993) has noted, sometimes a newscast or television documentary intends to debunk a circulating rumor but in so doing produces ironic results. As the rumors diffuse to a wide and partially inattentive audience the key observation about the falsity of the rumor falls by the wayside. All that's remembered by those who pass the story on is that they "heard it on the news." As a result, not only does the story spread more widely than it would have otherwise, but it is rendered more legitimate because of the media treatment it has received. On other occasions, urban legends become the plot lines of television or movie dramas. The films *Urban Legend, Urban Legends: Final Cut,* and *Candyman* are examples. Even the famous "kidney heist" legend discussed earlier was the basis for an episode of the popular television program *Law & Order.* Daytime talk shows or open line radio shows, which provide somewhat greater opportunity for members of the general public to express certain types of beliefs, can also facilitate the dissemination of rumor (Rosnow & Fine, 1976, p. 99).

In a somewhat different way, rumors and legends are often fuelled by media coverage of real-life events. One of the most famous examples of this aspect of rumor formation and diffusion can be found in an analysis of the story of "the Hook." This is perhaps the best known of all urban legends and is familiar to just about anyone who ever spent time telling spooky stories around a campfire or in some other adolescent setting. The most familiar form of the story is quoted by folklorist Jan Harold Brunvand (1981, p. 48) from a letter addressed to advice columnist Dear Abby:

> A fellow and his date pulled into their favorite "lovers' lane" to listen to the radio and do a little necking. The music was interrupted by an announcer who said there was an escaped convict in the area who had served time for rape and robbery. He was described as having a hook instead of a right hand. The couple became frightened and drove away. When the boy took his girl home, he went around to open the car door for her. Then he saw—a hook on the door handle.

In a detailed discussion of the hook legend, Ellis (1994) traces the origins of the present form of the story to 1950s California. Early tellings of the tale linked it to the very specific location of Mulholland Drive. According to Ellis, a likely influence on the development of the legend was the mass media publicity given to the notorious Chessman case during this same period. Caryl Chessman was arrested at the culmination of a citywide panic relating to a series of attacks on young couples on a local lovers lane. In one particular instance, the 17-year-old female victim was confined to a mental institution less than a year after the attack, presumably as a result of trauma relating to the victimization. According to Ellis (1994), the crimes (in a way that parallels the subsequent legend) produced "near hysteria in Los Angeles, and radio announcements were continually broadcast during the period" (p. 63). Chessman, who was eventually sentenced to death for the crimes, was nicknamed "Hooknose" in reference to deformities that resulted from a childhood accident. It can be suggested that the real-life episode provided the raw elements out of which this very enduring legend was constructed.

The complex character of the relationship between rumor and mass media is evident in the case of a one-person crime wave in Dallas in which, it was claimed, a young woman was endeavoring to kill random men by infecting them with the AIDS virus during sex (Bird, 1996). In 1991, an ABC news magazine program retold a story that had been circulating in Dallas for a couple of months by that point. *Ebony* magazine had published a letter from "CJ in Dallas" who said that she was infecting up to four men a week with the AIDS virus. The incident had led to a major scare in the Dallas area. It is important to ask how such a story finds its way into mainstream commercial media and why these media would have treated the incident so uncritically.

S. Elizabeth Bird (1996), who extensively examined the CJ legend, argues that while we think of news and folklore as opposites, the line between them is not all that clear. Although we tend to believe that news is "factual" while folklore is "fanciful," both reflect popular anxieties and both rely on good and effective story telling. There is no shortage of rumors and legends that focus on the threat of AIDS. By and large, these stories employ the same media values of drama, suspense, and irony that characterize so much news production. In addition to the rumor described at the start of the chapter, other stories circulating in the past several years include the following (see www.snopes2.com):

> American scientists created AIDS in a laboratory as a weapon to be used on enemies of the United States, and they began testing it on unsuspecting populations in Africa and Haiti, where they lost control of the experiment.

> A very good friend of mine is in an EMT certification course. There is something new happening that everyone should be aware of. Drug users are now taking their used needles and putting them into the coin return slots in public telephones. People are putting their fingers in to recover coins or just to check if anyone left change. They are getting stuck by these needles and infected with hepatitis, HIV, and other diseases. This message is posted to make everyone aware of this danger. Be aware! The change isn't worth it!
>
> P.S. This information came straight from phone company workers, through the EMT instructor. This did NOT come from a hearsay urban legend source.

The CJ story was in essence the story of a "supercriminal" striking randomly. Supercriminals provide excellent narrative themes and are often the basis of concerns about new kinds of crime threats. Through the personification of CJ as a "supercriminal," people came to understand her as a mass murderer. The attachment of a specific name to the threat allowed widespread fears about AIDS and random violence to come into sharp focus and made the threats these conditions pose seem less ambiguous and perhaps more manageable.

In this sense, it drew on the same media and folkloric themes that have focused public attention on missing children, serial killers, and home invasions. Bird concludes that the CJ story was not really a hoax in any simple sense, nor were the media simply wrong. Instead, the case represents the coming together of anonymous rumors and legends fed by both oral traditions and media practice. Cultural vulnerability is what the CJ story was all about and, like many legends, the CJ rumor grew out of fear and uncertainty.

TECHNOLOGICAL INNOVATION AND RUMOR TRANSMISSION

For most of human history, rumor transmission has relied primarily upon the spoken word. As new communication technologies have replaced or mediated the spoken word, however, they have provided alternative means for their diffusion (Donovan, 2004).

Brunvand (1995), for instance, used the term *faxlore* to describe the processes by the "lights out" rumor circulated widely in the 1990s. The rumor, which is widely known, concerned threats of random gang violence to which people subjected themselves by simply blinking their lights at an oncoming car (Donovan, 2004). The text of a recent version of the legend states,

> A police officer working with the DARE program has issued this warning: If you are driving after dark and see an on-coming car with no headlights on, DO NOT FLASH YOUR LIGHTS AT THEM! This is a common gang member "initiation game" that goes like this:
>
> The new gang member under initiation drives along with no headlights, and the first car to flash their headlights at him is now his "target." He is now required to turn around and chase that car, and shoot at or into the car in order to complete his initiation requirements. Make sure you share this information with all the drivers in your family!

The legend contains many familiar elements, including the wildness of youth and the irony of the good deed. To a considerable degree the narrative also reflects a concern with spreading gang activity and allows believers to blame local problems on organized conspiratorial others (Best, 1999; Fine & Turner, 2001; McCorkle & Miethe, 2002). The legend warns that gang members are leaving the "hood" and threatening "us" instead of anonymous others (Fine & Turner, 2001).

As well, the story reflects insecurities about those settings in which we believe we have every right to feel safe. Like concerns about crime in the home or at the mall, crimes in the car figure prominently in the more general anxiety about random violence (Fine & Turner, 2001). Indeed, several legends about cars and random violence circulated in the 1990s, including the story of the "killer in the backseat" and the "slasher under the car."

Brunvand's analysis highlighted the extent to which modern technology was central to the diffusion of the story. It was to a considerable degree through the use of fax machines that the legend spread nationally and internationally. It might be expected that such technologies would reduce the amount of leveling, sharpening, and assimilation that occurs with respect to rumor diffusion. Brunvand does note, however, that variations observed across versions of the "lights out" rumor were similar to those that characterize oral transmission. Thus, details are added or altered and aspects of the story are localized. Although the spread of the rumor depended on thousands of people copying and sending thousands of faxes rather than on word of mouth, there is a remarkable continuity between more modern and more traditional rumor transmission processes.

RUMORS OF WAR

There is no recent episode that more clearly illustrates the relationships involving new technologies, rumor processes, and the rapidly escalating threats of violence than the events of September 11, 2001. Within moments of the attacks on New York's World Trade Center, Internet servers became jammed. As typically occurs in disasters, there was a huge demand for news and information. E-mail, chat rooms, and Web page postings became a principal means by which "news" was improvised. The severity and the immediacy of the attack were unprecedented in the lives of Americans and almost everyone felt vulnerable. As well, there quickly developed in some quarters the perception that the "official version" of the events could not be trusted and that wider national and international conspiracies were somehow behind the attacks. All such factors combined to fuel a rapidly developing rumor mill that speculated, often wildly, on the meaning of the attacks and warned about the future. Online rumor collections list the following, many of which were in circulation within hours of the attack (http://www.snopes.com/rumors/rumors.htm; CSICOP Hoax Watch, 2002). All of these rumors are inconsistent with much more persuasive forms of empirical evidence:

- Although the government denied it, the plane in Pennsylvania was *shot* down because it was not responding to radio calls
- As many as eight airplanes were hijacked
- Some World Trade Center occupants were given advance warning of the attack and had 45 minutes to leave the building
- Westminster Abbey in London, England, was also destroyed by a hijacked plane
- Because all ports were closed and no oil would be available, it would be necessary for everyone to fill their automobile gas tanks as soon as possible
- Nostradamus, the French philosopher and seer, had predicted the 9/11 attacks

Another category of rumor, which did not arise in the immediate aftermath of the attacks, drew attention to new and even more threatening attacks that were imminent. According to one such rumor that circulated on the Internet,

> Just heard from Jackie—this is a very eerie story. A co-worker just told her that she and her husband were shopping at a Costco last night and they were checking out behind an Arab couple. The Arabs did not have enough money to pay their bill so she offered to give them the money. They said we can't pay you back but we can give you some information instead. They said to stay away from the Baltimore tunnels (specifically, the Harbor Tunnel) for the next few days. She called the FBI and they showed her the new Most Wanted list that just came out and he was one of them—the FBI has not been able to find him—he's apparently still living in Laurel. This woman was so upset that she came to work today and then went home.
>
> It's amazing that these people are living among us and even with their families and kids in our schools. Anyway, Jackie said they are checking all trucks going into and out of the Baltimore tunnels. She advised staying away from Baltimore period through this weekend at least. Tell anyone you think might be affected by this.

Another story that circulated in the month after the attack stated the following:

> Last week a gentleman of Middle Eastern descent opened up an account at the Hackensack Costco and purchased close to $7,000 worth of candy. I guess this was not particularly alarming because many small businesses purchase large amounts of items at Costco. What became alarming was that this same person (or someone using this person's card) purchased close to $15,000 worth of additional CANDY 2 days ago at the Wayne Costco. The cashier became alarmed at this large purchase of candy and more so when the person paid cash. I'm told she was fearful and did not alert anyone in the store until after the person left and then it was reported to authorities.
>
> I pass this along in case your children or grandchildren go trick or treating. I do not know the intentions of the person who purchased all this candy, but in today's time I do not think it is crazy to be overly cautious. The possibility of this candy being tainted and resold to unknowing discount distributors and then passed on to unknowing consumers is too great.

Clearly, this rumor reflects several interesting elements, including anxiety about the "ethnic other" and the fear of terrorism. It draws on much earlier folkloric traditions, however, by linking these concerns to the more durable problem of the Halloween sadist. Another rumor with similar content took the following e-mail form:

Hi:

I think you all know that I don't send out hoaxes and don't do the reactionary thing and send out just anything that crosses my path. This one, however, is a friend of a friend and I've given it enough credibility in my mind that I'm writing it up and sending it out to all of you.

My friend's friend was dating a guy from Afghanistan up until a month ago. She had a date with him around 9/6 and was stood up. She was understandably upset and went to his home to find it completely emptied. On 9/10, she received a letter from her boyfriend explaining that he wished he could tell her why he had left and that he was sorry it had to be like that. The part worth mentioning is that he BEGGED her not to get on any commercial airlines on 9/11 and to not go to any malls on Halloween. As soon as everything happened on the 11th, she called the FBI and has since turned over the letter.

This is not an e-mail that I've received and decided to pass on. This came from a phone conversation with a longtime friend of mine last night.

I may be wrong, and I hope I am. However, with one of his warnings being correct and devastating, I'm not willing to take the chance on the second and wanted to make sure that people I care about had the same information that I did.

Although the story was investigated by the FBI and found to be without substance, its impact was considerable. According to Rogers (2002), mall managers and owners across the United States in many cases cancelled their traditional Halloween festivities or, at the very least, greatly modified mall security.

The situation was further compounded, of course, by a series of crimes that involved the mailing of anthrax to media and government officials. Because these anthrax incidents began after the attacks of 9/11 and before Halloween, a further set of rumors circulated in cyberspace and contributed to the worries about terrorism and about Halloween. In some cases, these rumors represented variations on older themes, like the perfume robbers, presented at the beginning of the chapter:

I feel that it is important to inform you of very important information that I was told. Seven women have died after smelling a free perfume sample that was mailed to them. The product was poisonous. If you receive free samples in the mail such as lotions, perfumes, diapers etc. throw it away. The government is afraid that this might be another terrorist act. They will not announce it on the news because they do not want to alarm us of any danger.

Perhaps the most widely diffused of these rumors concerned the "Klingerman virus." While e-mail concerning this threat had actually circulated well before the terrorist attacks, the substance of the narrative assumed new saliency in the aftermath of the 9/11 attacks and in the wake of the anthrax mailing:

This is an alert about a virus in the original sense of the word . . . one that affects your body, not your hard drive.

There have been 23 confirmed cases of people attacked by the Klingerman Virus, a virus that arrives in your real mailbox, not your e-mail inbox. Someone has been mailing large blue envelopes, seemingly at random, to people inside the U.S. On the front of the envelope in bold black letters is printed, "A gift for you from the Klingerman Foundation." When the envelopes are opened, there is a small sponge sealed in plastic. This sponge carries what has come to be known as the Klingerman Virus, as public health officials state this is a strain of virus they have not previously encountered.

When asked for comment, Florida police Sergeant Stetson said, "We are working with the CDC and the USPS, but have so far been unable to track down the origins of these letters. The return addresses have all been different, and we are certain a remailing service is being used, making our jobs that much more difficult."

Those who have come in contact with the Klingerman Virus have been hospitalized with severe dysentery. So far seven of the twenty-three victims have died. There is no legitimate Klingerman Foundation mailing unsolicited gifts.

If you receive an oversized blue envelope in the mail marked, "A gift from the Klingerman Foundation," DO NOT open it. Place the envelope in a strong plastic bag or container, and call the police immediately. The "gift" inside is one you definitely do not want.

In response, several government organizations, including the Centers for Disease Control and the United States Postal Service, issued statements intended to discourage the spread of the rumor. Not only had none of the incidents occurred, but there did not even exist a Klingerman Foundation.

The Social Implications of Talk

In order to appreciate the social implications of talk about crime, it might be useful to address a question that has often been posed by sociologists and psychologists interested in the study of rumor or gossip: Is it more useful to think about rumors as social pathologies or to think about them as forms of problem solving (Donovan, 2004)? There is merit to both interpretations, depending on the nature of the rumor and the social context in which it is spread.

Most commonly, we think about rumors in the negative. Often they represent forms of character assassination or are misleading and error-ridden descriptions of problems or events. The intensification of talk that characterizes the social circumstances in which rumor and gossip are rife can create widespread anxiety. An important consequence might be people acting in ways that are not consistent with their best interests or that squander valued social and physical resources. In the aftermath of the attacks of September 11, 2001, rumors, as we have seen, fed such reactions. In small towns all across America, Halloween celebrations were cancelled, people avoided public places, and many refused to open their mail. As well, municipal, state, and federal government agencies directed money and human energy toward policies and programs intended to reduce risks that were in reality quite negligible. The sense that the threat of terrorism was rapidly escalating skewed perceptions of risk. Sociologist Pamela Donovon (2004) argues that a tendency to contain ominous warnings is a general feature of many crime rumors. This is because dominant themes in such narratives include (a) a strong sense of social disintegration and the decline of civil society, (b) a sense of lost guardianship, and (c) a comparatively high level of organization and systematic activity among criminals and predators.

At the same time, talk about crime can clearly be understood as a form of problem solving. For victims of crime, it is one of the ways in which they are able to work through the trauma caused by crime and to construct the personal meaning of what has happened to them. The kind of talk about crime that Skogan and Maxfield (1981) observed in their study of reactions to crime in three major American cities is clearly not without value. People do learn something about the local criminal environment and the kind of risks their neighbors face. In a more general way, talk about crime is a reflection of the most basic and celebrated democratic values. Public discussion of our problems and their potential solutions animate social life.

Even in the case of rumors, it must be recalled that the defining feature is not error but the lack of substantiation. Most of us know from our experiences in the workplace or in other settings that rumors often do prove to be true in the end. As forms of "improvised news," the spread of rumors suggests a way to understand our predicament or how to proceed in the absence of certainty. In some circumstances, rumors allow us to be proactive and to anticipate what it is we need to do. The problem with the rumor marketplace is the same as the problem with any marketplace—we may make bad decisions if we are not critical consumers.

Social scientists interested in the study of public reactions to crime suggest another context within which this issue can be addressed. For years, criminologists have attempted to determine whether public reactions to crime tend to drive people apart or pull them together. We will discuss this issue in greater detail in the next chapter. For the present it is sufficient to recognize that this theoretical question is in one sense a question about the sociological meaning of talk about crime. This is explicit in the work of the famous French sociologist with whom the examination of the relationship between crime and social solidarity originated. In *The Division of Labor in Society*, Durkheim (1893/1933) argued that the effects of crime are largely functional. In other words, as people react to crime, they are reminded of the moral sentiments they share in common. These reactions therefore tend to make society a more stable place than it might otherwise be. He acknowledges that talk about crime is really the means by which this effect is achieved:

> Crime brings together upright consciences and concentrates them. We have only to notice what happens, particularly in a small town, when some moral scandal has just been committed. [People] stop each other, they seek to come together to talk of the event and to wax indignant in common. (p. 102)

In contrast, a number of other writers have argued that the impact of crime is to reduce social solidarity. This is because as crime rates rise they generate fear, which is divisive. Much of the evidence we have reviewed in this chapter also suggests to us how talk is the medium through which such fear is activated. There is a tendency in much of the empirical literature to suggest that fear originates in our experiences with mass media presentations of crime. Interestingly, though, the research on this subject is rather inconsistent. One is hard pressed to make the case strongly that fear of crime is simply a product of reading too many newspapers or watching too much television. In part, the fallacy in this respect is thinking of audience members as passive dupes who parrot what the mass media tell them.

As we have seen in this chapter, people are much more active in this respect than they have been given credit for. In our conversations with each other we actively construct crime problems rather than passively reproduce media imagery. To be sure, media often provide the ideas, images, and language resources that we use to accomplish these constructions, but we are by no means restricted to what the mass media make available. Not surprisingly, while the research shows that media effects on fear of crime may be less strong than we popularly believe, it also shows that the effects of talking with others may be stronger than we popularly believe. One of the reasons for this, of course, is precisely because our conversations about crime tend to focus on local conditions and local victims, which are much more difficult to ignore.

Conclusion

"Money talks and bullshit walks." "Actions speak louder than words." "Stick and stones may break my bones but names will never hurt me." "Just ignore it. It's only talk." "Talk is cheap." Popular expressions of this sort encourage us to discount the importance of talk. This is especially true with respect to gossip and rumor. The former we often describe as "idle," the latter we qualify as *only* rumor. The position we have taken in this chapter is quite contrary. Everyday talk, despite its apparently inconsequential character, is pregnant with social significance.

The reason for this should be obvious by this point. The conversations we have with each other, the faxes and e-mails we send and receive, the messages we post on our Web sites, and all of the other ways in which interpersonal communication is accomplished constitute important means by which crime waves are constructed. The stories we tell encourage us to perceive problems as worsening, to believe that a new kind of criminal danger is making a sudden, if often mysterious appearance upon the social scene. As large numbers of stories with common themes flow through the information networks with which we are affiliated, we see problems spiraling out of control. The process by which this happens is a communal and not an individual one. Each of us contributes to and is influenced by processes of crime talk and rumor transmission.

6

Being Afraid

I t is ironic that criminologists seem to have paid so little attention to the role that is played by human emotions in crime and justice processes. After all, much of what concerns the student of crime has emotional content (Karstedt, 2002). We have always argued that anger is an important crime motivator, and recently we have become more and more interested in the role that "hate" or "rage" plays in crime commission. Increasingly, the justice system concerns itself with the proper role that offender shame or remorse might play in the judicial or rehabilitative process (Braithewaite, 1989). Various victim movements have encouraged the view that the pain and suffering of victims and their families are issues to which more attention needs to be paid by policy makers (Weed, 1995). In court, impact statements are thought by many to allow for a cathartic release of anger experienced by many victims. In a different way, many have come to recognize that the socialization of criminal justice professionals must be attentive to the kinds of "emotional work" that police, prosecutors, and others are required to routinely undertake (Goodrum & Stafford, 2003). As compared to other social scientists, criminologists have been content to make assumptions about, rather than to probe, the emotional character of the processes they are interested in studying (Burkitt, 1997; De Haan & Loader, 2002; Katz, 1999; Thoits, 1989).

There is, however, an important exception in this regard. For the past several decades, criminologists have been keenly interested in the study of the distribution, causes, and consequences of public fear of crime (Lee, 2001). Who is fearful of becoming criminally victimized and why? How does that fear affect the ways in which we live our lives? What is the larger social significance of fear? What is the most useful way in which we should try to think about fear for research purposes? Is fear a problem, and if so, what should we do about it? Since the 1960s, a large body of research has been accumulating that allows us to speak to these questions. Of course, the research is less consistent in some respects than we would like it to be. It is also less methodologically varied than we might like. Still, it is immensely useful in any attempt to make sense out of how fear structures reactions to crime.

The present chapter focuses on these kinds of issues as we investigate the role fear plays in the development and maintenance of crime waves. Of particular importance, though, is the way in which rising crime rates (or a perception of rising crime rates) increase public anxiety. This is not a peripheral matter. For the overwhelming majority of people who are not themselves directly victimized, it is through such an emotional response that crime waves are personally experienced. As we will see, however, these issues are complicated. While we might expect rising crime to create fear, it can also be argued that fear can cause crime levels to rise. Added to this mix are political pronouncements about proposed actions that it is claimed will quell widespread anxiety. Proponents advocate all manner of programs (often punitive) that they say the public demand. These programs suggest important questions about the relationships involving rising crime, fear, and public action that require our attention.

We begin with a discussion of what is meant by "public fear of crime" as a research concept. Next we address the way in which fear is socially distributed in society. Most especially, we want to know if levels of public fear are related to rising crime levels and to the media habits most likely to expose people to information about rising crime levels. We then consider some of the wider implications of public fear in the context of crime waves. The most important of these relate to the use of fear for political purposes and to what some have argued are the consequences fear can have for the subsequent crime rate increases. The chapter ends with a discussion of some episodes in which fear levels become so extreme that experts in collective behavior often refer to them as cases of mass hysteria.

The Meaning of Fear

What is the "fear of crime"? Despite the ease with which newspaper editorials and angry political speeches speak about fear, it may be surprising to learn that there really is no simple answer to this question. Fear can be understood in a variety of ways both within criminology and across the wide array of disciplines that comprise the social sciences.

Most of us tend to think about fear in terms of its physiological dimensions. Being afraid—in the face of some immediate danger, such as an impending attack by an animal or a human predator, in a car that is spiraling out of control, or in a plane that seems to be experiencing serious difficulty—is associated with quite distinct and easily recognizable changes to our bodily functions (Kovecses, 1990). These physical adaptations to threatening conditions are to some degree part of our physiological hard wiring and reflect our very long evolutionary past (Dozier, 1998).

From a physiological perspective, being afraid implies a series of complex changes to the endocrine system that alert us to danger and that allow us to react. These reactions, when the threat is immediate, typically involve "fight or flight" (Silberman, 1978). The heart rate increases rapidly and the systolic blood pressure goes up. Our faces blanch as blood flows to the brain and to the large muscle groups where it is most needed. The perception that everything is happening in slow motion provides a better opportunity to receive situational cues and react more carefully.

Most of what criminologists have had to say about the problem of fear has had little to do with these physical manifestations. The reason for this is quite obvious. Typically, researchers do not have access to people when they are actually afraid (and thus reacting physiologically). Instead, criminologists have focused on anticipated rather than actual fear. They have thus tended to think about fear more as an attitude or a perception than as a physical response. Most of this research has been conducted in the context of large standardized surveys in which hundreds, or sometimes thousands of people have been asked about their beliefs, feelings, or routine reactions regarding the threat of crime (Ferraro & LaGrange, 1987). In the context of social science, fear of crime is recognized as a "multidimensional concept" (Rountree, 1998). If one looks at the way in which fear has been defined for research for research purposes, it becomes clear that there are essentially three dimensions of the phenomenon in which investigators have been most interested.

COGNITIVE DIMENSIONS

Questions that focus on the cognitive dimension of fear of crime probe respondents' beliefs regarding crime and victimization. Survey items might therefore ask respondents to estimate subjectively the likelihood of being victimized (Forde, 1993; Rountree & Land, 1996). Or, respondents might be asked whether they think their neighborhoods have more crime or less crime than other neighborhoods in the city in which they live. In a manner that relates very directly to the study of crime waves, they might also be asked whether they think crime rates are going up or going down.

Measures that focus on the cognitive dimensions of fear have at least one very clear advantage over other types of measures. Because they ask about beliefs or judgments regarding empirical realities, it is reasonable to speak about such perceptions as being "correct" or "incorrect." In other words, if people say that crime rates are going up, when our various measures of the crime rate say that they are not, we are able to describe the public perception as essentially incorrect.

Research has documented, for instance, a tendency for people to overestimate both the amount of crime and the amount of crime that is violent (Kappeler, Blumberg, & Potter, 2000). It is also typically the case that people believe their own neighborhoods to have less crime than other places (even when this is not true). Given such errors in judgment, it is perhaps reasonable to think about the steps we might take to correct the misperception. This is not to say that the members of the public never get the facts right. Research by Mark Warr suggests that members of the general public can, for instance, accurately estimate the relative occurrence of criminal offenses. The principle that people use in this respect, according to Warr (1980), is the seriousness of crimes. In other words, they reason that more serious crimes occur less frequently than less serious crimes and thus that murders are less common than robberies and robberies are less common than shoplifting.

The problem with questions that focus on the cognitive dimension, however, is that they seem to have relatively little to do with our commonsense understanding of fear (Rountree & Land, 1996; Sparks & Ogles, 1990). The emphasis instead is on the actuarial calculations that people make of crime levels and personal risks. Indeed, these kinds of cognitive judgments do not dictate how people feel about the threats crime might pose to them. For many people, the sense that crime is going up may not have very much to do with being afraid. The individual who relishes danger, for instance, could view situations of enhanced risk as exciting rather than frightening.

AFFECTIVE DIMENSIONS

Researchers whose work focuses on the affective dimension of fear tend to be interested, explicitly, in the feelings people have about crime (Williams & Akers, 2000). In many surveys, respondents have been asked about how safe they might feel walking alone in their neighborhoods at night. Alternatively, they might be asked how much they worry about crime in general or about the possibility of being the victim of any of a number of specific crimes (Williams & Akers, 2000). Other surveys have asked about feelings of satisfaction with personal safety (Sacco & Nakhaie, 2001). In all cases, the intent is to get at something more like an emotional reaction than like a cognitive assessment.

An examination of the kinds of questions that researchers use to assess the affective dimensions of fear reveals that they approximate our everyday understanding of the concept. Unlike cognitive measures, however, there is no way we can really talk about which perceptions are correct or incorrect. Unlike an estimate of the probability of being victimized, our feelings about being victimized are not really right or wrong.

Interesting in this respect, though, is the widespread tendency of fear of crime researchers to talk about the rationality or irrationality of fear. The argument in this regard is that, given the real-world risks that some groups (like the elderly) actually face, they are behaving irrationally if they express high levels of fear. Of course, such reasoning is highly problematic. To charge that some given level of fear or anxiety is irrational is to argue, at least implicitly, that people are more afraid than they should be.

With respect to affectivity, it can be noted that personal fear (however it is defined) is not the only kind of feeling that people express about crime, although it is really the only one that has been thoroughly investigated. Some investigators have distinguished fear from concern (Furstenberg, 1971). Whereas the former relates to personal anxieties, the latter concept involves feelings about the significance of crime as a social problem. Clearly one can be concerned about crime, as a relatively abstract problem affecting society, without being personally worried about being a victim of crime.

In addition, one might be afraid of crime without being personally fearful. In this respect, it is possible to speak about what Mark Warr (1992) has identified as "altruistic fear." This refers to the fear that each of us might have for others. The father whose daughter is away at university may feel anxiety or worry when she informs him that she is going to a concert featuring a musical artist whose shows in the past have involved lethal violence. In a similar way, adults might fear for the safety of their elderly parents, or spouses might fear for the safety of each other.

In a very different way, Jason Ditton and his colleagues (Ditton, Bannister, Gilchrist, & Farrall, 1999) have written about how our almost exclusive attention to feelings of fear or anxiety has neglected other kinds of powerful feelings, most notably anger. Their research shows that when people are asked about their feelings of fear *and* their feelings of anger in the same survey, they are more likely to report the latter rather than the former type of emotion. Unfortunately, to date, very little research has been done on the subject of anger about crime or about related feelings like rage or the desire for retaliation (Craig, 1999).

BEHAVIORAL DIMENSIONS

It is possible to think about crime in terms of what people do rather than in terms of what people say (Sacco & Nakhaie, 2001). So, for example, when asked what they do in response to crime, people might say that they stay home at night rather than go out, that they carry a weapon to protect themselves, or that they refuse to make use of public transportation. We might interpret such responses as measures of fearful behavior.

If actions do speak louder than words, it might be argued that such reports give us a more rigorous assessment of who is afraid and who is not. After all, we are not dealing merely with "feelings" but with more consequential behavior. On the other hand, it is important to keep in mind that what we are usually dealing with is not really what we see people do but what they tell us they do. Dishonesty, bad memory, and a desire to gain the approval of the interviewer can all create a gap between actions and reports of actions.

How these three aspects of fear connect together is as much a theoretical problem as an empirical one. On the one hand, we can think about each of these dimensions as providing an alternative measure of the kind of underlying phenomenon in which we are interested. Alternatively, some researchers have argued that we can think about these dimensions as being related to each other in some kind of causal process (Warr & Stafford, 1983). In this way of thinking, for instance, our cognitive perceptions of the world around us influence our feelings and these feelings lead us to behave in certain ways. Or, we might want to try to argue that the routine crime precautions we take serve to reduce our feelings of crime anxiety so that the causal relationship runs in the opposite direction. This would suggest that taking precautions should make people feel safer. Of course, in the context of cross-sectional research (in which measures of perceptions, feelings, and behaviors are gathered at a single point in time), questions about the relative value of these interpretations are answered only with great difficulty—if at all.

What Are We Afraid Of?

Criminologists interested in fear have tended to focus on a relatively narrow range of crimes. Either implicitly or explicitly, they have emphasized anxieties relating to acts of physical and property victimization, which typically involve strangers and that often occur in public places. We know considerably less about how much people fear intimate violence or corporate victimization. Critics charge this narrow preoccupation with stereotypical street crimes reproduces the very "law and order" mentality it claims to investigate (Johnson & Wasielewski, 1982). In other words, our starting point for what kinds of fear need investigation is not the perspective of those who answer our surveys but our own sense of what they are probably afraid of. In this way, the actual experiences of members of the population and their lived sense of who victimizes them can easily fall between the cracks.

A more fundamental issue here relates to the socially constructed character of what it is that frightens us. Our tendency to think about fear as an emotion can lead us to assume that there is something unalterable or prepro-grammed about what or whom we see as dangerous. This is not the case. Our view of what threatens us is mediated by the cultural and historical context (Tudor, 2003). This is nicely illustrated in Sally Engle Merry's (1981) very insightful investigation of fear and danger in a Philadelphia public housing project. Merry's investigation revealed that the various ethnic groups that lived in the project had quite different understandings of whom to avoid and what sorts of places and situations threatened danger. In short, fearing crime is a social and cultural process.

Who Is Afraid?

Much research on the fear of crime elaborates what might be called the epidemiology of fear. Since the earliest studies it has been obvious that the tendency to worry about one's safety or to overestimate the risks of criminal victimization is not evenly spread in the population. Instead, some people seem much more likely than others to experience fear as a problem. Of course, the research literature is very broad and not always consistent, especially given the wide variety of ways in which fear has been defined for research purposes. Still, a judicious use of this literature supports some broad generalizations regarding the kinds of factors that seem to discriminate between those who are more and those who are less fearful.

GENDER

At the individual level, there is a strong research consensus that supports the view that women are much more likely than men to express concern about personal safety (LaGrange & Ferraro, 1989; Ortega & Myles, 1987; Pain, 1995). This appears not to be just a result of some tendency on the part of men to be stoic in interview sessions. Rather, the consistency of the findings indicates that there really is something quite different about the ways in which men and women think about their personal safety (Gordon & Riger, 1989).

There is no single explanation as to why these differences exist. In part, they reflect the simple biological truth that on average men tend to be stronger and bigger than women. When woman, as compared to men, contemplate the typical (male) offender, they contemplate someone who is likely to be bigger and more physically intimidating. A second factor has to do with the uniqueness of rape (or other forms of sexual assault) as a threatening crime. This is a form of victimization that almost exclusively affects women. Even if men and women feared other crimes equally, the addition of rape to the female fear equation would create an imbalance (Warr, 1985). Even more generally, we can recognize that processes of female and male socialization differ markedly in the lessons that are taught regarding sexual vulnerability. In short, the sexual socialization of adolescent females, much more than the sexual socialization of adolescent males, stresses the potential for physical danger of many types (Hamner & Saunders, 1984; Sacco, 1990).

The unique vulnerability of women to violence generally and sexual violence specifically was pointedly illustrated by press reports of the escalating levels of fear among Iraqi women as "major hostilities" concluded in 2003. According to a report in the *Boston Globe,* women in Iraq were staying indoors, avoiding schools, and donning veils in response to widespread reports of kidnappings and rapes (Milligan, 2003). The degree of change in actual levels of predatory crimes targeting women is of course not easily documented under the kinds of conditions that prevailed in Iraq at the time of the report.

AGE

It is commonly believed that "the elderly" comprise one of the most fearful groups in the population (Clarke, 1984; Yin, 1980, 1982). Indeed several fear-of-crime surveys of the general population have shown that when the responses of older Americans are compared with those of younger Americans on standardized questions, older people tend to give more fearful responses. Many gerontologists have been quick to point out why this might be the case. Older people may feel less physically capable, may be less trusting, and may have much greater fear of the consequences that can emerge out of what others might consider a relatively minor victimization.

Some critics, however, have suggested that the matter is much more complicated (McCoy, Wooldredge, Cullen, Dubeck, & Browning, 1996). They contend that the tendency to find higher levels of fear among older Americans is a product of the kinds of questions that are used in such surveys (LaGrange & Ferraro, 1987). As stated, fear is often measured by asking respondents how safe they feel walking alone in their neighborhoods after dark. Yet for a variety of reasons (many of which are unrelated to crime) older people tend to make only infrequent use of city streets at night. This means that questions that use city streets after dark as the reference point may not yield a terribly accurate picture of how older people really feel. The suggestion that ageing brings with it a generalized fear of the world, a diminished sense of capacity, and irrational fears may themselves reflect an ageist understanding of the relationship between age and perceptions of safety (Pain, 1997).

RACE AND INCOME

Indicators of membership in an economic or ethnic minority group are associated with higher levels of fear of crime (Parker, Smith, & Murty, 1993; Will & McGrath, 1995). The differences involving minority status are not as strong as those involving sex and age, however (Skogan, 1995). Among those with lower incomes and among African Americans, for instance, the concerns for personal safety and for the safety of property emerge as more significant problems. In part, minority group membership can be read as an indicator of lower levels of access to the kinds of resources other people can use to make themselves feel safe. Those without substantial disposable income may, for instance, be more reliant on public transportation and less able to purchase the locks or lights that might provide a greater sense of security. As well, income and race can be read as indicators of residence. The high degree of economic and racial segregation in American cities and differential distribution of crime problems across neighborhoods can mean that minority group membership brings with it a higher likelihood of residence in an area where the threats to person and property may indeed be more substantial (Taylor & Covington, 1993).

COMMUNITY OF RESIDENCE

Fear of crime varies across physical locations as well as across categories of people (Akers, La Greca, Sellers, & Cochran, 1987; Bankston, Jenkins, Thayer-Doyle, & Thompson, 1987). At the most micro level, we can recognize "hot spots of fear" (Nasar & Jones, 1993). These could include places that are poorly lit, where individuals might feel trapped, or where the environment offers many opportunities for a potential offender to hide. The movie cliché of a cluttered dark alley located off a deserted city street clearly illustrates what such a hot spot might look like. In general, the fear of crime is higher in more urban places (Belyea & Zingraff, 1988; Fischer, 1984). Cities tend to have higher rates of crime than small towns or rural regions. In addition, city life, by its nature, involves life in a world of strangers (Merry, 1981). In the public spaces of cities we typically encounter people who are strangers to us in two distinct ways. On the one hand, they are strangers in a personal sense in that we lack any sort of detailed biographical information about them. But often they are strangers in a cultural sense as well. This means that they are people whose public demeanor, style of dress, language, or ethnic membership may differ dramatically from our own (Lane & Meeker, 2000). Claude Fischer (1984), the famous urban sociologist, has argued that because strangers are less predictable than those about whom we have more knowledge, the public realm of the city quite naturally increases our apprehension about safety.

Fear of crime also varies across neighborhoods within cities (Akers et al., 1987; Austin, Furr, & Spine, 2002; Moeller, 1989). We tend to find more fear where we find more crime. However, crime is not the only environmental condition that has been linked to fear. Several researchers have argued that a whole range of conditions called "incivilities" or "disorders" also tend to increase feelings of anxiety (Kanan & Pruitt, 2002; LaGrange, Ferraro, & Supancic, 1992; Taylor & Hale, 1986; Skogan, 1990). Such conditions include abandoned houses, public drug use, aggressive panhandling, graffiti, and loud music. In particular, gangs and gang crime represent especially troubling forms of disorder for the residents of many neighborhoods that already suffer from a variety of social and physical ills (Lane, 2002). According to one interpretation, such conditions are read by residents as signaling that no one really cares about these places and no one is in charge. It is this perceived lack of order and a widespread sense that there are few limits on what the environment will tolerate that make people feel more insecure.

VICTIM STATUS

It might be assumed that being a victim of crime is a major factor explaining the distribution of fear in the population. Once again, however, the effects are somewhat more complicated by both the meaning of victimization and by the research methods used to investigate such effects (Miethe, 1995; Sacco & Macmillan, 2001). Most important, much of what we count as victimizations in any of our tallies tends to be at the less serious end of the seriousness continuum. Simply put, theft is common, and murder is rare. There really is no reason why we should expect relatively minor crimes against property to have important implications for how we feel walking alone in neighborhood streets at night. Yet, as we would expect when we look at the effects of serious predatory crimes such as assaults, rapes, or robberies on fear, more significant effects of victim experience on feelings of fear do emerge.

Yet, direct experiences with (serious) victimization do not take us very far in explaining fear of crime in society. This is because there are many more people who are likely to report being afraid than who report being a recent victim of serious predatory violence. For statistical reasons this condition places limits on the possible size of the correlation between these variables.

ACCESS TO CRIME NEWS

As discussed in the previous chapter, it is popularly believed that the mass media are the major determinants of fear of crime, even though researchers have had a very difficult time documenting any clear and obvious relationship in this regard (Heath & Gilbert, 1996; Sacco, 1995). It appears that, overall, how much television people watch or how many newspapers they read doesn't have much to do with their levels of worry about crime. There are good reasons for this. A major one has to do with the essential irrelevance of much media content to the personal concerns of the average media consumer. In other words, reading about major gang crimes in Los Angeles may have little to do with the assessment of personal safety made by the reader living in, for instance, Middlebury, Vermont.

In contrast, as we have seen, much of the information that flows through our interpersonal networks may strike much closer to home. Hearing about the victimization of neighbors, friends, or family members cannot be easily dismissed as something that happens to some anonymous victim living in some distant place (Skogan & Maxfield, 1981). This is not to say that the effects of media on fear are irrelevant. It is just that they are more specific and more conditional than many glib observations have suggested (Heath & Gilbert, 1996). When media coverage, for instance, focuses on randomly occurring violent crimes that occur locally, media consumers are likely to express higher levels of concern about their personal safety (Liska & Baccaglini, 1990).

Do Rising Crime Levels Cause Fear?

So much of the research on the fear of crime conceptualizes fear as a kind of characteristic that some people have and others do not. In psychological terms, fear is treated more like a trait than a state (Gabriel & Greve, 2003). This tendency to view fear as a kind of enduring psychological characteristic that some people have and others do not simplifies a much more complex reality. More realistically, we might think about fear in situational terms (Charles, 1983). In other words, there are some circumstances in which we feel more afraid and others in which we feel less afraid. The point is perhaps most obviously made by comparing fear to other kinds of emotions. We probably all know people who always seem to be happy and others who never seem to be happy, although most of the people we know are happy in some circumstances but not in others. The same is probably true with respect to fear (Bursik & Grasmick, 1993). Mark Warr (1990) has shown that both the novelty of a situation and the level of darkness can be potent signs of danger, and in combination they can have a powerful effect on fear. The presence of others, however, can be frightening or reassuring depending on who these others are. Those who are perceived as dangerous others and thus whose presence promotes fear rather than feelings of security are more likely to be young males—especially young males of minority status.

An important situational contingency in which we are especially interested involves the context of escalating crime rates. How are levels of public anxiety about crime affected when the levels of crime rise? Once again, the relationship is not as straightforward as we might expect. While some studies do in fact suggest that rising crime rates are associated with rising levels of fear (Baker, Nienstedt, Everett, & McCleary, 1983), other studies do not (Forde, 1993; Miethe 1995). A common problem, in this respect, relates to the finding that people always tend to think crime rates are going up—even when they are not. For instance, 38% of people interviewed as part of the British Crime

Survey in 2001 reported a belief that crime had risen "a lot" in the previous 2 years. A further third of the population thought that it had gone up a little, and only about 4% expressed the "correct" view that crime had fallen ("Britain: Fear Itself, Crime," 2003).

Upon closer examination, we might not be all that surprised by such a finding. This is because any attempt to understand the relationship between crime levels and fear levels needs to consider the nature of the mechanisms that mediate any effects the former might have upon the latter. Crime levels, of course, do not affect feelings directly but do so only through some sort of channel that spreads the word that crime is on the rise.

The most obvious such mechanisms, as we have seen, are the mass media. The relationships involving rising crime levels, media coverage of crime, and fear levels are quite complicated, however. Overall, it appears that the processes that drive the crime level are quite independent from whatever processes drive media coverage of crime (Lowry, Nio, & Leitner, 2003). One is not merely a reflection of the other. Mark Fishman's (1978) study of a crime wave against the elderly in New York City, for instance, showed that intensified media coverage of such crimes in a number of newspapers and television newscasts was not inspired by any actual increase in the rate at which such crimes occurred. Overall, we do not really expect there to be much of a relationship between the amount of measured crime (as indicated, for instance, by the UCR) and the amount of crime we find in the news.

As we have seen, crime news coverage can have profound effects on fear—under particular conditions. Variations in coverage reflect news production dynamics, and not the dynamics that move the crime levels. Dennis Lowry and his colleagues (2003) studied the relative effect of network news variables and "objective" crime rates on perceptions of crime as the most important problem facing America. Their overall finding was that network television news variables accounted for almost four times as much variance in perception as did actual crime rates. They conclude that crime scares can have more to do with the ways in which crime is being covered than with shifts in crime levels.

Another complication concerns the fact that changing fear levels over time may be related to shifts in other kinds of conditions that might be related to but are in fact quite separable from changing crime levels (Skogan, 1986, 1990; Taylor & Covington, 1993). So, for example, over time as social disorder increases, people are more likely to become worried about their safety and the safety of others. As abandoned buildings, public drug use, panhandling, and other forms of physical and social incivility increase, they can steadily undermine the confidence people have in the local social order. Of course, levels of social disorder and levels of more serious crime are related both in space and over time, though they represent separate forms of community problems.

Even more broadly, the fear of crime may increase over time as a result of more diffuse kinds of social change (Bankston et al., 1987; Krannich, Berry, & Greider, 1989). In particular, as neighborhoods become more socially heterogeneous, anxieties about safety in public might be aggravated. In this respect, some writers have discussed the ways in which increases in levels of ethnic or racial heterogeneity contribute to a sense of discomfort on the part of neighborhood residents who feel that their neighborhood is undergoing a decline. Dramatic increases in the numbers of "strangers" make the environment seem less familiar and perhaps more threatening. Once again, we might expect these changes to correlate with changes in the crime level, but the correlation is far from perfect. The implication is that these more diffuse changes may themselves exaggerate problems of personal security.

Some analysts have suggested that, to a considerable degree, the fear-of-crime discourse in contemporary society is discourse about race and a fear of racial change (Bursik & Grasmick, 1993). Thus, while it may be "politically incorrect" to express racist attitudes openly, expressions of anxiety about crime and criminals are usually regarded as perfectly appropriate forms of public discussion. What troubles critics, though, is the extent to which these fears and the political legitimacy that is attached to them are code words for anti-minority sentiment. Not surprisingly, much of this research has focused on the ways in which white neighborhood residents respond to the presence of and the crimes committed by members of minorities. There is strong evidence to support the conclusion that white encounters with black citizens provoke a strong fear of victimization (Anderson, 1999; Lane & Meeker, 2000; St. John & Heald-Moore, 1996). Several studies show that the presence of racial minorities in neighborhoods is associated with higher levels of fear among white residents (Moeller, 1989; St. Johns & Heald-Moore, 1996; Skogan, 1995). In her study of perceptions of and reactions to crime in a Philadelphia public housing project, Sally Merry (1981) found that concerns about safety were to a considerable degree rooted in the misunderstanding and distrust that characterized relations among the large number of ethnic groups that inhabited the project. The documentation of such patterns raises much larger questions about the historical tendency of media and culture more generally to associate particular ethnic identities with criminal stereotypes (Bursik & Grasmick, 1993).

Does Fear Cause Rising Crime Levels?

There is a less conventional way of understanding the relationship between rising crime levels and fear. While the traditional view emphasizes how increasing crime can contribute to increasing fear, another form of the argument directs our attention to the reciprocal process (Bursik & Grasmick, 1993; Skogan, 1986). In other words, how might fear actually contribute to crime levels?

One version of this argument emphasizes an understanding of how crime causes crime (Conklin, 1975; Goodstein & Shotland, 1982). In such a model, fear is conceptualized as the mechanism that intervenes over time between lower crime rates at one stage and higher crime rates at a later point. The process could be said to have several distinct phases. At stage one we observe an initial increase in crime levels, attributable to any of a number of demographic or cultural factors. At a second stage, news about the increased crime levels or details about the character of some kind of "new" crime circulate via mass media or word of mouth. At stage three we observe that a general escalation in fear occurs as people learn about the new threats in their environments. As they grow more afraid, they withdraw from their communities. Perhaps they become less trusting of others and less willing to speak to strangers. They stay home at night rather than go out. In general, they are less likely to make use of the numerous social and cultural opportunities their communities make available to them. At the next stage, we note that as people withdraw from the social life of their communities, the delicate social ties that bind community residents to each other are disrupted. This has severe consequences for the informal social controls that routinely regulate behavior—especially public behavior. As streets become deserted, for instance, they are less likely to be subject to informal community control. As the levels of social control decline, the opportunities for crime become more abundant. Less control thus allows more crime to take place, which further aggravates the sense of fear and worry. Thus, as the cycle repeats itself, crime levels can be expected to rise.

The so-called broken windows argument involves a similar kind of logic, except that the kinds of acts that precipitate the cycle seem more innocuous (Kelling & Coles, 1998; Skogan, 1990; Wilson & Kelling, 1982). When the various kinds of disorder that we have already discussed—like public drinking, panhandling, noisy neighbors, or graffiti—go unchecked, a message is sent to the lawful as well as the lawless that no one really cares about the need to maintain public order (Skogan, 1990). The law-abiding will find the situation threatening and as they become more and more afraid, they will seek to avoid the kinds of public environments in which disorder is pervasive. Those who are inclined to engage in lawbreaking will, however, view the disorder differently. To them it is a sign that the local social order seems most willing to tolerate widespread disobedience of traditional norms of urban civility. It might also communicate that any environment that tolerates widespread disorder will also tolerate more serious breeches of the criminal law. For the potential offender, then, declining social order signals greater opportunity to do whatever one wants to do, irrespective of what the law or traditional public morality might seem to require.

Thus, problems of disorder become more serious crime problems through the intervening processes of crime and withdrawal from city life. It is in this way that one broken window in an abandoned building becomes many broken windows (Wilson & Kelling, 1982).

How might such spirals, once set in motion, come to an end? One answer to this question has been provided by Alan Liska and Barbara Warner (1991). Their starting point is routine activities theory (Cohen & Felson, 1979). In a very general way, they argue, routine activities theory maintains that social patterns that separate people from their property and that keep them away from family and friends create greater opportunity for predatory crime. Liska and Warner agree that public reactions to crimes like robbery may be that people avoid going out. Worry about the danger of the public sphere may lead people to seek out those environments (especially the home) in which they are more like to feel at ease. Of course, when people do this in large numbers, the cumulative effect is to undermine community and to exacerbate the problems that characterize public space. At the same time, however, the cumulative effect of such actions is to increase the levels of guardianship that household members exert over their property (and over each other). The consequence may thus be an increase in social control and a probable stabilization of crime rates. The process is an ironic one. As the levels of some kinds of crime (like robbery) rise, so does fear. The effect, however, may be to stabilize or lower the rate of robbery as well as other kinds of crime.

In addition, it has become fashionable to argue that it is possible to undertake deliberate policy interventions directed toward the breaking of these fear-crime spirals. Some of the implications of and problems with these policy approaches are discussed in Chapter 7.

While these arguments are certainly interesting, they are problematic in some important respects. Perhaps most important, they lack a sufficient degree of empirical support (Harcourt, 2001; Taylor, 2001). In a very important examination of the broken windows argument, Robert Sampson and Stephen Raudenbush (1999) found little supporting evidence. Their analysis of data gathered from Chicago neighborhoods revealed that it was not possible to conclude that disorder leads to more serious crime problems in a manner consistent with the kind of model just described. Instead, both disorder and more serious crime have the same kinds of common causes—most notably structural poverty and the lack of a strong sense of community efficacy.

The (Ir)Rationality of Fear

Researchers who study the fear of crime, as well as many policy makers, tend to think about the fear of crime as some sort of pathology. In other words, they emphasize how the fear of crime lowers the quality of life. There are two major ways in which this approach is apparent.

The first concerns the focus that researchers place on the negative outcomes that fear has for social life. A large number of studies have investigated the relationships that link fear to decreases in trust, in fondness for the community, and in levels of community activity (Conklin, 1975; Hartnagel, 1979). Fear is thus seen to undermine the stability and cohesion of social life.

There are a couple of problems with this approach, however. The first, as we have seen, is a tendency toward hyperbole on the part of many who have written about the consequences that the fear of crime has for social life. The stereotypical image of the urban dweller, beset by powerful anxieties that make communal living next to impossible, lacks any real generalizability (Hindelang, Gottfedson, & Garofalo, 1978). To be sure, there are people who are affected in this way, but for most people the adaptations that fear requires are more subtle. Overall, it seems, the effects of fear have more to do with the ways in which people do things, than what it is they do (Miethe, 1995). So, for example, fear is less likely to stop people from going out at night than it is to affect where they go or whether they go with others instead of by themselves.

Another problem concerns the lack of attention paid to what might be considered the positive aspects of fear. The definition of fear as a problem neglects a consideration of its potential benefits. After all, in a world that objectively threatens us, a certain degree of fear is useful. Fearfulness might be problematic, but so might be an absence of fear. The opposite of fearfulness may not be fearlessness, but recklessness. To the degree that fear keeps us safe, it must be seen to be somewhat adaptive.

A second major way in which researchers and others have tended to focus on the pathological character of fear concerns the attention paid to questions of rationality and irrationality. These questions concern the apparent gap between measured levels of fear and measured levels of victimization for certain demographic categories, particularly for the elderly and for women. In each case, it has been argued, fear seems to outstrip actual experiences with crime and as a result older Americans and women are actually "more afraid than they should be," given the real threats they face. Ideologically speaking, arguments about the irrationality of the fears expressed by the elderly and women come dangerously close to ageism and sexism. The argument seems to be that the fears of older people and women have more to do with an unfounded hysteria than with real-world experiences. How these groups end up being described in this literature is uncomfortably reminiscent of traditional descriptions by, for instance, many health care specialists who have complained about the unfounded concerns of women and older people.

These arguments about irrationality are highly problematic. In large part, this is because such arguments seem to suggest that we know how fearful people *should* be. Realistically, there seems to be no reasonable way in which such a judgment can be made. How afraid should I be if I face a very low risk of a victimization incident that has very severe consequences? How about if I face a very high risk of an incident with somewhat less serious consequences? Both the risk and the seriousness of the outcomes are very relevant to how frightened people feel (Warr & Stafford, 1983).

The difficulties involved in any attempt to assess the rationality of fear are illustrated in the notorious case of the Washington, D.C.,-area sniper killings. In October of 2002, two individuals later identified as Lee Boyd Malvo and John Allen Muhammad were responsible for the murder of 10 people and the wounding of three others in a series of commando-style shootings. The randomness of the shootings combined with the fact that the victims were typically going about the performance of everyday tasks like shopping or filling their gas tanks created considerable fear in the population. Not surprisingly, the media coverage was almost hysterical. Halloween festivities were cancelled, schools went into "code blue lockdowns," and many people stopped doing anything that would expose them to a potential sniper in a public place. Were people behaving rationally or irrationally?

There is no simple answer to this question ("United States: The Logic of Irrational Fear," 2002). The murders took place in five counties with a total population of 3.1 million people. Over the period during which the sniper was active, there was one chance in 310,000 of becoming a victim. While the risks appear slim, they would have (had the sniper remained active) resulted in an annualized murder rate more than twice the rate of these Washington-area counties. Moreover, it is important to ask how people assess the risk of being killed by a sniper. There are several problems involved in any effort to make such an assessment. For one thing, the sniper was a novel threat, and people really had no basis for evaluating the risks of their own victimization. For another, one of the victims was a child and there is a tendency for people to overestimate the risks of uncommon threats involving children. Finally, there did not really appear to be any way to mitigate the risks of victimization. Routine precautions (not talking to strangers, locking car doors, etc.) provided no protection. Clearly, the issue of the rationality of fear is quite complex.

Another problem with these irrationality arguments is that the gaps that are assumed to exist between victimization levels and fear levels may be more illusory than actual (Donovan, 2004). In the case of the elderly, it is true that according to the best empirical evidence, older Americans, in the aggregate, have the lowest victimization rates of any group in the population (Cook & Skogan, 1990). As well, with respect to fear, we have already discussed how efforts to research fear among the elderly are characterized by some serious measurement problems. Yet when fear is measured in ways that employ terms of reference relevant to the lives of older people, the levels of elderly fear are much less extreme. As a result, the paradox involving victimization and fear among the elderly becomes much less paradoxical (Fattah & Sacco, 1989).

With respect to women's fear, the paradox requires a somewhat different resolution. Unlike in the case of the elderly, the problem does not seem to involve the ways in which fear is measured since findings about the higher levels of crime-related anxiety among women are pretty robust. Instead, the problem involves the ways in which traditional counts of female victimization have been tallied (Sacco, 1990). In short, the estimates of female victimization that have been used in the construction of arguments about the irrationality of women's fear have tended to underestimate victimization levels (Stanko, 1985). As many critics have noted, traditional victimization survey methodologies are not terribly good at counting crimes that involve intimate offenders or crimes that occur in private places. Of course, these are two very common features of crimes—such as domestic assault and much sexual assault—that rather uniquely victimize women. In addition, there is a whole range of fear-inducing events that, again, tend to disproportionately victimize women and that have not typically been asked about in the context of traditional victim surveys (Hamner & Saunders, 1984). Such events include, for instance, the encounter with the obscene telephone caller or the exhibitionist. When women's victimization experiences are measured more accurately, levels of victimization rise and the paradox is made less puzzling.

Indeed, the point about the irrationality of fear is more generally problematic. Efforts to map the social location of fear and the social location of victimization risk, "objectively measured" suggest several points of correspondence. Fear tends to be more of a problem for racial minorities and for the poor (for whom victimization risks are also higher). Fear tends to be higher in more urban places, where crime rates of most types tend to be higher. It is also more of a problem among victims of serious crime and within settings where levels of uncivil behavior are more common. All such relationships suggest the rationality of fear.

When Fear Goes Wild

Despite the rational character of much fear, episodes do occur in which fear appears to be out of control. Sometimes it is fed by the occurrence of real-world events, when for instance a serial killer or other type of predatory offender seems to strike at will and to defy apprehension. The public reaction to Jack the Ripper in 19th-century London (Curtis, 2001), to the Mad Butcher of Kingsbury Run in Cleveland of the 1930s (Badak, 2001), or to the Atlanta child killings in the 1980s (Headley, 1998) provide vivid examples of how community life can be fundamentally altered, at least for brief periods of time, by an ominous criminal threat.

In other cases, however, fear levels dramatically escalate in response to threats that by all empirical indicators simply do not exist. Such incidents have been described as "collective delusions" (Bartholomew, 2001). These delusions typically involve the rapid, spontaneous, and temporary spread of some false belief within a population. The term *delusion* in this context does not imply any kind of psychological pathology on the part of those who are involved in this process. Rather it refers to the socially constructed character of the delusion. Among the best known cases of collective delusions are those involving the "phantom anesthetist of Mattoon" (Johnson, 1945; Rosnow & Fine, 1976) and the "monkey man of New Delhi."

The episode of the phantom anesthetist or phantom prowler of Mattoon began on a late August night in 1944 in Mattoon, Illinois. At around midnight, a Mattoon resident had her neighbor phone the police to report that a prowler had opened her bedroom window and sprayed her and her daughter with a paralyzing gas. The police, however, upon investigation were unable to find any sign of an intruder. A couple of hours later, the woman's husband returned home and notified the police that he had just seen a man running from the vicinity of their bedroom window. A second investigation by the police revealed nothing. The news coverage the next day was sensationalist and referred to the woman and her daughter as the "first victims" and warned of an "Anesthetic Prowler on the Loose." No doubt the phrase "first victims" established a strong set of expectations and over the course of the following week, several reports of victimization by a phantom gasser were made to the police. The symptoms usually included temporary paralysis, eye and mouth irritation, dizziness, and nausea. In a few cases it was even claimed that the family dog had obviously been gassed since the pet had not barked at the intruder. Some residents, armed, silently waited for the offender to strike again. Others reported that they had seen him in the act of victimizing others.

As the number of reports increased, the state police were invited into the case in the hope that their advanced technology and greater investigatory experience might facilitate its resolution. Worried servicemen from Mattoon who were stationed overseas as part of the war effort, wrote letters home to inquire about the safety of their families. Within a week, "the city was in a state of fright" (Bartholomew, 2001) and vigilantes and volunteers began to patrol city streets. The episode reached its peek on the weekend of September 8 and 9 "as the gasser was seemingly everywhere" (Bartholomew, 2001, p. 101).

Within a couple of weeks, the episode came to a rather unsatisfactory conclusion. No prowler was caught and the number of cases being reported rapidly declined. It became increasingly apparent to almost all observers that there had never been a prowler. Several aspects of the case seemed curious

(Rosnow & Fine, 1976). First, the symptoms of the victims resembled what have widely been reported in the psychological literature as the classic symptoms of hysteria. These include nausea and vomiting, sudden and temporary paralysis, palpitations, and dryness of the mouth. In addition, the police investigation was unable to find any physical evidence of the prowler. Finally, the anesthetic would have to have had some quite contradictory properties. On the one hand, it must have been potent and stable enough to act quickly and yet so unstable that it produced dramatic differences in its toxic effects. It was powerful enough to produce paralysis and vomiting and yet left no visible trace.

While it is difficult to determine with precise accuracy exactly why the episode occurred, several explanatory factors might be suggested, including widespread war-related tension and a general malaise and fear of the future. More specifically, the incident coincided with a wave of anxiety about the use of poison gas during World War II, a search for some escaped Nazis, and a local increase in burglaries (Bartholomew & Radford, 2003). It seems clear that following the sensationalist coverage of the initial incident, a number of people began to reinterpret more routine occurrences such as nighttime shadows, common illnesses, and unusual odors as evidence of the presence of the mad gasser (Bartholomew & Goode, 2000).

How can we explain the observation that almost all of the gasser's victims were women? A partial answer may involve the recognition that the women of Mattoon were acutely worried about the safety of husbands, sons, and brothers involved in the war effort. In addition, it may be that the representation of women was inaccurately portrayed by the researcher who investigated the incident. A subsequent analysis of the episode suggests that the extent to which men may have succumbed to the delusion was minimized by a research assumption that it is women much more than men who were likely to exhibit hysterical symptoms.

In May of 2001, CNN (http://edition.cnn.com/2001/World/asiapcf/south/05/16/india.monkeyman) and a large number of international media outlets began to report on a somewhat similar, but much more fanciful series of events that were occurring in East Delhi, India. The episode involved widespread reports of a "monkey man" who was attacking and generally terrorizing local residents. Over several nights, media reports indicated that dozens of people had been injured and at least two had died. In both cases, the deaths resulted from injuries sustained in falls, as in one incident a man and in another a pregnant woman attempted to flee the monkey man.

Those who claimed to have seen the attacker offered wildly varied physical descriptions. Many described him as hairy and ape-like. Others said he was an agile feline-like creature. Still others claimed that the attacker was very obviously human—an individual covered from head to toe with bandages or wearing a helmet. He was variously described as having razor-like claws, super-human strength, and an ability to leap across rooftops. The rapidity of reports in highly disparate locales led some to conclude that perhaps more than one person (or more than one creature) was involved in the attacks. While rank-and-file police officers may have not taken the reports all that seriously, the official response suggested otherwise. The commissioner of police told American news reporters, for instance, that officers would be posted on rooftops and that public areas would be kept well lit. As well, they had planned to fortify checkpoints at entrances to the city and to hold a series of public meetings. Such steps, it was hoped, would keep public panic under control. The police also posted a reward for information leading to the monkey man's capture and, perhaps most dramatically, they issued an order to "shoot on sight." All the while, armed vigilante groups patrolled the streets.

As in the case of the phantom gasser of Mattoon, the monkey man seems to have been the product of a collective delusion (Bartholomew & Radford, 2003). Despite the very high levels of real fear in the population, a detailed police investigation, an examination of forensic evidence, and inconsistencies in victims' statements all supported the conclusion that there really was no offender—human or otherwise—on the loose.

How then do we explain a city in the grip of fear over the threat of a non-existent monkey man? Once again several factors seem relevant. To begin with, chronic power outages and stifling heat put large numbers of people on dark-ened rooftops at night. In addition, the superstitions of rural immigrants com-bined with unrestrained media coverage to promote a climate of rumor and worry. The sight of real monkeys running free on the outskirts of urban areas (and occasionally attacking people) was not unknown and provided further grist for the rumor mill. As in the case of the Mattoon gasser, it is likely that early reports encouraged widespread reinterpretation of ambiguous stimuli like nighttime shadows, animal bites, and other injuries of unknown origin.

The cases involving the phantom gasser and the monkey man are not isolated examples of the phenomenon of collective delusions. The research lit-erature on the sociology of collective behavior suggests numerous episodes throughout history. Surely the medieval witch craze and the satanic crime wave of the 1980s provide additional examples of widespread fear developing in response to predatory threats that did not exist. Other scares have revolved around the following:

- A Puerto Rican creature known as "El Chupacabras" that is thought to attack and prey upon farm animals (Bartholomew & Goode, 2000)
- "Spring-Heeled Jack," the scourge of early 19th-century London, whose preda-tory style anticipated that of the New Delhi monkey man (Polidor, 2002)
- A phantom slasher in Taiwan in 1956 who was thought to be indiscriminately attacking people with a sharp razor (Jacobs, 1965).

- Widespread reports of mutilated cattle and sheep in the 1970s and 1980s
- (Another) mad gasser in Virginia in the 1930s (Bartholomew & Radford, 2003)

In all cases, the fear that was generated was real and tangible, although the threat to which the fear was directed was not.

Conclusion

It seems rather evident that the fear of crime is a central feature of crime waves. As people begin to develop the perception that crime is on the increase or that crime is changing in qualitative ways that suggest greater danger or greater viciousness, an increase in anxiety is likely. To a degree, of course, the term *public anxiety* or *public fear* is somewhat of a misnomer. Evidence that we have examined suggests that the burden of fear does not fall equally on the shoulders of everyone. People who live in high crime neighborhoods, the poor, ethnic minorities, women, and city-dwellers fear for their safety more than the members of other social and demographic categories and will contribute disproportionately to fear increases. Moreover, people who share several of these characteristics may find fear a particular problem.

Of particular interest to those involved in the study of the relationship between crime waves and the fear of crime are the implications that rising crime has for fear. Several models available in the literature suggest that these relationships might be more complicated than criminologists have traditionally believed. One intriguing argument focuses on the way the fear response to rising crime waves (or rising levels of disorder) becomes an unraveling thread in the social fabric, which facilitates additional increases in rates of crime and disorder. While the argument demands attention, evidence to support the view that this process might be operating in any clear and obvious way is lacking.

A broader perspective on the consequences of fear requires attention to the political uses to which it can be put. Those who favor particular social policies or legal interventions often do so in the name of public fear. Politicians portray themselves as prisoners of such fear. Their approaches to the problem of crime, they tell us, are meant to assuage a terrified public that demands punishment. The argument is of course wrong on several counts. As we have seen, rising crime levels do not necessarily even mean rising fear. In addition, however, there is no strong body of evidence to support the conclusion that fear promotes punitiveness (Beckett, 1997; Stinchcombe et al., 1980).

Finally, it is important to note that fear itself—as distinct from crime—has been defined as a policy problem. Often within the context of community policing initiatives, program planners have asked what steps can be taken to reduce fear in the population (Scheider, Rowell, & Bezdikian, 2003). Indeed, many of the specific strategies associated with community policing are intended to calm a worried public. Foot patrols, the aggressive policing of misdemeanors in public places, and crime awareness workshops have the alleviation of fear as their objective, at least to the same degree that they have stopping crime as their objective (Scheider et al., 2003; Thurman, Zhao, & Giacomazzi, 2001). Moreover, the evaluations of such programs often demonstrate success (Williams & Pate, 1987). Overall, it seems, it is easier to reduce fear than to reduce crime. Indeed, one might cynically suggest that the relative ease with which success can be demonstrated is one of the reasons why it became a policy objective in the first place.

Critically, it should be pointed out that "fear prevention" as a social strategy seems to proceed from assumptions that may not be correct. In the first instance, it is difficult to think of any other situation in which government resources are deemed necessary to change a widespread public mood. In addition, the implicit suggestion that fear is too high assumes that we somehow know what appropriate levels of fear are (we do not). We are also asked to assume that fear is irrational (which it may not be). Otherwise, why would we seek to reduce it?

7

Crime Waves and Public Policy

When we perceive that crime is getting worse, our collective response is to try to do something about it. How do we manage climbing crime rates? What steps might we take to pull these rates down or soften the impact that crime has on victims or on society at large? These are important questions and our efforts to answer them require a discussion of the sources, roles, and consequences of crime policy. In a very general way, we can think about crime policy as whatever it is that governmental (or other relevant) organizations do (or do not do) with respect to crime. Such a definition leaves us with a great deal of latitude. Within the framework provided by such a definition, we need to understand that there are more useful and less useful policies; policies that help resolve problems and policies that make problems worse; policies that are well thought out and policies that are hastily devised; policies that might work and policies that quite simply cannot work.

Thus, in order to make sense of crime waves, we need to pay attention to what it is we think we are doing about them. Our goal, however, will not be to review the hundreds of different kind of policies and the thousands of empirical studies that have as their goal the evaluations of such policies. Several excellent reviews of these issues are readily available (Lab, 1992; Rosenbaum & Lurigio, 1998; Sherman et al., 1997). Instead, the focus here is on the broader context of the processes by which crime policies are developed, implemented, and evaluated.

Our starting point is the recognition that social policies involve the making of choices and decisions, often directed toward the management of crises (Best, 1999). What is of real interest to us, however, is the way in which these choices and decisions are shaped by social, cultural, economic, and historical contexts. Implicit in the perception that a crime wave is under way is the judgment that something needs to be done quickly. This need to respond quickly might very well promote decisions that are ineffective, inefficient, or that even create more problems than they solve.

But this is not the only complexity. It is also true that social policies, like all complex institutional decisions, are usually intended to achieve more than one objective. Crime policy may have reining in the crime problem as its manifest goal, but there might be other goals as well. For instance, those responsible for the policy might seek to gain political advantage over rivals or to achieve more pragmatic bureaucratic advantages.

Yet our attempt to make sense of the relationship between crime waves and public policy resists any simple explanation for another quite interesting theoretical reason. Our commonsense assessment of crime waves and public policy suggests that the latter is a reaction to the former. In other words, crime rates go up and crime policy is the response. However, there is another way of conceptualizing this relationship. Some scholars maintain that the relationship might run in the opposite direction. From this perspective, crime rates reflect our policy decisions. How could this happen? Most simply, it can be argued that more aggressive or new styles of policing could result in the certification of more criminal behavior. A casual observer might notice at any point in time that crime is going up and that the police are working harder (or at least differently). While it is easy to conclude that crime rates precipitate changes in policing, it is obvious that the argument requires more scrutiny.

The Political Context

The development and implementation of crime policy must be understood as a political process (Gest, 2001). Political parties declare their identities and seek to curry voter favor in large part when they support (or when they oppose) particular crime policies. That there is often much at stake politically is clear to even the most casual observer. As John Conklin (2003) notes, when crime gets worse, politicians and justice system bureaucrats rarely accept responsibility. Instead, they typically blame the actions of their political opponents or a range of causal factors that any reasonable person would see as lying well beyond the control of politicians. When crime rates fall, these same politicians are usually quick to accept credit. In some cases, those on the same side of the political fence might even conclude that there is not enough praise to go around, and the mayors or police chiefs might argue about who really is most entitled to bragging rights. This was the case, for instance, in New York in the 1990s when Mayor Rudolph Giuliani and Police Chief William Bratton each sought to present themselves to a thankful public as the man responsible for the New York City crime crash (Parenti, 1999).

While we take for granted in the early 2000s that federal elections do focus, at least to some degree, on questions of crime and justice, this has not always been the case. Indeed, the "nationalization of crime" as a political issue really emerged only in the late 1950s and early 1960s (Caplan, 1973; Finckenauer, 1978; Gest, 2001). In a simple way, the placement of crime on the political agenda was a function of rising postwar crime rates, but the reasons are somewhat more complicated and relate to the increasing political salience of crime during this period. As crime rates climbed, victimization became an increasingly common experience for many people who had always thought of themselves as insulated from such risks. As the politically involved middle class became more anxious, either because of their personal experiences with crime or because of more general uneasiness about city life, the political marketability of crime became more apparent.

Crime is often referred to as a "valence issue" (Nelson, 1984). This means that it is the kind of social problem that tends to elicit a rather limited range of emotional responses from members of society. Stated differently, nobody is really in favor of crime, and everyone opposes it. As a result, political points can be easily won by taking a strong position against crime. In doing so, the politician can be pretty confident that no effective political opposition will be mobilized. No "pro-crime" lobbies will demand equal time and no newspaper editorial will demand even more victimization.

But the nationalization of the crime issue during the 1960s had other, less apparent dimensions. The concern about crime developed and political rhetoric intensified when the nation was deeply divided along a number of fault lines. Protests in opposition to the war in Vietnam, racial conflict and riots in the inner cities, various youth movements, the feminist movement, and a number of political assassinations suggested to many people that American society was coming apart. As convenient catchphrases, "crime in the streets" and "law and order" summarized a range of issues that called into question traditional social and political authority. The need to "crack down" on "hoodlums" and "troublemakers" and "outside agitators" conveniently conflated the concern about "street crime" and many forms of political dissent (Beckett, 1994).

Several decades later, we continue to see presidential candidates and others who populate the national political scene rail against a range of crime and drug problems. Importantly, though, this rhetorical activity is often more expressive than instrumental. This is because there are serious limitations to what the federal government can really accomplish with respect to many of the problems that occupy the attention of criminal justice officials. To paraphrase the famous Boston politician Tip O'Neil, much crime (like all politics) is local.

At all levels of government, crime seems to fit more closely with a conservative than with a liberal political agenda. In general, a series of federal crime bills passed since 1968 have tended to make laws tougher and penalties more severe (Donziger, 1996). The conservative politician is likely to argue that crime doesn't really result from racism or poverty or joblessness (Beckett & Sasson, 2000); instead, crime is seen to be the product of poor moral choices, an inefficient criminal justice system, an overly indulgent welfare system, or a general moral decline that fuels drug abuse and sexual promiscuity. While liberal politicians might oppose these conclusions, they are often reluctant to counter with progressive arguments that speak about the "root causes" of crime. To do so is to risk the political charge that one is insensitive to victims or, worst of all, "soft on crime."

One need only look to the actions and rhetoric of recent liberal politicians to find examples. President Bill Clinton, for instance, ran for the office as the more liberal alternative to Republican George Bush (senior) in 1992 and Robert Dole in 1996. On questions of crime, however, his sensibilities seemed more political than reformist. He supported the hiring of more police, so-called three-strikes legislation, the death penalty for 160 violent crimes, and tougher punishment overall. Even more recently, in the 2004 race for the presidency, Democratic nominee John Kerry was painted by many in the conservative media and by his Republican opponents as a "Massachusetts liberal." That term was generally meant to discredit Kerry's policies by suggesting that they were irresponsible, hypocritical, and out of step with those in the "heartland." On the questions of crime and justice, however, Kerry's election Web site presented him as anything but a Massachusetts or any other type of liberal. Rather than describing the need for social reforms that might address the root causes of crime, we were told that

> John Kerry is a former prosecutor for one of the country's largest counties. He personally prosecuted armed robbers, rapists and mob bosses. He learned firsthand the importance of putting resources in the community so that tough laws lead to arrests and convictions. In the United States Senate, he was an early advocate of laws that cracked down on international drug dealers and money laundering and he wrote the Community Oriented Policing System Act which dedicated federal resources to hiring and deploying thousands of cops-on-the-beat throughout the country. Kerry has continued the fight to provide real Homeland Security. (Retrieved December 12 from http://www.johnkerry.com/issues/crime/)

One of the major reasons, of course, why "liberals" sound so much like "conservatives" is because these labels and the distinctions to which they refer are very relative. Despite much name calling (like "Massachusetts liberal"), the Democratic and Republican parties tend to merge on some (but certainly not all) policy questions. This political pragmatism sometimes means that they occupy positions only a short distance from each other near the middle of any political continuum running from the far Left to the far Right. This gives political decision making, political discourse, and candidate selection a character in the United States that differs dramatically from many European countries.

It is important to appreciate that all aspects of the policy process have political dimensions. Even criminological researchers, who like to think of themselves as objective scientists and therefore above the pettiness of politicians, are in reality often part of the problem rather than part of the solution. Our discussion in Chapter 3 of how ideology and interests color crime statistics is consistent with this conclusion. The issue is even larger, however. Questions about what kind of research gets done, how it gets done, and the uses to which it is to be put typically have political answers.

It would probably be wrong to think that there is anything overtly conspiratorial about this situation. Instead, we need to understand that the relationship between the researcher and the policy maker can be quite complex (Walters, 2003). One important aspect of this complexity relates to the researcher's need for research funding. While private foundations do make research finding available, most criminological and criminal justice research is supported by state agencies. In the majority of cases, the funder is interested in asking particular kinds of policy-relevant questions that, as we have seen, might reflect particular kinds of political priorities (Savelsberg, King, & Cleveland, 2002). This is not to say that state agencies force researchers in universities or in the private sector to produce particular kinds of findings. It is only to suggest that these agencies are more willing to fund research that answers some kinds of questions and not others. The overall impact of these structural arrangements can be to draw the attention of the criminological community toward some kinds of crime problems and away from other kinds of problems.

The war on drugs, for instance, produced a mountain of research on drugs and drug users—most of which accepted implicitly dominant political views of the kind of problem drugs represented. In a similar way, the post–9/11 period led to a dramatically increased willingness on the part of government agencies to fund research on terrorism. The tendency once again, however, is to think about terrorism in the relatively narrow terms of conventional political discourse. As Philip Jenkins (1999, 2003) has noted, the conservative political forces that want to see something done about terrorism fail to see some kinds of behaviors as subject to that label. Conservative religious groups, for instance, that blockade women's clinics or threaten abortion providers might be seen as criminal—but rarely are they considered terrorist. The distinction is arbitrary. These groups (like others that are considered terrorists) use violence and the threat of violence to try to achieve political goals. Neither policy makers nor the researchers they typically fund have such groups in mind when they consider the need for informed policy about terrorism.

Such political influence can extend well beyond the funding of research, however. Joachim J. Savelsberg and his colleagues (2002) argue that the effects can be much more fundamental and can involve a rather comprehensive restructuring of academic fields. Broad trends toward professionalization in many fields and the need for universities and colleges to maintain enrollments have underwritten the widespread proliferation of criminology and criminal justice programs in recent years at both the undergraduate and graduate levels.

In many cases, these multidisciplinary programs developed at the expense of more traditional disciplinary programs, especially sociology programs, in which criminology courses were housed. The most rapid growth of the programs occurred in the early 1970s when the federal Law Enforcement Assistance Administration made funds available to enable law enforcement agencies to upgrade educational requirements. One concern that is often expressed about these developments concerns the ways in which the traditionally critical posture of the academy might be undermined by a more technocratic approach that some types of criminal justice programs might encourage.

We're Going to War

A common political and policy response to the problem of crime is the declaration of war. Wars are not really specific crime policies so much as a general orientation toward the problem of crime. The approach is a venerable one, and over the last few decades several such wars have been declared (Dubber, 2002; Gest, 2001; Hawdon, 2001; Herman, 1991; Lock, Timberlake, & Rasinski, 2002; Walker, 2001). President Johnson declared a war on crime in 1965 and President Nixon did the same in 1969. President George Herbert Walker Bush declared a war on drugs in 1988 and his son George W. Bush declared a war on terrorism after the attacks of September 11, 2001. In between the Bush wars, President Bill Clinton declared a war on gangs (Lane & Meeker, 2000). Of course, with respect to all such wars, the object of our attention is less clearly defined than in the case of more conventional wars. This is in part because crime or drugs or terrorism is somewhat more abstract than are warring nations. As a result, clarity of purpose is perhaps less easily achieved. The war on drugs was of course also a war on all drug-related crime.

In an even more interesting way, in the aftermath of the attacks of September 11, the war on drugs merged with the war on terrorism. In particular, a public information campaign launched by the White House antidrug office suggested that anyone who buys drugs (even what might many call "soft" or "recreational" drugs) might be contributing to the coffers of terrorists. The term *narco-terrorist* suggests a similar kind of perhaps intentional confusion. In September 2004 a Drug Enforcement Administration traveling museum exhibit titled "Target America: Drug Traffickers, Terrorists and You" premiered in Times Square, New York City. In addition to drug paraphernalia, barrels of chemicals used to make methamphetamines, and toys representing the children of neglectful drug-addicted parents, the exhibit included large displays of debris from both the World Trade Center and the Pentagon attacks of September 11, 2001 (http://www.usatoday.com/travel/destinations/2004-09-12-dea-museum_x.htm).

The popularity of war analogies and rhetoric derives from several sources. First, to declare war is to suggest an all-out commitment to tackling the problem. Wars imply major investments of our resources and our energy. To tell a worried nation that we are about to wage war on a problem like crime is to announce that we take the problem most seriously. After all, what could be MORE serious than war?

Second, to declare war is to express certainty about what needs to be done. When war is declared, lines are drawn in the sand. In our minds, war is closely connected to patriotism. If war is declared, our moral duty seems clear. We must choose sides, and to oppose the war or to question the sincerity of those who have declared it seems wrong. If criminal justice policy can take the form of a war on crime, then to question or to critique that policy can seem an awful lot like treasonous conduct. The call for such moral clarity was never clearer than when President George W. Bush in his speech to the joint session of Congress shortly after the events of September 11, 2001, said, "Either you are with us, or you are with the terrorists" (http://www.whitehouse.gov/news/releases/2001/09/20010920-8.html). While in the first instance these comments were directed toward other nations, many read them as a deliberate attempt to create a chilly climate for even those domestic critics who would call his administration's policies into question. A detailed analysis of the coverage by CNN of the breaking events of September 11, 2001, by Amy Reynolds and Brooke Barnett (2003) suggests that the march to war was under way within hours of the terrorist attacks. The character of the coverage, the kinds of experts who were consulted, and the framing of the need for a rapid response pointed to an inevitable conclusion. According to the authors,

> CNN's breaking coverage of September 11 contained a plethora of keywords, images, sources of information, sentences and thematic elements that, in the end, created a powerful, dominant frame—that a U.S. military-led international war would be the only meaningful solution to prevent more terrorist attacks. (Reynolds & Barnett, 2003, p. 91)

Third, when wars are declared, resources typically flow toward those agencies that are charged with (or that seek) the task of waging the war. The windfall, financial and otherwise, can be considerable. William Chambliss (1994) wrote in the mid-1990s that for first time in history state and municipal governments were spending more money on crime than they were spending on education. Fostering war rhetoric can produce very tangible benefits for those agencies that are understood as occupying the front line.

Finally, wars can produce benefits for some occupants of political or bureaucratic office by virtue of their visibility. Statements about war allow politicians to produce ideal "sound bites." Headlines about wars have an immediacy and urgency that is difficult to dispute. The fighting of wars against crime, drugs, or terrorism often makes possible thrilling and graphic video.

Reports of raids on crack houses, stories about drug-sniffing dogs at airports, and descriptions and demonstrations of new police technologies that allow the police to more efficiently capture or disarm suspects have very real media appeal. The "perp walk" and the display of captured weapons and drug paraphernalia have become visual clichés. Quite obviously, the newsworthiness of such items derives from their drama, novelty, and televisuality. Unfortunately, stories about job retention programs that might produce no immediate success despite longer-range promise lack the elements that are likely to garner the attention of those involved in news construction.

For all of these reasons, the tendency to speak about crime in militaristic terms becomes commonplace (Best, 1999) and no rhetorical flourish seems out of order. In 1940, Winston Churchill delivered a speech to the British House of Commons that was intended to rally all of England to the cause of war with the Nazis. Churchill told his fellow citizens, "We shall fight on the landing grounds, we shall fight in the fields and in the streets, we shall fight in the hills; we shall never surrender" (http://uk.geocities.com/pillboxesuk/onthe beaches.html). In 1993, just before William Bratton was sworn in as the police chief of New York City, he said of his impending war on crime, with equal fervor, "We will fight for every house in the city. We will fight for every street. We will fight for every borough. And we will win" (http://www.savannahnow.com/stories/012503/OPEDOpedLetters.shtml; Parenti, 1999).

Politicians and criminal justice officials, like military planners, speak of strategies and tactics. Other terms, like *campaign, battlefronts,* and *neighborhoods under siege,* figure prominently in policy discussions about crime. We speak of raids and of fighting the "enemies within." Much of this language and imagery is deeply rooted in the history of the justice system. Until relatively recently, for instance, policing has largely been organized in terms of a military model. The emphasis has been on weapons, combat, and tactics, and policing has been organized in ways that suggest strong military parallels. There is even a common tendency in much public and organizational discourse to distinguish police officers from "civilians." However, this distinction is more rhetorical than real since police officers, unlike members of the military, are not subject to the dictates of a separate system of military law.

Despite their commonplace character, these war analogies are highly problematic for several reasons. First, it can be suggested that the notion that we are at war with crime can raise false expectations of victory (Walker, 2001). In the case of "real wars," victory is generally understood as an actual and definable moment. A treaty is signed, hostilities cease, or troops are withdrawn. There are no analogous events in the case of our wars with crime, so in a very real way it is not at all clear how we win such wars or how we know we have won them.

A second quite significant problem with the war analogy relates to the fact that wars imply enemies to be defeated. In the case of national wars, the matter is more straightforward. The enemies are the members of the military (or perhaps even the civilians) of the combatant nation. In the case of wars on crime, though, enemies are less readily identifiable. In this sense, wars on crime remind us of the words that cartoonist Walt Kelly put in the mouth of his character Pogo—"We have met the enemy and he is us." Enemies in these wars are distinguishable not by their citizenship or by their uniforms or allegiances, but by their behavior. In other words, the wars on crime or the wars on drugs become wars on "criminals" or wars on "drug dealers" and "drug users." The problem here is that these behavioral categories can easily morph into social ones. It has been argued that most of the recent wars on crime and wars on drugs have really been wars on inner-city minorities (Nelson, 2000). During the 1980s, arrest and imprisonment became extremely common occurrences in so-called underclass neighborhoods (Goode, 2002). The consequences of this approach, in the minds of many, have been catastrophic. The justice system has been overloaded, and entire communities have been alienated by what seems a cruel and unfair system of punishment (Reinarman, 1997; Rosenbaum, 1991; Walker, 2001).

Finally, many critics have questioned what the real value of these wars might be. While the wars serve as highly visible evidence that the problem is being addressed, their real utility is often more difficult to document (Cunneen, 1999). Because crackdowns and other military style tactics don't address the root causes of crime, their success (if there is success) is more likely to be short term than long term (Reinarman & Levine, 1995).

In addition, the crackdowns, zero-tolerance policies, sweeps, and aggressive policing often associated with crime wars can create serious problems (Eck & Maguire, 2000). The war on drugs, for instance, resulted in very high rates of arrest (Reinarman, 1997). In 1970s, the American prison and jail population stood at around 300,000. But in the early years of the 21st century, it topped two million with another four million under some form of carceral control (Dubber, 2002, p. 4). If current rates of incarceration remain unchanged, 6.6% of all persons born in the United States in 2001 will go to state or federal prison during their lifetime. This figure is up from 5.2% in 1991 and 1.9% in 1974. The areas most affected by these efforts are the inner-city communities already wracked by poverty, racism, and social disorganization (Anderson, 1999). The consequences for such communities and for the relationships between the police and communities have been severe (Parenti, 1999).

Policy and Problem Image

Crime policies that are intended to resemble wars and those that are not all proceed from certain assumptions about the problem that needs to be addressed. The social constructionist position, of course, is that these policies are never really directed toward a problem, per se, they are directed toward the image of a problem (Gusfield, 1981; Loseke, 1989). Such imagery is always implicit, however, and we rarely pause to think that the problem we are trying to solve could be constructed in other ways. Nothing could seem more logical or correct than hiring more police, or making laws tougher as ways of dealing with crime. What is important to keep in mind at this point, though, is the commonsensical character of the solutions. The taken-for-granted assumptions about the nature of the problem suggest that the solutions we develop are practically inevitable.

Of course, the "true nature" of crime problems isn't really "discovered," it is constructed. As we have already seen at various points, there is a wide range of social, political, and economic interests that encourage us to think about problems in particular ways. This is no less relevant in the policy realm than in any other (Hawdon, 2001; Welch, Fenwick, & Roberts, 1997). At the most basic level, when we construct a troubling situation as a crime, we suggest that it is the criminal justice system and its traditional bureaucracies and policies that should be mobilized to deal with it. If my neighbor is drunk every day and drunkenness is understood as a sickness, then I might try to help by calling a doctor. But if drunkenness is a crime, I will likely call the police instead. Neither of these constructions is somehow "more right" than the other, but each represents a very distinct way of thinking about how we should go about correcting the situation that troubles us.

Of course, crime policies take a variety of shapes and forms because crime problems can be understood in a variety of different ways for policy purposes. Victim organizations, political parties, and crime industry associations endeavor to give the policy process particular content (Stolz, 2002). What we learn to see as the inevitable solution to crime problems is to a large degree a product of effective lobbying with respect to criminal justice policy outcomes (Stolz, 1985). A central task involved in the critical analysis of crime policy, therefore, is to make explicit the assumptions from which policies proceed. Doing so helps us to understand the policy process by getting "outside the box." Several examples might help clarify what is at stake here.

The sociologist Donileen Loseke (1989) has written about the assumptions that underlie mandatory arrest policies in cases of domestic violence. As a result of effective claims-making on the part of feminist intellectuals, politicians, journalists, academics, and others, a particular view of the problem of wife assault has come to dominate policy discourse. This view proceeds from the assumption that (a) the violence that occurs in homes is serious violence and has already taken place when the police typically arrive on the scene; (b) the male party involved in the typical domestic violence episode is completely guilty and the woman is completely innocent; (c) many women do not call the police or request arrest if the police are on the scene because they are afraid to do so. In a sense, such assumptions became a kind of stereotype of the domestic violence episodes and come to represent an important part of the image that domestic violence police need to address. Given such assumptions, mandatory arrest appears as a logical solution. In other words, when the police are called to a domestic violence episode, the level of harm, the status of the victim, and the need for arrest should be obvious. It makes sense, therefore, to mandate such arrests rather than to leave them to the discretion of individual police officers.

Loseke, however, argues that there are some fundamental flaws in this logic. First, real-life domestic situations are often more complicated than this image would suggest. For example, sometimes when the police show up, it is not so obvious that the man is "completely guilty" and that the woman is "completely innocent." Both might have injuries and they might tell quite conflicting stories about how the incident started and how it unfolded. In addition, sometimes women call the police *before* rather than after a violent episode because what they want the police to do is to prevent a bad situation from getting worse. In such cases, police on the scene would see no evidence of obvious harm or injury. Finally, it is sometimes the case that the woman does not want the police to arrest her partner. This might be because she feels that, all things considered, she would be even worse off if her husband goes to jail and loses his job; or, among many women of color, there is a real concern about what might happen to their partners if they are arrested. These examples suggest that mandatory arrest is only a very partial solution to a complex problem. As public policy, it has little to offer many women, and several cases that require intervention of some kind fall by the wayside.

Kenneth Adams (2003) has written about the policy assumptions that underlie juvenile curfews. Like many popular policies, curfews are highly visible but of questionable effectiveness. Typically, they are intended to keep children off public streets during nighttime hours. Violation of curfews can result in penalties for the youth as well as for the parents or guardians. In a simple way, the assumption behind curfews is that if children are kept off the streets they are less likely to become involved in crime as either offenders or as victims. Once again, however, the implicit assumptions need to be questioned. For example, the policy assumes that young people have potentially effective parents or guardians who can be motivated by the law to watch over them and keep them out of trouble. It also assumes that children have safe and secure places to live and they are better off at home than they are on the streets. For children who live under threats of parental sexual or physical abuse this is clearly not the case. Finally, the policy assumes that the effect of curfews is to stop youth from being delinquent rather than merely to shift their delinquencies to times and places not covered by the curfew.

One of the most powerful policy ideas of recent years, the so-called broken windows theory of policing, provides a third example. The idea, which originated in the writings of James Q. Wilson and George Kelling (1982), maintains that there is a need to take seriously the consequences of small criminal or noncriminal (but deviant) behaviors in public places. As we have seen, the argument maintains that if seemingly trivial forms of "disorder" like loitering, public drinking, and panhandling are ignored by local residents and by the police, the message is sent to more serious offenders that no one really cares about what goes on in the neighborhood. Thus, an environment is created in which offenders might be emboldened to engage in more serious crimes, and over time local crime problems will worsen. In summary, the theory asks, How does one broken window in an abandoned building become many broken windows? Advocates of this argument maintain that if a broken window is not fixed, the message is sent that nobody cares and anybody who wants to break a window can go ahead and do so.

The implications of the broken windows theory for policing seemed obvious to policy makers. What police needed to do was respond in an assertive way to those forms of disorder that they had previously ignored. By taking care of untended people and untended places, it would be possible to create an environment inhospitable to more serious crime. During the 1980s, the idea became central to the philosophy known as "community policing," and many journalists and police spokespersons have claimed that efforts to police the quality of life was largely responsible for the reductions of crime in New York City in the 1990s.

Just what are we being asked to assume here about the meaning of social disorder? Bernard E. Harcourt (2001) argues that the theory, and the policy that derives from it, asks us to accept that it is possible to make a clear distinction between orderly and disorderly people. The former care about their neighborhoods and their families but the latter do not. Perhaps, Harcourt says, this distinction is a little simplistic. As well, we are asked to believe that the differences between these kinds of people somehow intrinsically shape the ways in which people respond to disorder. Orderly people are cowed by disorder and seek to vacate disorderly settings. Disorderly people see disorder as an enhancement of the opportunity structure that allows them to behave badly.

In addition, Harcourt says, the theory assumes that it is really only the poor inner-city resident whose life is plagued by disorder. What about those forms of disorder that don't occur on the street, such as paying cash "under the table" to avoid sales taxes, or other everyday forms of tax evasion? They are not discussed by advocates of the broken windows thesis. More fundamentally, the argument assumes that the forms of disorder identified in the relevant policy discussions are pretty evident. But are they? What is loitering, after all? In some neighborhoods, young people who lack other options gather on street corners to socialize. They may get loud and obstreperous. Is this disorder? What about graffiti? Is it the defacement of public property? Maybe, but others suggest that it is one of the cornerstones of a rich, vibrant hip-hop culture that has transformed urban blight into bright and colorful artwork.

Organized crime provides a final example of how unspoken assumptions are embedded in our crime policies. A central strategy in dealing with organized crime, from the earliest days of federal enforcement to the present, has been "headhunting" (Geary, 2002; Kappeler, Blumberg, & Potter, 2000). In brief terms, this policy involves the employment of criminal justice resources to catch the bosses and the managers of organized crime enterprises. The taking down of "mob bosses" is the stuff of legend and provides powerful narratives that are the bases for numerous novels, films, and television programs. The policy proceeds from the assumption that organized crime operates like some sort of alien conspiracy and that removing the leadership should debilitate the organization. Just as the capture of the head of state of a combatant nation should make that nation less able to function, the capture of an organized crime boss should weaken the criminal conspiracy.

Of course, the logic of this position is problematic. While removing bosses might create large numbers of headlines (as in the case of John Gotti), the effectiveness of the strategy is limited. In the case of Al Capone, for example, his arrest and incarceration for income tax evasion did not destroy the "Chicago Outfit." Indeed, the historical record suggests that organized crime in Chicago prospered in the decades after Capone's forcible removal from the scene. Quite obviously, just as the sale and distributions of computers, shoes, or books would continue even if the president of the respective company dies, goes to jail, or quits that job, so does the manufacture and sale of illegal commodities. The same principle applies at lower levels of organization within illicit markets. Grabbing drug dealers in crackdowns, for instance, can create the economic conditions that simply draw more dealers into the business. As the business becomes riskier, the prices charged for illicit goods and services will rise. These increases make illegal entrepreneurial opportunities even more tempting to a wider range of potential offenders.

Searching for the Panacea

Efforts to develop crime policy when perceptions are rampant that the problem is spiraling out of control can lead to the search for quick fixes to what may be very complicated problems. James Finckenauer (1982) terms this the "panacea phenomenon." Indeed, he argues, somewhat cynically that "the highway of delinquency prevention is paved with punctured panaceas" (p. 3). For Finckenauer, the story of crime policy development is both sad and familiar. The need to do something about the problem of crime leads to the search for some kind of cure-all that advocates hope will take care of the problem. The hype that surrounds any new panacea promotes unrealistic and unsound expectations. The proposal is implemented and meets with failure. The result is widespread frustration and the search for a new panacea.

Finckenauer (1982) contends that the panacea process is fed by two distinct but related kinds of "isms" that afflict those responsible for the public policy process. One type, *Doism*, reflects the belief that it is always better to do something than to do nothing. Doism can lead to a rush to judgment about potential success. Insufficient research might be undertaken prior to implementation or too little thought might be given to possible negative consequences that could result from a new policy. The other ism is *Newism*. This reflects the appeal of new policies just because they are new. As in the area of fashion, that which is novel or untried often appears more interesting that that with which we are familiar. As older programs fail, new ones seem so much more attractive. Policies thus become "ideas du jour." In the area of juvenile crime, for instance, a number of policy ideas—boot camps, "scared straight," school uniforms, and many others—have produced disappointing results despite the promise they apparently held.

Yet the mythical promise of a panacea is not the only explanation of why some policy approaches have so much more appeal than others. Several other relevant factors can be identified.

COST-EFFECTIVENESS

In general, those responsible for the development of public policy would like to solve the problem in the cheapest possible way. Norris and Kaniasty (1992), for instance, argue that one of the reasons why governments are so eager to promote citizen crime prevention efforts, despite their ineffectiveness, is because they require little in the way of coordinated effort or financial output.

A problem in this respect is that in many cases new programs are mounted even though no new resources are made available. One important consequence of this action, however, is that those resources that do exist in the system often need to be redeployed in order to accommodate the new policy. Such redeployment might create serious problems.

For instance, in response to the family violence crises (child abuse or elder abuse), many jurisdictions adopted mandatory reporting policies (Crystal, 1988). In the case of child abuse, such policies required professionals (teachers or physicians, for instance) to report suspicious circumstances to child welfare authorities. Critics argue that these laws promote conservative decision making. A teacher who sees a scratch or scar on a child may take the safest route and report the incident. The teacher may seriously doubt that anything happened, but when the failure to act in prudent fashion could have legal repercussions, reporting makes more sense than nonreporting. Many people acting this way will mean that a large number of new cases will have to be investigated; if several teachers make a large number of very conservative decisions, the overwhelming majority of these cases will be "unfounded." If no new resources are put into the child welfare system, where will the resources come from to fund the investigation and unfounding of all of these cases? Usually they come from the "back end" of the system. This means that money that might have been used for treatment or other forms of intervention is diverted to the "front end" because of the mandatory reporting law. Without more resources, victims who need support and services may find them unavailable. Quite ironically, change that is championed with arguments about the need to help more people might end up disadvantaging those most in need.

IMMEDIATE GAINS

Problem solutions have greater appeal when they can show results in the near term. As stated, the development of crime policy is, in a fundamental way, a political process. This means that any current administration will look to the potential political gains or losses a particular policy might hold. There is little incentive for a president, mayor, or governor to take the very long view of things or to develop policies that might pay political dividends to his or her successor.

CLEAR LOGIC

The marketability of a crime policy depends to some degree on the clarity of its logic. At some broadly understood level, policies must make common sense. In many quarters, the opposition to ideas such as drug legalization, offender reintegration, or job creation springs from the fact that their link to pressing crime problems sometimes seems less than obvious. In contrast, the potential relevance of boot camps or more police on the streets seems more straightforward. The effectiveness of these policies aside, the assumption that they *should* be effective is nonproblematic.

In part, the appeal of school uniforms as a tool in the arsenal against crime derives from the logic of the approach. Advocates of mandatory school uniforms have long argued that the benefits that flow from the policy are obvious. If children and adolescents are not allowed to wear expensive clothes and jewelry, then victimization incidents prompted by envy or by the practical desire on the part of some to take by force what others have are made less likely. As well, if everyone (meaning students but not teachers) wears a uniform, it will be much easier to identify intruders in the school. In addition, because gangs will not be able to display their colors, the risks of gang-related violence will be reduced.

A great deal of anecdotal evidence has been marshaled by a large number of school administrators and teachers, and some early research evaluations seem to support the commonsense view that uniforms can reduce school crime (Brunsma & Rockquemore, 1998; Stanley, 1996). Indeed, in his 1996 State of the Union Address, President Bill Clinton was able to point to these successes as he lent presidential legitimacy to the idea that school uniforms are an effective policy option. Despite the strength of the case made for uniforms, however, more recent and more careful evaluations of the crime prevention value of uniforms can be called into serious question (Brunsma & Rockquemore, 1998; "A Mixed Bag of Uniform Research," 2000).

GOOD INTENTIONS

Policy options are preferred when they broadly communicate the goodwill of those who are charged with doing something about the problem. This observation recognizes that policies are intended to serve symbolic as well as instrumental purposes (Stolz, 1985). One symbolic purpose of policy is to provide tangible evidence that something is being done by people who care (Pfuhl & Henry, 1993).

This may be one of the reasons why mass media campaigns emerged as such a popular way to "fight crime" in the 1980s and 1990s (Sacco & Silverman, 1982). Evaluations of many of these campaigns suggest that they may not be terribly effective as a way of communicating crime prevention skills to the general population or changing public behavior. Still, campaigns of this sort are highly visible and communicate in effective fashion that officials are concerned about the problem of crime and are working in our interests to do something about it.

Some critics have suggested, for instance, that many kinds of so-called hate crime laws also serve this function. Some such laws provide enhanced penalties for offenses that are judged to be motivated by bias or hatred of the victim's "race, religion, color, disability, sexual orientation, national origin or ancestry" (Bureau of Justice Assistance, 1997, p. 27). While this seems like a reasonable way to stem the tide of hate crime, those who question such laws raise a number of objections. First, the statistical case in support of a rising tide of hate crime is made only with difficulty. Second, it is not at all clear that laws that create enhanced penalties for hate crime really accomplish anything of a practical nature. The crimes they promise to punish usually already carry quite severe penalties. Finally, it has been argued that these laws create or reinforce certain inequalities. If the enhanced penalties are intended to provide an additional level of protection, then why is this protection extended only to people who fall into certain social and demographic categories? Why aren't short people, or tall people, or Republicans, or believers in UFOs named in hate crime legislation? Because they are not, it is implicitly argued that attacking a member of such a category is less serious and (from the point of view of the offender) less costly than attacking members of groups identified in such legislation.

Given these shortcomings, it may be that the "real" purpose of the hate crime laws is to communicate good intentions on the part of lawmakers (Jacobs & Potter, 1997). Advocating such laws gives politicians a powerful opportunity to denounce bigotry and to send a message of concern and compassion to actual and potential constituents.

Often the symbolic content is encoded in the name of the law. Laws like, for instance, Megan's Law, which ostensibly speaks to the interests of children, bear the name of the child whose tragic story inspired the law. Aligning oneself with the law can be confused with the support of or sympathy for a particular victimized child. In a related way, while civil libertarians express sincere doubts about the scope and potential for abuse of the legislation, the name of the USA PATRIOT (Uniting and Strengthening America by Providing Appropriate Tools Required to Intercept and Obstruct Terrorism) Act is obviously intended to send a strong political message to both the supporters and the opponents of the legislation. In other cases, laws might be given names that hide their real purpose. It has been argued, for instance, that the "California Child Protection Act of 1984" really did nothing to protect the interests of children. What it did do, was allow the state to confiscate property derived from the profits of child pornography, as well as the cameras, lights, and other equipment (McShane & Williams, 1992).

EVIDENCE OF SUCCESS

Policies are more likely to garner support when their advocates can point to demonstrable proof that they work. In the area of public policy, as in business, it is often true that nothing succeeds like success. However, the evaluation of social programs is a complex undertaking not only methodologically but also ethically and politically. Research that would allow us to determine with some degree of certainty whether a particular policy is working and if so, why it is working, can be very costly and can take a long time to complete. Too often, the crisis environment within which decisions are made allows inadequate research or even anecdotes to substitute for sound, methodologically rigorous evaluations. What works comes to be understood as matter of common sense and, as a consequence, particular policies can be widely adopted long before the evidence is in (Lempert, 1989).

One of the big crime control success stories is, of course, New York City. As has been documented now in both scholarly and popular literature, the 1990s saw a dramatic decline in rates of predatory crime in New York. Most accounts stress the important role played by the police in bringing these changes about (Kelling & Bratton, 1998). A highly laudatory 1996 *Time* magazine cover story of the "New York City miracle" refers to New York City Police Commissioner William Bratton as "one good apple" who "set out to prove that cops really can cut crime. The experts scoffed—but felony rates have dropped so far, so fast that no other explanation makes sense" (Pooley, 1996, p. 24).

Specific attention, in this respect, is focused on the role played by aggressive quality-of-life policing styles associated with the broken windows theory discussed earlier. Many researchers, however, argue that there has been a tendency to give the police too much credit too soon. While the police may have had something to do with the decline, they surely were not the only—or maybe even the principal—cause of the decline (Karmen, 2000). A large number of circumstances, including shifts in the economy, the demographic structure of the population, and the social organization of the drug market, no doubt also contributed to the decline (Conklin, 2003; Karmen, 2000).

Harcourt (2001) claims that arguments that emphasize the role played by the police suffer from two major deficiencies. First, crime rates declined not only in New York but also in many other large cities in the 1990s, including Boston, Houston, Los Angeles, and San Diego (LaFree, 1999), though many of the cities experiencing declines did not adopt the aggressive quality-of-life strategies assumed to have produced the changes in New York. Second, even if the police did contribute importantly to the decline, there is reason to doubt that the broken windows philosophy could be credited with the decline. Instead Harcourt and others (Parenti, 1999) suggest that different mechanisms might have been at work. The aggressive misdemeanor policing may not have "fixed" broken windows so much as it allowed the police to undertake more gun searches, to locate people with outstanding warrants, and to increase the general level of surveillance in the urban population.

The problem in this respect is a more general one. There is a conflict between the need to do something quickly and the need to take the time to evaluate carefully what does and does not really work. Can hiring more police reverse a crime wave? Perhaps, but perhaps not. After all, we will find the pressure to hire more police to be most intense when crime rates are at their highest. When more police are hired, the crime rate might fall. Statisticians use the term "regression to the mean" to refer to the phenomenon in which extreme scores on a measure are likely to be followed by less extreme scores (Gilovich, 1993). Regression toward the mean explains why very tall parents tend to have children who are shorter than they are. It also explains why the very high mark a student receives on one essay may be followed by a somewhat lower mark. As well, it helps us understand why very high crime rates might be followed by somewhat lower crimes—even if the recently hired police had no impact on the decline. In addition, Eck and Maguire (2000) argue that because several other things will also be going on while crime rates are falling and more police are being hired, it is always difficult to separate out the independent influence of policing strength and policing styles.

HUNGRY FOR A SOLUTION

Samuel Walker (2001) suggests that in a very general way our approach to crime policy is a little like our approach to weight loss. Serious weight loss experts are consistent in their advice about how one goes about losing weight and keeping the weight off. The emphasis is always on long-term results and broad changes in lifestyle. For most people, however, the time horizon is much shorter. They want to lose a lot of weight quickly. It is this desire that gave rise to the huge market in diet drugs, cookbooks, and exercise machines that promise fast results. Of course, these crash diets don't work. Often there is no weight loss, and in those cases where there is weight loss, the weight is quickly regained once one stops dieting. For many people, the effort to lose weight is best understood as a series of unsuccessful crash diet episodes. In a similar way, as we search for the panacea for crime reduction we move from one highly hyped fad to another. As in the case of weight loss, the results in crime prevention are often equally unimpressive.

The dietary analogy has even greater applicability, however. The social theorist George Ritzer (2001) has written extensively about a social process he calls the McDonaldization of society. Ritzer's argument is that our major social institutions are organized increasingly along the same principles as the fast food restaurant. According to Ritzer, McDonaldization is characterized by four organizing principles:

Efficiency. The organizational purpose of McDonald's or any other fast food restaurant is to feed people in the most direct and immediate way possible. Customers are served quickly, and there is little in the way of wasted energy or effort.

Calculability. Fast food restaurants emphasize quantity over quality. Advertising emphasizes the amount of food the customer gets rather than the nutritional value. The practice of "supersizing" and the names given to burgers—BIG MAC and WHOPPER—reflect the importance of calculability.

Predictability. One of the defining features of the fast food meal is its consistency. The burger we buy from the fast food outlet in Duluth, Minnesota, tastes precisely like the one we buy in Richmond, Virginia. The use of brand names, logos, and familiar signage provoke feelings of the familiar and remove feelings of uncertainty.

Control. Fast food restaurants are all about control. Most pointedly, the organization of employees minimizes the degree to which they are allowed to make independent decisions. Uniform, rigid store policies and close employee supervision maximize the levels of workforce control. At the same time, customers are also subject to high levels of control. The menu offers relatively few choices, and customers are expected to line up and briefly make their food requests at the counter. Unlike a full-service restaurant, we are expected to pay before we eat, carry the food to the table ourselves, eat quickly, and clean up after ourselves when we are done.

While efficiency, calculability, predictability, and control are clearly in evidence in fast food restaurants, Ritzer's point is that they infuse most aspects of the social order. McDonaldization is not an all-or-none proposition, however, and we can think about the relative degree of McDonaldization that characterizes particular social institutions. For instance, it can be argued that the typical contemporary university or college is highly McDonaldized. Like the fast food restaurant, the goal is to process as many customers (students) as possible. Multiple-choice exams, televised lectures, and the extensive use of teaching assistants make the delivery of the educational experience more efficient. Our institutions of higher education also stress calculability. Students are often less interested in what they have learned and more interested in what their numeric mark will be. No matter what one has learned, higher marks are better than lower marks. Students in one program are often offered options by which they can pursue other certificates, diplomas, or course credits in ways that allow them to "supersize" their degrees. College and university programs have become more standardized, as have entrance examinations for many programs. Such measures are of course intended to ensure predictability. Finally, concerns about academic dishonesty and competitiveness among students have resulted in greater and greater levels of control over the academic enterprise. Assignments are more highly structured, and independent work, which is more difficult to monitor, is increasingly discouraged.

How does this argument relate to crime control processes? Matthew B. Robinson (2001) suggests that crime control also has become highly McDonaldized. As the system of criminal justice becomes focused on catching, convicting, and punishing criminals in assembly-line fashion, the goal of efficiency can be seen to override the goal of justice. As wars on crime emphasize "more police on the streets," more laws, additional penalties, and longer sentences, the attention to calculability becomes clear. In the justice system, as in the fast food restaurant, various measures are put in place to reduce uncertainty. Efforts to ensure predictability include the use of profiling methods by police and a variety of risk assessment techniques. The expansion of control is perhaps most vividly illustrated by the growth over the past couple of decades of the prison industry. Robinson argues that the so-called supermax prison epitomizes this control dimension. In a way that clearly parallels the use by fast food restaurants of terms like *giant, jumbo,* or *huge* to describe "average" food portions, we have escalated the language of control. Technically, Robinson states, nothing can be more maximum than maximum—except of course "supermaximum."

One especially ironic aspect of Ritzer's McDonaldization argument is that while the processes he describes are intended to make institutions function in more rational ways, they actually generate high levels of irrationality. So, for instance, the fast food restaurant is so successful at serving people quickly that it generates long lines, which mean that people will be served much more slowly. In a different way, we can see how the efficiencies of the restaurant result in inefficiencies for the customer. Thus, it is the customer who serves the food and disposes of the trash. In addition, the ability to serve food cheaply and quickly compromises the quality of the food and the health of the customer (Schlosser, 2001).

In the field of crime control, the so-called three-strikes laws provide perhaps the best example of how the McDonaldization that is supposed to produce rationality results in high levels of irrationality. Since the passage of California's "Three Strike Law" in 1994, 25 states and the federal government have passed some similar form of legislation (Clark, Austin, & Henry, 1997; Gest, 2001). The law in California requires that the sentence for a felony be doubled for offenders who have committed a prior serious or violent felony (http://www.justicepolicy.org/article.php?id=395). It also requires a 25-year-to-life sentence for any felony for offenders with two prior serious or violent felonies. In addition, a person convicted under the law is not eligible for parole until 80% of the sentence has been served. Quite obviously, such laws reflect the influence of McDonaldization. They are intended to emphasize efficiency in the processing of offenders. As well, they emphasize the quantity of punishment, aim to increase the predictability of punishment, and expand the level of state control exerted over actual and potential lawbreakers.

At the same time, as David Shichor (1997) has written, such laws span troubling irrationalities. Most notably, they have produced very dramatic increases in the size of prison populations, often for relatively nonserious crimes (Glaser, 1997). Recent analyses of the California Three Strikes Law concluded that, despite the rhetoric surrounding such laws, they have failed to produce significant declines in crime rates. It has been argued that they operate on the basis of what is known in the retail trades as "bait and switch." In other words, people are promised one set of goods but sold another set. The support for three-strikes laws emerged largely out of the concern among citizens about violent crime (Glaser, 1997). However, much of the prison expansion that has resulted from these laws has involved drugs and nonviolent offenses (Donziger, 1996). Further irrationalities involve the observation that the three-strikes laws appear to some degree at least to impose differential burdens on minority populations, which undermines the principles of justice upon which the entire system is supposedly predicated. As well, despite promises of great efficiency, the ways in which these laws have fed prison growth have imposed substantial burdens on taxpayers.

When Social Control Becomes the Problem

Arguments about the irrationalities of crime policy require us to consider alternative interpretations of the relationships between crime waves and social control. The naïve and commonsense interpretation of course is that crime levels rise and in response new (perhaps more coercive) policies are put in place. There is another way of thinking about this relationship, though. Some writers argue that crime level increases are the result—not the cause—of intrusive and aggressive social control. From this perspective, it is the refocusing or perhaps the redirection of social control that produces higher crime levels. This implies that the media and other public sources of information about crime create an illusion. As we read the paper, we might learn that crime is up and that the criminal justice system is becoming more aggressive. We assume the second empirical fact follows from the first, but it could be—at least in some cases—the other way around.

We can certainly find cases in which crimes waves seem to involve mostly shifts in control (rather than shifts in criminal behavior). The satanic crime wave of the 1980s, for instance, seems to have been almost completely the product of very proactive policing on the part of "cult cops" and irresponsible—if sometimes well-intentioned—therapists (deYoung, 1997; Hicks, 1991; Victor, 1993). While a large number of effective prosecutions of satanic abuse in day care centers were undertaken, it seems extremely unlikely that there was anything to any of these charges in the overwhelming majority of cases. In a similar way, the crime waves involving medieval witchcraft and various delinquency episodes suggest instances of excessive control fed by "moral panic" (Goode & Ben-Yehuda, 1994). As Michael Shermer (1997) argues, many of these events are "epidemics of accusations" rather than epidemics of crime.

In a classic work on the sociology of deviance, Kai Erikson (1966) argued that crime waves as control waves represent important ways in which societies establish their unique moral character. Such waves are precipitated by boundary crises in which the members of society grow increasingly insecure about who they are, as a people, and what it is that separates them from others. The widespread policing and public denunciation of particular kinds of deviants provide highly dramatic ways in which boundaries can be rearticulated. Erikson's argument was based on an analysis of the 17th-century Massachusetts Puritan colony. Over a 60-year period, Erikson wrote, the colony experienced three distinct crime waves, each of which emerged out of historically specific threats to collective moral boundaries.

The best known of these crime waves revolved around the Salem witchcraft trial and executions that were immortalized in Arthur Miller's play, *The Crucible*. The episode began in 1692 when a small group of young girls began to spend time with a slave from Barbados by the name of Tituba, who was known to be a practitioner of magic. As time went on, the girls began to engage in some rather aberrant behavior. These behaviors included screaming, convulsing, the hurling of Bibles, and even barking like dogs. As the bizarre behavior spread throughout the colony, it appeared to defy rational explanation. Many in the colony came to the conclusion that Satan had come to Salem and an epidemic of witchcraft was under way. Pressed to identify the sources of their tormentors, the girls named Tituba and two other women. The persecution of those suspected of, and unable to deflect accusations of, witchcraft spiraled out of control. Before the episode was over, hundreds faced charges and dozens languished in jail. Perhaps most tragically, at least 22 deaths could be directly linked to the witchcraft crime wave.

Erikson (1966) argued that the witchcraft crime wave followed a number of significant developments that had threatened the cohesion of the colony. Several land disputes had created divisions among the leadership of the colony. In addition, a long and very costly war with neighboring Indian nations had demoralized and frightened colonists. Finally, and perhaps most notably, the English monarch had withdrawn the charter of the colony. In short, the residents of Salem seemed to have lost their way. In such a context, the presence of the devil and the evils of witchcraft emerged as convenient and readily understandable explanations of why things were going as badly as they were. Importantly, the nature of the threat that witchcraft represented helped colonists reestablish moral boundaries. Surely, they could tell themselves, their original spiritual zeal and singularity of moral purposes must still have been intact if Satan himself came to the Colony to try to do them in.

How well arguments about boundary maintenance generalize to complex and heterogeneous societies like the contemporary United States is debatable. Still, cases like those discussed above do suggest that sometimes crime waves seem to be a response to rather than a reason for more expansive control. But of course this is not always the case. Perhaps a more balanced interpretation recognizes the interactive character of crime waves and public policy. In such a model, more aggressive and more inclusive control measures might be a response to rising crime, but these measures might cast a wider and finer net. Thus, if an increase in school crime is already under way and policies of zero tolerance are put into place, the rates will, because of enhanced enforcement, rise even more than they otherwise would have.

In a different way, Hawdon (1996) has argued that the rates of objective behavior and the rate at which that behavior is labeled criminal might vary inversely. Based on a historical analysis of two drug epidemics, he suggests that the central variable in unraveling this paradox is social mobility. When rates of social mobility are high, there is, as a result of greater exposure to alternative lifestyles, a reduction in social control and a greater willingness on the part of people to experiment socially. This means that rates of drug use increase. At the same time, these conditions encourage a culture of toleration that results in a decrease in the tendency to police such behavior. Conversely, when the rate of social mobility slows, the willingness of people to experiment with drugs lessens and so does the tolerance of such conduct. Thus Hawdon argues that, in the 1960s, for instance, rates of many kinds of drug use were high but so was public toleration. By the late 1980s when the number of drug users was in decline, enforcement efforts directed against drug use intensified.

Conclusion

There is, to be sure, a need to be critical of the steps we take to do something about crime waves. A major concern in this respect is the highly political character of the policy-making process. Programs and interventions directed against crime are intended to serve a variety of functions, only some of which have anything to do with getting the crime rate down. The errors that might be made, by accident or by intention, are numerous. The appeal of many policies—based on their cost-effectiveness, their emotional content, on common sense, or on any number of other factors—can compromise the development of rational and effective policy. Much of the political, media, and interest group rhetoric mystifies the process by which policy is made, and it is, therefore, necessary to look more deeply.

One of the more interesting questions in this respect concerns the nature of the relationship between crime waves and public policy. While it is usually assumed that policies are developed in response to rising crime, this might not be the case. Indeed, rising crime might develop in response to policies, or each might develop in response to the other. The idea that social control amplifies rather than dampens the amount of crime in society is one that has fallen into discredit in recent years but that still might have real value.

8

Crime Waves

A Skeptic's Guide

In the previous chapters the case has been made for a "social constructionist" view of crime waves. This means that we have been thinking about crime waves as social episodes in which large numbers of people come to believe that crime is getting worse. As we have seen, this can happen for several reasons:

- Crime levels might really be going up, and the widespread belief that crime is increasing really just reflects this
- Shifts in the ways in which we count crime can produce new tallies that suggest that crime is rising
- Crime-saturated media can lead audience members to believe that crime is getting worse
- Rumor, gossip, and other forms of improvised news can be dominated by particular types of narratives that help establish the collective premise that new and virulent strains of crime are taking hold
- More than one or any number of the above processes can be involved in any particular crime wave

Social constructions are powerful and obstinate creations. Once they are established, they acquire a kind of taken-for-grantedness. In this sense, social constructions are like physical constructions. The homes and other buildings that exist in your neighborhood were the products of someone's labor. They had to be built, and the process by which that happened was messy and untidy. Indeed, in some cases you may have even contributed to their construction. Once they are built, however, they become a part of the landscape and we rarely if ever bother to contemplate the complex process that put them in place. They are somehow just there.

In the same way, as consensus builds around particular social constructions, a parallel process unfolds. The widespread view that a crime wave is under way comes from somewhere, and is a product of human action. Once in place, though, like the houses on the street it becomes part of the background.

It is easy to become immersed in the taken-for-granted reality of crime waves. Everybody seems to agree—the problem is getting worse. Furthermore, it is difficult to avoid getting swept along by events. We might find ourselves becoming more and more fearful, or more and more willing to adopt solutions to the crime problem that we think might promise us some kind of immediate relief.

Of course, one of the objectives of criminological or any other kind of social scientific education is the development of a set of skills that allows us to subject such social constructions to incisive and prolonged critical scrutiny. When we think critically, we call into question much of what others take for granted. What is involved in such critical thinking? Several specific elements have been identified, including (Wade & Tavris, 1990) the following:

- The skill to interpret and analyze complex empirical evidence
- The willingness to reconsider one's views in light of evidence that calls established views into question
- A readiness to examine the assumptions and biases on which our views are predicated
- An ability to recognize that our emotions and feelings are not necessarily very good guides to the empirical world; in other words, just because we feel that things should be a particular way doesn't mean that they are that way
- A willingness to tolerate uncertainty and to recognize that not every issue we seek to understand can be sufficiently understood given the current fund of knowledge

Perhaps most basic to critical thought, however, is the ability to ask probing questions. To a considerable extent the previous chapters have been devoted to an examination of what these questions might be. In summary form they include the following.

Are Crime Rates Really Going Up?

In many ways, this is the most basic question. In popular usage, we equate the term *crime wave* with rising crime rates. In previous chapters the argument has been made that widespread beliefs that a crime wave is under way and action that proceeds from that assumption (i.e., a socially constructed crime wave) is not necessarily synonymous with rising crime rates.

Who says that crime rates are going up? We have seen that there are many sectors of society—the media, politicians, the security industry, victim organizations, and even offenders—who might want us to believe that crime is increasing. There is no need to evoke a conspiracy theory or to attribute bad will to those who try to convince the rest us that we are in the midst of a crime wave. We all seek to convince others of the rightness of our view (especially if it advances our interests). There is, however, good reason to question the claim itself. How do they know that crime is increasing? What sorts of evidence leads them to this conclusion? What, if anything, do they stand to gain from the pressing of such claims?

Of course, in the age of the Internet it is easy to undertake some independent investigation. We can check FBI crime data and read what a wide range of newspapers and magazines have to say about the supposed crime wave. The bottom line, though, is that we should always maintain some degree of skepticism when those who have our attention sound a call to arms. Just because a mayor or a president, a police chief or an academic says something is so does not make it so.

What Causes the Sudden Shifts in Crime Levels?

If crime rates are indeed going up, it is logical to ask "why?" We know from the study of criminology more generally and from our discussion in Chapter 2 that the answer to this question is not likely to be simple. As discussed, in order to understand upturns (and downturns) in crime levels we need to focus our attention on the kinds of social change that have the same rhythms as the crime trends we seek to analyze. We discussed three broad kinds of social process that have some relevance in this regard: social dislocation, social diffusion, and social innovation.

It is important to emphasize that the world is often a much more complex place than our explanations suggest. While we can discuss these processes separately from each other, in reality they are correlated over time and across space. War, a major form of social dislocation, correlates with technological and social innovation. Similarly, technological innovation makes possible greater degrees of cultural diffusion. In addition, the effects of any of these processes will be conditioned by the historical context and exacerbated or moderated by the demographic structure of the population at any particular point in time. As well, we cannot expect all "crime" to have a single explanation. Gang violence, corporate crime, and domestic homicide are all crimes, but they differ from each other as categories of behavior. We should not expect, therefore, that an explanation that serves us well in one circumstance would necessarily serve us well in another.

There is no shortage of opinion makers in society who will seek to convince us that factor x or variable y is a cause of crime rate increases. Day care, poverty, too much religion, too little religion, abortion, bad parenting, video games, rap music, and a host of other conditions have been identified as key causes of crime. In this respect, Marcus Felson (2002) warns us to be wary of the "agenda fallacy" in which people nominate as a cause of crime what they already seek to control for quite unrelated reasons. In other words, if I think that tattoos are a bad thing and that tattoo parlors should all be closed down, one way in which I might enlist your support in this undertaking is by trying to convince you that tattoos cause crime. In general, however, anecdotes, glib generalizations, and moral outrage are poor substitutes for rigorous theorizing and empirical evidence. It is important that we set a high standard with respect to the evaluation of the usefulness of our explanations of crime level increases (or of any social phenomena, for that matter).

Finally, as Felson (2002) also warns us, we should not necessarily expect to find moral symmetry in the social world. It is, of course, comforting to believe that "bad" things have "bad" causes and "good" things have "good" causes. This fallacy would lead us to be more receptive to some kinds of arguments than others regarding crime rate increases. As we have seen, however, arguments about moral symmetry are often difficult to sustain. It can be argued that the post–World War II crime rate increase in part reflects increases in the standard of living and the diffusion of technological marvels like the automobile. Of course, the need for moral equivalence can never substitute for rigorous analysis.

Can We Really Trust Crime Statistics?

This depends entirely upon what we mean by "crime statistics." There are two kinds of issues here that concern us. The first has to do with the nature of the statistics and the second has to do with their source.

We always need to be wary of raw numbers. They tell us very little unless we have some understanding of the population (people, cars, houses, etc.) at risk. To be told that there were 1,000 crimes of a certain sort committed in a particular community last year and 1,100 committed this year really tells us very little. We also need to know something about the size and character of the population of potential offenders and potential victims in each year.

As well, it is important to be cautious of small numbers, whether they are presented in a raw form or as percentages. It is too easy to find what look like meaningful patterns where none really exist. One murder in my town last year and two this year should be described as a 100% increase only if one seeks to mislead.

It is important as well for the skeptical consumer of crime wave information to remember that the production of crime statistics is a social process involving a large number of decision makers. The content of these decisions can create a considerable disparity between the processes of measurement and the things being measured.

In particular, we need to make sure that we are clear on the definition of the phenomenon being counted. Especially in the case of newly emerging problems, the behaviors at issue may be defined rather loosely. What exactly is "computer crime" or "home invasion" or "school violence"? Researchers are often free to define these problems as they see fit. When those doing the counting have a vested interested in keeping the numbers large, we want to ask some especially hard questions about how the phenomenon is defined.

Most commonly we will encounter statistics about crime level increases in media reports. Too often journalists themselves are uninformed about the subtleties and complexities of statistical data. The need to conform to journalistic and other media conventions can cause those involved in news production to try to find the most exciting and shocking hook on which to hang what they see as rather drab news stories.

None of this to say that crime statistics are always wrong or completely unreliable. Indeed, some kinds of crime data (e.g., homicide data) are quite reliable. We need to be patient enough and careful enough to separate the statistics in which we can have confidence from "advocacy numbers" and "junk science."

Are My Own Experiences (and Those of My Friends) a Useful Guide as to Whether Crime Levels Are Increasing?

It is often difficult to contextualize our own experiences. Despite this we sometimes try to use our own experiences as a basis for generalizing about various aspects of social life. Perhaps I have recently been victimized. When I mention this to people, they tell me about related experiences they have had. Other people who have heard about what happened to me have made a point of coming to tell about their own unfortunate encounters with crime. I hadn't noticed this before, but since I was victimized it sure seems like a lot of people have been having a problem with crime, and even more people seem concerned about crime. It might not be too long before I conclude, based on my experiences, that yes, a full-blown crime wave is indeed under way.

There are problems with my logic, though. In short, my "evidence" for the crime wave is anecdotal and impressionistic—always dangerous bases for generalizing about what might really be going on both within and beyond our own social circles. Hearing about others' experiences may of course be prompted by my own experience rather than coincident with it. In a similar way, my own tendency to notice so much more crime content in my own environment might really be a reflection of the way in which my own criminal victimization has sensitized me, rather than of any real changes in this environment.

Of course, what happens to me or to friends or family members has great personal salience. Moreover, it might suggest some important hypotheses about what is going on in society. Before we reach any conclusions in this respect, however, we need to gather more systematic observations.

What Are We to Make of the Media Obsession With Crime?

As we have seen, crime is a dominant feature of contemporary commercial mass media. This is true whether the focus is news or entertainment (assuming that this distinction is a valid one), and whether the point of reference is print or electronic. There is more crime content in the media than there used to be, and it often seems as well that the kinds of crimes we read about are more lurid than they used to be. Very often, all major media will focus our attention upon the same specific problems. At various points these problems have included satanism, child abuse, serial murder, gang violence, and domestic terrorism. The sort of pack mentality that characterizes much media coverage can lead us inescapably to the conclusion that the problem in question is getting worse and worse.

The points about which we need to be reminded when we jump to such conclusions are simple ones. First, the world of crime "out there" and the world of crime in the media bear only a tenuous relationship to each other. To say this differently, the mechanisms that drive the amount of crime in society are different from the mechanisms that drive the amount of crime content in the media. Because each can vary relatively independently of the other we need not assume that there is more crime just because there is more coverage of crime.

Second, we need to remind ourselves about the importance of separating "fantasy" from "reality." Docudramas, reality television, and movies "based on true stories" are not simply reflections of a real world. Instead, they are cultural products that pick and choose those aspects of empirical reality that are thought to serve journalistic or dramatic purposes best.

These Stories I Have Been Hearing From So Many People Have to Be True, Don't They?

Often our views of increasing crime are fed by stories that friends and others we trust tell us about unsafe people or unsafe places. They come via e-mail or are told over coffee or around campfires. They are rich in specific details regarding places we have been and people like ourselves. Sometimes they are even accompanied by pictures.

A careful assessment of these stories, however, often makes us suspicious. The narrative structure is too melodramatic, certain details don't make sense, and there is a little too much irony. We recognize such stories as urban legends, and as in the case of much media content, they can encourage perceptions about the escalation of criminal danger.

There are Internet sites that can be of real assistance in the identification of such legends. For instance, the Urban Legend Reference page (www.snopes2.com) or Hoaxbusters (www.hoaxbusters.ciac.org) describe, classify, and debunk large numbers of traditional and current legends. Increasingly, they also make clear how video and digital technologies have been used to lend visual credibility to rumors. Contrary to the popular truism, pictures do sometimes lie.

The Fear of Crime Is Irrational, Right?

The use of the term *irrational* in this context can point us in one of two directions. The first relates to the frequent observation that fear is rampant and that people panic easily. The second involves the idea that fear is distributed in society in ways that suggest inconsistency with the ways in which actual risks are distributed.

With respect to the first issue, it is of course possible to point to many isolated examples in which fear seems to spiral out of control. Our discussion of the "monkey man of New Delhi" and the "phantom gasser of Mattoon" are illustrations. Of course, even in these cases, there is an unspoken assumption that we somehow know what the correct level of fear is supposed to be. To say that people are too afraid suggests an appropriate level of fear. Yet, how we do the math in this respect is unclear.

More generally, however, there has been a marked tendency on the part of many observers to overestimate the ease with which the members of society can be frightened by crime or other kinds of threats. The sociologist Andrew Greeley (2002) has written, for instance, about how journalists reporting on the Twin Tower terrorist attacks of September 11, 2001, emphasized the fear and panic among the residents of New York City. While some people did react this way, most did not, according to Greeley. Indeed, it is the absence of widespread panic that is most noteworthy. Greeley states that the waterborne evacuation by as many as one million people from Manhattan (the largest such evacuation in American history) on the morning of September 11 is testimony to the ability of people to remain calm and orderly under the most trying of circumstances. Greeley also notes, however, that the evacuation was practically invisible to television viewers, who were much more likely to see scenes of frightened New Yorkers fleeing the scene as the buildings collapsed. Panic expert Lee Clarke (2003) has argued that this tendency to overestimate fear and panic is prevalent in media and much scholarly work. Ironically, even people who do not themselves feel afraid might have little trouble believing that everyone else does. The situation suggests an example of what psychologists sometimes refer to as "pluralistic ignorance." In other words, each of us thinks, "Well, I am not afraid but everyone else seems to be."

A second aspect of the irrationality argument, as stated, relates to the various "fear paradoxes" identified by several researchers. Such arguments make it easy to disregard the fears of women, for instance, which seem to greatly outstrip measured risks. As we have discussed, this logic is flawed. For one thing, it assumes that we have tended to measure women's risks accurately (which we have not). For another, it assumes that the only kinds of factors of which people need to take account in deciding how afraid to be is the level of risk they face. In contrast, we have learned that fear is a complex reaction that is sensitive to and expressive of a wide range of personal and environmental conditions.

In addition, there is a wealth of contrary evidence suggesting that the fear of crime and the real risks of crime map rather closely. Fear, for example, is higher for urban dwellers, residents of high crime neighborhoods, and victims of predatory crimes.

It's Fear That Drives the Justice System Response, Isn't It?

As we have discussed, policies directed toward crime wave problems always arise in a political context. Often, the purpose of such policies is to achieve a variety of both practical and symbolic aims. Very often, these policies are marketed through the use of strategies that claim that a fearful public *demands* that something drastic be done quickly. These claims require careful attention.

As discussed above, much of what is said in the media and in political discourse about public fear is characterized by hyperbole. In addition, we need to recognize that evidence regarding some kind of link between public fear and support for punitive policies is less consistent than we might naïvely assume.

Of course, we can cynically suggest that these arguments about fear as a driving force behind justice system responses serve an important political end. In articulating such arguments, political decision makers are able to construct themselves as both responsive to and restrained by the greater public will. There is a need to act quickly, decisively, and perhaps even harshly not because those who do so see that such action serves their own ends, but because their actions are a response to the deeply held sentiments of constituents. The position can pass a commonsense test of plausibility for most of us: Even though

I am not afraid, I might read a state of pluralistic ignorance as indicating that other people are.

A Rising Crime Level Is a Simple Problem With a Simple Solution, Right?

As we have discussed, there is a powerful tendency in much popular culture to portray social problems in simplistic terms. Crime waves are no exception. Tougher laws, more laws, and more police are often championed as "all we need to do." Often, as well, there is a "flavor of the month" quality as policy makers and academic entrepreneurs champion new, one-size-fits-all solutions. School uniforms, lifestyle policing, zero-tolerance, juvenile curfews, and scared straight programs are all examples of the kinds of trendiness that sometimes characterize our approach to what we believe to be worsening crime conditions. The heavy use of war analogies is perhaps the best illustration of this tendency. Wars suggest moral clarity and simplicity of approach. As well, wars imply battles to be won, enemies to be defeated, and moments of victory to work toward.

At issue are the social constructions of the problems to which these solutions are directed. Of course, solutions are directed toward an image of what the problem is, rather than toward what the problem might actually be. When problems are portrayed in simplistic terms, as much popular culture and political discourse tends to do, we are more likely to be content with simple solutions. We would always do well to recognize though that social reality tends to be complex, and social interventions that assume that it is not, may not only fail, they may produce other, unanticipated problems.

When Interventions Are Followed By Falling Crime Levels, Can We Assume Cause and Effect?

It is as difficult to determine why crime levels fall as it is to determine why they rise. We must be careful not to draw unwarranted conclusions regarding what does or does not work in our efforts to stem a rising tide of crime.

There is serious potential for error here. Those who wish to sell us on certain strategies might point to what they describe as obvious evidence. We are told that crime levels fell in the immediate aftermath of favored policies. Assuming that crime rates did indeed fall, how valid is the attribution? We know, for instance, that when crime problems are at their worst we are likely to respond most harshly. But does crime fall afterward because of the harshness of our response, or because, as the principle of statistical regression would suggest, extreme scores on a variable tend to be followed by less extreme scores?

To answer this question we need to know more than whether the rates fell. Do they fall every year at this time, irrespective of the policies in place? Did the levels fall in places that did have and in places that did not have the policy in place? Was the fall a significant change or was it just a random fluctuation? Was the falling of the crime levels consistent with the implementation of the policy?

Before we decide to lend our vocal or moral support to specific actions intended to deal with rising crime problems, we should set the methodological bar pretty high. Conclusions about what works and what doesn't have to be based on solid research evidence and not just on "common sense" or on superficial assessments.

In closing, it is perhaps useful to recall C. Wright Mills's (1959) view that a fundamental value of the perspective of much social science is that it helps us to understand the relationship between our own experiences and conditions in the wider society. Clearly, this view has special relevance to the study of the social phenomena we refer to as crime waves.

References

Adams, D. B., & Reynolds, L. E. (2002). *Statistics 2002 at a glance.* Washington, DC: U.S. Department of Justice. Retrieved December 12, 2004, from http://www.ojp.usdoj. gov/bjs/pub/ascii/bjsg02.txt

Adams, K. (2003). The effectiveness of juvenile curfews at crime prevention. *Annals of the American Academy of Political and Social Science, 587,* 136-159.

Adler, F. (1975). *Sisters in crime: The rise of the new female criminal.* New York: McGraw-Hill.

Adler, J. S. (1996). The making of a moral panic in 19th-century America: The Boston garroting hysteria of 1865. *Deviant Behavior: An Interdisciplinary Journal, 17,* 259-278.

Akers, R. L., La Greca, A. J., Sellers, C., & Cochran, J. (1987). Fear of crime and victimization among the elderly in different types of communities. *Criminology, 25*(3), 487-505.

Allen, R. (1996). Socioeconomic conditions and property crime: A comprehensive review and a test of the professional literature. *American Journal of Economics and Sociology, 55,* 293-308.

Allport, G. W., & Postman, L. J. (1947). *The psychology of rumor.* New York: Holt.

Alterman, E. (2003). *What liberal media? The truth about bias and the news.* New York: Basic Books.

Altheide, D. L., & Johnson, J. M. (1980). *Bureaucratic propaganda.* Boston: Allyn & Bacon.

Anderson, D. C. (1995). *Crime and the politics of hysteria: How the Willie Horton story changed American justice.* Toronto: Times Books.

Anderson, E. (1999). *The code of the street: Decency, violence and the moral life of the inner city.* New York: Norton.

Archer, D., & Gartner, R. (1984). *Violence and crime in cross national perspective.* New Haven, CT: Yale University Press.

Armstrong, E. G. (2001). Gangsta misogyny: A content analysis of the portrayals of violence against women in rap music, 1987-1993. *Journal of Criminal Justice and Popular Culture, 8*(2), 96-126.

Austin, D. M., Furr, L. A., & Spine, M. (2002). The effect of neighborhood physical and social conditions on perceptions of safety. *Journal of Criminal Justice, 30*(5), 417-427.

Badak, J. J. (2001). *In the wake of the Butcher.* Kent, OH: Kent State University Press.

Bagdikian, B. H. (2000). *The media monopoly* (6th ed.). Boston: Beacon.

Baker, M. H., Nienstedt, B. C., Everett, R. S., & McCleary, R. (1983). The impact of a crime wave: Perceptions, fear, and confidence in the police. *Law and Society Review, 17*(2), 319-334.

Bankston, W. B., Jenkins, Q. A. L., Thayer-Doyle, C. L., & Thompson, C. Y. (1987). Fear of criminal victimization and residential location: The influence of perceived risk. *Rural Sociology, 52*(1), 98-107.

Barnett, C., & Mencken, F. C. (2002). Social disorganization theory and the contextual nature of crime in nonmetropolitan countries. *Rural Sociology, 67*(3), 362-393.

Barr, A. (1999). *Drink: A social history of America.* New York: Carroll and Graf.

Barra, A. (1998). *Inventing Wyatt Earp: His life and many legends.* New York: Carroll and Graf.

Bartholomew, R. E. (2001). *Little green men, meowing nuns and head-hunting panics: A study of mass psychogenic illness and social delusion.* Jefferson, NC: McFarland.

Bartholomew, R. E., & Goode, E. (2000). Mass delusions and hysterias [Electronic version]. *Skeptical Inquirer, 243,* 20-28. Retrieved December 12, 2004, from http://csicop.org/si/2000-05/delusions.html

Bartholomew, R. E., & Radford, B. (2003). *Hoaxes, myths, and manias: Why we need critical thinking.* New York: Prometheus.

Bayley, D. H., & Shearing, C. D. (2001). *The new structure of policing: Description, conceptualization, and research agenda.* Washington, DC: National Institute of Justice.

Becker, E. (2001, February 9). As ex-theorist on young "super-predators," Bush aide has regrets [Electronic version]. *New York Times.* Retrieved December 12, 2004, from http://www.crimelynx.com/dilulio2.html

Becker, H. (1963). *Outsiders: Studies in the sociology of deviance.* New York: Free Press of Glencoe.

Beckett, K. (1994). Setting the public agenda. *Social Problems, 41*(3), 425-447.

Beckett, K. (1997). *Making crime pay: Law and order in contemporary American politics.* New York: Oxford University Press.

Beckett, K., & Sasson, T. (2000). *The politics of injustice: Crime and punishment in America.* Thousand Oaks, CA: Pine Forge Press.

Behr, E. (1997). *Prohibition: Thirteen years that changed America.* New York: Arcade.

Belyea, M. J., & Zingraff, M. T. (1988). Fear of crime and residential location. *Rural Sociology, 53*(4), 473-486.

Bennett, W. J., DiIulio, J. J., Jr., & Walters, J. P. (1996). *Body count.* New York: Simon & Schuster.

Best, J. (1988). Missing children, misleading statistics. *Public Interest, 92*(Summer), 84-92.

Best, J. (1990). *Threatened children.* Chicago: University of Chicago Press.

Best, J. (1991). "Road warriors" on "hair-trigger highways": Cultural resources and the media's construction of the 1987 freeway shootings problem. *Sociological Inquiry, 61*(3), 327-345.

Best, J. (1995). *Images of issues: Typifying contemporary social problems* (2nd ed.). New York: Aldine de Gruyter.

Best, J. (1999). *Random violence: How we talk about new crimes and new victims.* Berkeley: University of California Press.

Best, J. (2001a). *Damned lies and statistics: Untangling numbers from the media, politicians, and activists.* Berkeley: University of California Press.

Best, J. (2001b). The diffusion of social problems. In J. Best (Ed.), *How claims spread: Cross-national diffusion of social problems.* New York: Aldine de Gruyter.

Best, J. (2003). Monster hype. *Education Next.* Retrieved December 12, 2004, from http://www.educationnext.org/20022/50.html

Best, J., & Horiuchi, G. (1985). The razor blade in the apple. *Social Problems, 32*(5), 488-499.

Best, J., & Hutchinson, M. M. (1998). The gang initiation rite as a motif in contemporary crime discourse. In G. W. Potter & V. E. Kappeler (Eds.), *Constructing crime: Perspectives on making news and social problems.* Prospect Heights, IL: Waveland.

Best, J., & Thibodeau, T. M. (1998). Measuring the scope of social problems: Apparent inconsistencies across estimates of family abductions. In G. W. Potter & V. E. Kappeler (Eds.), *Constructing crime: Perspectives on making news and social problems.* Prospect Heights, IL: Waveland.

Biagi, S. (1998). *Media/impact: An introduction to mass media* (4th ed.). Belmont, CA: Wadsworth.

Bird, S. E. (1996). CJ's revenge: Media, folklore and the cultural construction of AIDS. *Critical Studies in Mass Commercialism, 13*(1), 44-58.

Black, D. (1970). Production of crime rates. *American Sociological Review, 35,* 733-747.

Blakely, E. J. (1997). *Fortress America.* Washington DC: Brookings Institution.

Blumstein, A. (2002). Why is crime falling—or is it? In A. Blumstein, L. Steinberg, C. C. Bell, & M. A. Berger (Eds.), *Perspectives on crime and justice: 2000-2001 lecture series.* Washington, DC: U.S. Department of Justice, National Institute of Justice.

Bogart, L. (1995). *Commercial culture: The media system and the public interest.* New York: Oxford University Press.

Box, S. (1981). *Deviance, reality and society.* London: Holt, Rinehart & Winston.

Braithwaite, J. (1979). *Inequality, crime and public policy.* Boston: Routledge & Kegan Paul.

Braithwaite, J. (1989). *Crime, shame and reintegration.* New York: Cambridge University Press.

Brantingham, P., & Brantingham, P. (1984). *Patterns in crime.* New York: Macmillan.

Britain: Fear itself, crime. (2003, July 19). *The Economist, 368*(8333), 25.

Brownstein, H. H. (1996). *The rise and fall of a violent crime wave: Crack cocaine and the social construction of a crime problem.* New York: Criminal Justice Press.

Brunsma, D. L., & Rockquemore, K. A. (1998). Effects of student uniforms on attendance, behavior problems, substance abuse, and academic achievement. *Journal of Education Research, 92*(1), 53-62.

Brunvand, J. H. (1981). *The vanishing hitchhiker: American urban legends and their meanings.* New York: Norton.

Brunvand, J. H. (1989). *Curses! Broiled again!* New York: Norton.

Brunvand, J. H. (1993). *The baby train and other lusty urban legends.* New York: Norton.

Brunvand, J. H. (1995). "Lights Out!": A faxslore phenomenon. *Skeptical Inquirer, 19*(2), 32-37.

Bullock, C. F., & Cubert, J. (2002). Coverage of domestic violence fatalities by newspapers in Washington State. *Journal of Interpersonal Violence, 17,* 475-499.

Bureau of Justice Assistance. (1997). *A policymaker's guide to hate crime.* Washington, DC: U.S. Department of Justice.

Bureau of Justice Statistics. (2002). *Homicide trends in the United States.* Washington, DC: U.S. Department of Justice. Retrieved December 12, 2004, from http:// www.ojp.usdoj.gov/bjs/homicide/homtrnd.htm

Bureau of Justice Statistics. (2003). *Criminal victimization, 2003.* Washington, DC: U.S. Department of Justice. Retrieved December 12, 2004, from http://www.ojp.usdoj.gov/bjs/abstract/cv02.htm

Burkitt, I. (1997). Social relationships and emotions. *Sociology, 31*(1), 37-55.

Bursik, R. J., Jr., & Grasmick, H. G. (1993). *Neighborhoods and crime: The dimensions of effective community control.* New York: Lexington Books.

Burton, V. S., Cullen, F. T., Evans, T. D., Alarid, L. F., & Dunaway, R. G. (1998). Gender, self-control, and crime. *Journal of Research in Crime and Delinquency, 35*, 123-147.

Canada, G. (1995). *Fist stick knife gun: A personal history of violence in America.* Boston: Beacon.

Cantor, D., & Land, K. C. (1985). Unemployment and crime rates in post World War II United States: A theoretical and empirical analysis. *American Sociological Review, 50*(June), 317-332.

Caplan, G. (1973). Reflections on the nationalization of crime, 1964-1968. *Arizona State University Law Journal, 58*, 583-635.

Cavender, G. (1998). In "The shadow of shadows": Television reality crime programming. In M. Fishman & G. Cavender (Eds.), *Entertaining crime.* New York: Aldine de Gruyter.

Chambliss, W. J. (1994). Policing the ghetto underclass: The politics of law and law enforcement. *Social Problems, 41*(2), 177-194.

Chandler, K. A., Chapman, C. D., Rand, M. R., & Taylor, B. M. (1998). *Students' reports of school crime: 1989 and 1995.* Washington, DC: U.S. Department of Education and U.S. Department of Justice.

Chapman, C. R., & Harris, A. W. (2002). A skeptical look at September 11th: How we can defeat terrorism by reacting to it more rationally [Electronic version]. *Skeptical Inquirer.* Retrieved December 12, 2004, from http://www.csicop.org/si/2002-09/9-11.html

Charles, J. R. (1983). The situational relationship between age and the fear of crime. *International Journal of Aging and Human Development, 17*(2), 103-111.

Chasteen, A. L. (2001). Constructing rape: Feminism, change, and women's everyday understandings of sexual assault. *Sociological Spectrum, 21*, 101-139.

Chermak, S. (1995). *Victims in the news: Crime and the American news media.* Boulder, CO: Westview.

Clark, J., Austin, J., & Henry, D. A. (1997). "Three strikes and you're out": A review of state legislation. *NIJ Research in Brief.* Washington, DC: U.S. Department of Justice. Retrieved December 12, 2004, from http://www.ncjrs.org/pdffiles/165369.pdf

Clarke, A. H. (1984). Perceptions of crime and fear of victimization among elderly people. *Aging and Society, 4*(3), 327-342.

Clarke, L. (2003). Conceptualizing responses to extreme events: The problem of panic and failing gracefully. *Research in Social Problems and Public Policy, 11*, 123-141.

CNN. (2001). *"Monkey man" fears rampant in New Delhi.* Retrieved December 12, 2004, from http://archives.cnn.com/2001/WORLD/asiapcf/south/05/16/india.monkey man/index.html

Cohen, L., & Felson, M. (1979). Social change and crime rate trends: A routine activities approach. *American Sociological Review, 44*, 588-608.

Cohen, P. C. (1998). *The murder of Helen Jewett.* New York: Vintage.

Cohen, S. (1972). *Folk devils and moral panics: The creation of the Mods and Rockers.* London: MacGibbon and Kee.

Cohen, S., & Young, J. (1981). *The manufacture of news: Social problems, deviance and the mass media.* London: Constable.

Cohl, H. A. (1997). *Are we scaring ourselves to death? How pessimism, paranoia, and a misguided media are leading us toward disaster.* New York: St. Martin's Griffin.

Coleman, C., & Moynihan, J. (1996). *Understanding crime data: Haunted by the dark figure.* Philadelphia: Open University Press.

Conell, C., & Cohn, S. (1995). Learning from other people's actions: Environment variation and diffusion in French coal mining strikes, 1890-1935. *American Journal of Sociology, 101*(2), 366-403.

Conklin, J. E. (1975). *The impact of crime.* New York: Macmillan.

Conklin, J. E. (2003). *Why crime rates fell.* Boston: Allyn & Bacon.

Cook, F. L., & Skogan, W. G. (1990). Agenda setting in the rise and fall of policy issues: The case of criminal victimization of the elderly. *Environment and Planning C: Government and Policy, 8,* 395-415.

Corbett, C. (2003). *Car crime.* Devon, UK: Willan.

Corn, D. (2003). *The lies of George W. Bush.* New York: Crown.

Coser, L. A. (1956). *The functions of social conflict.* London: Routledge & Kegan Paul.

Courtwright, D. T. (1998). *Violent land: Single men and social disorder from the frontier to the inner city.* Cambridge, MA: Harvard University Press.

Craig, K. M. (1999). Retaliation, fear, or rage: An investigation of African American and white reactions to racist hate crimes. *Journal of Interpersonal Violence, 14*(2), 138-151.

Critcher, C. (2003). *Moral panics and the media.* Philadelphia: Open University Press.

Cross, W. E., Jr. (2003). Tracing the historical origins of youth delinquency and violence: Myths and realities about black culture. *Journal of Social Issues, 59*(1), 67-82.

Crossen, C. (1994). *Tainted truth: The manipulation of fact in America.* New York: Simon & Schuster.

Crouch, B. M., & Damphousse, K. R. (1992). Newspapers and the antisatanism movement: A content analysis. *Sociological Spectrum, 12*(1), 12-20.

Crutchfield, R. D., Glusker, A. N., & Bridges, G. S. (1999). A tale of three cities: Labor markets and homicides. *Sociological Focus, 32,* 65-83.

Crystal, S. (1988). Elder abuse: The latest "crisis." *Public Interest, 88,* 56-66.

CSICOP Hoax Watch. (2002). CSICOP tracks misinformation and hoaxes in the wake of the terrorist attacks. Retrieved December 12, 2004, from http://www.csicop.org/hoaxwatch/

Cullen, F. T., Wozniak, J. F., & Frank, J. (1985). The rise of the elderly offender: Will a "new" criminal be invented? *Crime and Social Justice, 23,* 151-165.

Cunneen, C. (1999). Zero tolerance policing and the experience of New York City. *Current Issues in Criminal Justice, 10*(3), 299-313.

Curtis, L. P., Jr. (2001). *Jack the Ripper and the London press.* New Haven, CT: Yale University Press.

DeFleur, M. (1988, January/February). Diffusing information. *Society,* pp. 72-81.

De Haan, W., & Loader, I. (2002). On emotions of crime, punishment and social control. *Theoretical Criminology, 6*(3), 243-253.

Dewdney, A. K. (1993). *200% of nothing: An eye-opening tour through the twists and turns of math abuse and innumeracy.* New York: John Wiley.

deYoung, M. (1997). Another look at moral panics: The case of satanic day care centers. *Deviant Behavior: An Interdisciplinary Journal, 19,* 257-278.

Ditton, J., Bannister, J., Gilchrist, E., & Farrall, S. (1999). Afraid or angry? Recalibrating the "fear" of crime. *International Review of Victimology, 6,* 83-99.

Donovan, P. (2004). *No way of knowing: Crime, urban legends, and the Internet.* New York: Routledge.

Donziger, S. R. (Ed.). (1996). *The real war on crime: The report of the National Criminal Justice Commission.* New York: HarperPerennial.

Doob, A. (1995). Understanding the attacks on Statistics Canada Violence against Women Survey. In M. Valverde, L. MacLeod, & K. Johnson (Eds.), *Wife assault and the Canadian criminal justice system.* Toronto: University of Toronto, Centre of Criminology.

Douglas, J. (1967). *The social meaning of suicide.* Princeton, NJ: Princeton University Press.

Dozier, R., Jr. (1998). *Fear itself.* New York: St. Martin's.

Dubber, M. D. (2002). *Victims in the war on crime: The use and abuse of victims' rights.* New York: New York University Press.

Durkheim, E. (1933). *The division of labor in society.* Glencoe, IL: Free Press. (Original work published 1893)

Durkheim, E. (1951). *Suicide: A study in sociology.* Glencoe, IL: Free Press. (Original work published 1897)

Eck, J., & Maguire, E. R. (2000). Have changes in policing reduced violent crime: An assessment of the evidence. In A. Blumstein & J. Wallman (Eds.), *The crime drop in America.* New York: Cambridge University Press.

Ehrlich, M. C. (2004). *Journalism in the movies.* Champaign: University of Illinois Press.

Ellis, B. (1994). "The hook" reconsidered. *Folklore, 105,* 61-75.

Ericson, R. V., Baranek, P. N., & Chan, J. B. L. (1989). *Negotiating control: A study of news sources.* Toronto: University of Toronto Press.

Erikson, K. T. (1966). *Wayward puritans: A study in the sociology of deviance.* New York: John Wiley.

Fabianic, D. (1997). Television dramas and homicide causation. *Journal of Criminal Justice, 25*(3), 195-203.

Farrell, G., & Pease, K. (Eds.). (2001). *Repeat victimization.* Monsey, NY: Criminal Justice Press.

Fattah, E. A. (1986). Some visible and hidden dangers of victim movements. In E. A. Fattah (Ed.), *From crime policy to victim policy: Reorienting the justice system.* New York: St. Martin's.

Fattah, E. A., & Sacco, V. F. (1989). *Crime and victimization of the elderly.* New York: Springer.

Federal Bureau of Investigation. (2002). *Crime in the United States.* Washington, DC: U.S. Department of Justice. Retrieved December 12, 2004, from http://www.fbi.gov/ucr/cius_02/pdf/4sectionfour.pdf

Felson, M. (2002). *Crime in everyday life* (3rd ed.). Thousand Oaks, CA: Sage.

Ferraro, K. F., & LaGrange, R. (1987). The measurement of fear of crime. *Sociological Inquiry, 57,* 70-101.

Ferrell, J. (1998). Criminalizing popular culture. In F. Y. Bailey & D. C. Hale (Eds.), *Popular culture, crime, and justice.* Belmont, CA: West/Wadsworth.

Finckenauer, J. O. (1978, January). Crime as a national political issue: 1964-76: From law and order to domestic tranquility. *Crime and Delinquency,* pp. 13-27.

Finckenauer, J. O. (1982). *Scared straight! and the panacea phenomenon.* Englewood Cliffs, NJ: Prentice Hall.

Fine, G. A., & Turner, P. A. (2001). *Whispers on the color line: Rumor and race in America.* Berkeley: University of California Press.

Fine, G. A., & Whyte, R. D. (2001). Creating collective attention in the public domain: Human interest narratives and the rescue of Floyd Collins. *Social Forces, 81*(1), 57-85.

Fischer, C. S. (1984). *The urban experience* (2nd ed.). San Diego, CA: Harcourt Brace Jovanovich.

Fischer, C. S. (1995). The subcultural theory of urbanism: A twentieth-year assessment. *American Journal of Sociology, 101*(3), 543-577.

Fischer, C. S. (1980). The spread of violent crime from city to countryside, 1955 to 1975. *Rural Sociology, 45,* 416-434.

Fischer, C. T. (1984). A phenomenological study of being criminally victimized: Contributions and constraints of qualitative research. *Journal of Social Issues, 40*(1), 161-178.

Fishman, M. (1978). Crime waves as ideology. *Social Problems, 25,* 531-543.

Fishman, M. (1998). Ratings and reality: The persistence of the reality crime genre. In M. Fishman & G. Cavender (Eds.), *Entertaining crime.* New York: Aldine de Gruyter.

Fishman, M., & Cavender, G. (Eds.). (1998). *Entertaining crime: Television reality programs.* New York: Aldine de Gruyter.

Flowers, R. B. (1989). *Demographics and criminality: The characteristics of crime in America.* New York: Greenwood.

Forde, D. R. (1993). Perceived crime, fear of crime, and walking alone at night. *Psychological Reports, 73,* 403-407.

Forst, M. L., & Blomquist, M. (1991). *Missing children: Rhetoric and reality.* Toronto: Lexington Books.

Fox, J. A., & Levin, J. (2001). *The will to kill: Making sense of senseless murder.* Boston: Allyn & Bacon.

Freeman, R. B. (1995). The labor market. In J. Q. Wilson & J. Petersila (Eds.), *Crime.* San Francisco: ICS Press.

Fumento, M. (1998). Road rage versus reality [Electronic version]. *Atlantic Monthly.* Retrieved December 12, 2004, from http://www.fumento.com/atlantic.html

Furstenberg, F. (1971). Public reactions to crime in the streets. *American Scholar, 40,* 601-610.

Gabler, N. (1998). *Life: The movie: How entertainment conquered reality.* New York: Knopf.

Gabriel, U., & Greve, W. (2003). The psychology of fear of crime: Conceptual and methodological perspectives. *British Journal of Criminology, 43,* 594-608.

Gans, H. J. (1979). *Deciding what's news: A study of CBS Evening News, NBC Nightly News, Newsweek and Time.* New York: Pantheon.

Geary, W. R. (2002). The legislative recreation of RICO: Reinforcing the "myth" of organized crime. *Crime, Law and Social Change, 38,* 311-356.

Gest, T. (2001). *Crime and politics: Big government's erratic campaign for law and order.* New York: Oxford University Press.

Gilbert, J. B. (1986). *A cycle of outrage: America's reaction to the juvenile delinquent in the 1950s.* New York: Oxford University Press.

Gilbert, N. (1994). Miscounting social ills. *Transaction: Social Science and Modern Society, 31*(3), 18-26.

Gilbert, N. (1997). Advocacy research and social policy. *Crime and Justice: A Review of Research, 22,* 101-148.

Gillespie, D. L., & Leffler, A. (1987). The politics of research methodology in claims-making activities: Social sciences and sexual harassment. *Social Problems, 34*(5), 490-500.

Gilovich, T. (1991). *How we know what isn't so: The fallibility of reason in everyday life.* New York: Free Press.

Gilovich, T. (1993). *How we know what isn't so* (Rpt. ed.). New York: Free Press.

Glaser, D. (1997). *Profitable penalties: How to cut both crime rates and costs.* Thousand Oaks, CA: Pine Forge Press.

Glassner, B. (1999). *The culture of fear: Why Americans are afraid of the wrong things.* New York: Basic Books.

Glynn, K. (2000). *Tabloid culture: Trash taste, popular power and the transformation of American television.* Durham, NC: Duke University Press.

Golianopoulos, T. (2004, March). Black Steele in the hour of chaos. *The Source,* pp. 120-121.

Goode, E. (1999). *Paranormal beliefs: A sociological introduction.* Prospect Heights, IL: Waveland.

Goode, E. (2002, July-August). Drug arrests at the millennium. *Society, 39,* pp. 41-45.

Goode, E., & Ben-Yehuda, N. (1994). *Moral panics: The social construction of deviance.* Cambridge, MA: Blackwell.

Goodrum, S., & Stafford, M. C. (2003). The management of emotions in the criminal justice system. *Sociological Focus, 36*(3), 179-196.

Goodstein, L., & Shotland, R. L. (1982). The crime causes crime model: A critical review of the relationship between fear of crime, bystander surveillance and changes in the crime rate. *Victimology, 5*(2-4), 133-151.

Gordon, M. T., & Riger, S. (1989). *The female fear.* New York: Free Press.

Gottfredson, M. R., & Gottfredson, D. (1988). *Decisionmaking in criminal justice* (2nd ed.). New York: Plenum.

Gottfredson, M. R., & Hirschi, T. (1990). *A general theory of crime.* Stanford, CA: Stanford University Press.

Grant, D. S., II, & Martinez, R., Jr. (1997). Crime and the restructuring of the U.S. economy: A reconsideration of the class linkages. *Social Forces, 75*(3), 769-799.

Gray, H. (1989). Popular music as a social problem: A social history of claims against popular music. In J. Best (Ed.), *Images of issues.* New York: Aldine de Gruyter.

Greek, C. (1993). *Attacks on Florida tourists.* Retrieved December 12, 2004, from University of South Florida, School of Criminology Web site: http://www.fsu.edu/~crimdo/tourists.html

Greeley, A. (2002, September 6). Media ignored claim amid 9/11 chaos [Electronic version]. *Chicago Sun Times.* Retrieved December 12, 2004, from http://www.leeclarke.com/docs/interviews/Greeley.html

Gurr, T. (1981). Historical trends in violent crime: A critical review of evidence. In M. Tonry & N. Morris (Eds.), *Crime and justice: An annual review of research* (Vol. 3, pp. 295-353). Chicago: University of Chicago Press.

Gusfield, J. R. (1963). *Symbolic crusade: Status politics and the American temperance movement.* Urbana: University of Illinois Press.

Gusfield, J. R. (1981). *The culture of public problems: Drinking-driving and the symbolic order.* Chicago: University of Chicago Press.

Hagan, J. (1995). *Crime and inequality.* Stanford, CA: Stanford University Press.

Hagan, J., Simpson, J., & Gillis, A. R. (1988). Feminist scholarship, relational and instrumental control and a power-control theory of gender and delinquency. *British Journal of Sociology, 39*(3), 301-336.

Hall, S., Critcher, C., Jefferson, T., Clark, J., & Roberts, B. (1978). *Policing the crisis: Mugging, the state, and law and order.* London: Macmillan.

Hamner, J., & Saunders, S. (1984). Well founded fear: *A community study of violence to women.* London: Hutchinson.

Harcourt, B. E. (2001). *Illusion of order: The false promise of broken windows policing.* Cambridge, MA: Harvard University Press.

Hartnagel, T. F. (1979). The perception and fear of crime: Implications for neighborhood cohesion, social activity, and community affect. *Social Forces, 58,* 176-193.

Hawdon, J. E. (1996). Cycles of deviance: Structural change, moral boundaries, and drug use, 1880-1990. *Sociological Spectrum, 16,* 183-207.

Hawdon, J. E. (2001). The role of presidential rhetoric in the creation of a moral panic: Reagan, Bush and the war on drugs. *Deviant Behavior: An Interdisciplinary Journal, 22,* 419-445.

Headley, B. D. (1998). *The Atlanta youth murders and the politics of race.* Carbondale: Southern Illinois University Press.

Health, L., & Gilbert, K. (1996). Mass media and fear of crime. *American Behavioral Scientist, 39*(4), 379-386.

Helmer, W., & Mattix, R. (1998). *Public enemies: America's criminal past 1919-1940.* New York: Checkmark Books.

Helmer, W. J., & Bilek, A. J. (2004). *The St. Valentine's Day massacre: The untold story of the gangland bloodbath that brought down Al Capone.* Nashville, TN: Cumberland House.

Herman, E. S. (1991). Drug wars: Appearance and reality. *Social Justice, 18*(4), 76-85.

Hicks, R. D. (1991). *In pursuit of Satan: The police and the occult.* Buffalo, NY: Prometheus.

Hindelang, M. J., Gottfredson, M. R., & Garofalo, J. (1978). *Victims of personal crime: An empirical foundation for a theory of personal victimization.* Cambridge, MA: Ballinger.

Hochstetler, A. (2002). Sprees and runs: Opportunity constructions and criminal episodes. *Deviant Behavior: An Interdisciplinary Journal, 23,* 45-73.

Hochstetler, A. L., & Shover, N. (1997). Street crime, labor surplus, and criminal punishment. *Social Problems, 44*(3), 358-368.

Hoffman, D. E. (1993). *Scarface Al and the crime crusaders: Chicago's private war against Capone.* Carbondale: Southern Illinois University Press.

Holstein, J. A., & Miller, G. (Eds.). (2003). *Challenges and choices: Constructionist perspectives on social problems.* New York: Aldine de Gruyter.

Hope, T. (1995). The flux of victimization. *British Journal of Criminology, 35*(3), 327-341.

Horowitz, R. (1987). Community tolerance of gang violence. *Social Problems, 34*(5), 437-450.

Howitt, D. (1982). *The mass media and social problems.* Elmsford, NY: Pergamon.

Howitt, D. (1998). *Crime, media and the law.* New York: John Wiley.

Huff, D. (1954). *How to lie with statistics.* New York: Norton.

Illouz, E. (1998). What role for emotions in sociological theory. *Body and Society, 7*(1), 97-102.

Jackson, K. T. (1985). *Crabgrass frontier: The suburbanization of the United States.* New York: Oxford University Press.

Jacobs, J. B., & Henry, J. S. (1996). The social construction of a hate crime epidemic. *Journal of Criminal Law and Criminology, 86*(2), 366-391.

Jacobs, J. B., & Potter, K. A. (1997). Hate crimes: A critical perspective. *Crime and Justice: A Review of Research, 22,* 1-50.

Jacobs, N. (1965). The phantom slasher of Taipei: Mass hysteria in a non-Western society. *Social Problems, 12,* 318-328.

Jenkins, P. (1992). *Intimate enemies: Moral panics in contemporary Great Britain.* New York: Aldine de Gruyter.

Jenkins, P. (1994). *Using murder: The social construction of serial homicide.* New York: Aldine de Gruyter.

Jenkins, P. (1999). Fighting terrorism as if women mattered: Anti-abortion violence as unconstructed terrorism. In J. Ferrell & N. Websdale (Eds.), *Making trouble: Cultural constructions of crime, deviance, and control.* New York: Aldine de Gruyter.

Jenkins, P. (2003). *Images of terror: What we can and can't know about terrorism.* New York: Aldine de Gruyter.

Jenkins, P., & Maier-Katkin, D. (1992). Satanism: Myth and reality in a contemporary moral panic. *Crime, Law and Social Change, 17,* 53-75.

Johnson, B., Golub, A., & Dunlop, E. (2000). The rise and decline of hard drugs and drug market violence in inner city New York. In A. Blumstein & J. Wallman (Eds.), *The crime drop in America.* New York: Cambridge University Press.

Johnson, D. M. (1945). The "phantom anesthetist" of Mattoon: A field study of mass hysteria. *Journal of Abnormal Psychology, 40,* 175-186.

Johnson, H. (1996). *Dangerous domains.* Scarborough, ON: Nelson Canada.

Johnson, K. A., & Wasielewski, P. L. (1982). A commentary on victimization research and the importance of meaning structures. *Criminology, 29*(2), 205-222.

Kanan, J. W., & Pruitt, M. V. (2002). Modeling fear of crime and perceived victimization risk: The (in)significance of neighborhood interaction. *Sociological Inquiry, 72*(4), 527-548.

Kappeler, V. E., Blumberg, M., & Potter, G. W. (2000). *The mythology of crime and criminal justice* (3rd ed.). Prospect Heights, IL: Waveland.

Karmen, A. (2000). *New York murder mystery: The true story behind the crime crash of the 1990s.* New York: New York University Press.

Karstedt, S. (2002). Emotions and criminal justice. *Theoretical Criminology, 6*(3), 299-317.

Katz, C. M. (2003). Issues in the production and dissemination of gang statistics: An ethnographic study of a large midwestern police gang unit. *Crime and Delinquency, 49*(3), 485-516.

Katz, J. (1999). *How emotions work.* Chicago: University Of Chicago Press.

Kay, J. H. (1998). *Asphalt nation: How the automobile took over America and how we can take it back.* Berkeley: University of California Press.

Keller, T. (1993). Trash TV. *Journal of Popular Culture, 26*(4), 195-206.

Kelling, G. L., & Bratton, W. J. (1998). Declining crime rates: Insiders' views of the New York City story. *Journal of Criminal Law and Criminology, 88,* 1217-1231.

Kelling, G. L., & Coles, C. M. (1998). *Fixing broken windows.* New York: Free Press.

Kennedy, L. W., & Sacco, V. F. (1998). *Crime victims in context.* Los Angeles: Roxbury.

Kidd, P. B. (n.d.). One-man crime wave. *Crime Library.* Retrieved December 12, 2004, from http://www.crimelibrary.com/serial_killers/weird/cooke/wave_7.html

Killias, M. F., & Aebi, M. F. (2000). Crime trends in Europe from 1990 to 1996: How Europe illustrates the limits of the American experience. *European Journal on Criminal Policy and Research, 8*(1), 43-63.

Killingbeck, D. (2001). The role of television news in the construction of school violence as a "moral panic." *Journal of Criminal Justice and Popular Culture, 8*(3), 186-202.

Klinenberg, E. (2003). *Heat wave: A social autopsy of disaster in Chicago.* Chicago: University of Chicago Press.

Kooistra, P. G., & Mahoney, J. S., Jr. (1999). The historical roots of tabloid TV crime. In J. Ferrell & N. Websdale (Eds.), *Making trouble: Cultural constructions of crime, deviance, and control.* New York: Aldine de Gruyter.

Kovecses, Z. (1990). *Emotion concepts.* New York: Springer.

Krajicek, D. J. (1998). *Scooped! Media miss real story on crime while chasing sex, sleaze and celebrities.* New York: Columbia University Press.

Krannich, R. S., Berry, E. H., & Greider, T. (1989). Fear of crime in rapidly changing rural communities: A longitudinal analysis. *Rural Sociology, 54*(2), 195-212.

Lab, S. P. (1992). *Crime prevention: Approaches, practices and evaluations* (2nd ed.). Cincinnati, OH: Anderson.

LaFree, G. (1998a). *Losing legitimacy: Street crime and the decline of social institutions in America*. Boulder, CO: Westview.

LaFree, G. (1998b). Social institutions and the crime "bust" of the 1990's. *Journal of Criminal Law and Criminology, 88,* 1324-1368.

LaFree, G. (1999). Declining violent crime rates in the 1990s: Predicting crime booms and busts. *American Review of Sociology, 25,* 145-168.

LaGrange, R. L., & Ferraro, K. F. (1987). The elderly's fear of crime: A critical examination of the research. *Research on Aging, 9,* 372-391.

LaGrange, R. L., & Ferraro, K. F. (1989). Assessing age and gender differences in perceived risk and fear of crime. *Criminology, 27*(4), 697-719.

LaGrange, R. L., Ferraro, K. F., & Supancic, M. (1992). Perceived risk and fear of crime: Role of social and physical incivilities. *Journal of Research in Crime and Delinquency, 29*(3), 331-334.

Lane, J. (2002). Fear of gang crime: A qualitative examination of the four perspectives. *Journal of Research in Crime and Delinquency, 39*(4), 437-471.

Lane, J., & Meeker, J. W. (2000). Subcultural diversity and the fear of crime and gangs. *Crime and Delinquency, 46*(4), 497-521.

Lane, R. (1997). *Murder in America: A history*. Columbus: Ohio State University Press.

Leanza, C., & Feld, H. (2003). More than a "toaster with pictures": Defending media ownership limits. *Communications Lawyer, 21*(3), 17-22.

Lee, M. (2001). The genesis of "fear of crime." *Theoretical Criminology, 5*(4), 467-485.

Lejeune, R., & Alex, N. (1973). On being mugged: The event and its aftermath. *Urban Life and Culture, 2*(3), 259-283.

Lempert, R. (1989). Humility is a virtue: On the publicization of policy-relevant research. *Law and Society Review, 23*(1), 145-161.

Levin, J., & Arluke, A. (1987). *Gossip: The inside scoop*. New York: Plenum.

Levitt, S. D. (1999). The limited role of changing age structure in explaining aggregate crime rates. *Criminology, 37*(3), 581-597.

Lewis, T. (1997). *Divided highways. Building the interstate highways, transforming American life*. New York: Viking.

Liska, A., & Baccaglini, W. (1990). Feeling safe by comparison: Crime in the newspapers. *Social Problems, 37*(3), 368-374.

Liska, A. E., & Warner, B. D. (1991). Functions of crime: A paradoxical process. *American Journal of Sociology, 96*(6), 1441-1463.

Locher, D. A. (2002). *Collective behavior*. Upper Saddle River, NJ: Prentice Hall.

Lock, E. D., Timberlake, J. M., & Rasinski, K. A. (2002). Battle fatigue: Is public support waning for "war"-centered drug control strategies. *Crime and Delinquency, 48*(3), 380-398.

Lombardo, R. M. (2002). The Black Hand: Terror by letter in Chicago. *Journal of Contemporary Criminal Justice, 18*(4), 394-409.

Loseke, D. R. (1989). "Violence" is "violence"—or is it? The social construction of "wife abuse" and public policy. In J. Best (Ed.), *Images of issues*. New York: Aldine de Gruyter.

Loseke, D. R. (1999). *Thinking about social problems: An introduction to constructionist perspectives*. New York: Aldine de Gruyter.

Loseke, D. R., & Best, J. (2003). *Social problems: Constructionist readings*. New York: Aldine de Gruyter.

Lowry, D. T., Nio, T. C. J., & Leitner, D. W. (2003, March). Setting the public fear agenda: A longitudinal analysis of network TV crime reporting, public perceptions of crime, and FBI crime statistics. *Journal of Communication*, pp. 61-73.

Lule, J. (1993). Murder and myth: *New York Times* coverage of the TWA 847 hijacking victims. *Journalism Quarterly, 70*(1), 26-39.

MacKenzie, D. L., Baunach, P. J., & Roberg, R. R. (1990). *Measuring crime: Large-scale, long-range efforts.* Albany: State University of New York Press.

Mahiri, J., & Conner, E. (2003). Black youth violence has a bad rap. *Journal of Social Issues, 59*(1), 121-140.

Maier, M. H. (1991). *The data game. Controversies in social science statistics.* New York: M. E. Sharpe.

Marks, C. (1991). The urban underclass. *Annual Review of Sociology, 17*, 445-466.

Marks, P. M. (1989). *To live & die in the West: The story of the O. K. Corral gunfight.* New York: Simon & Schuster.

Marriott, R. (1999). Gangsta, gangsta: The sad, violent parable of Death Row Records. In A. Light (Ed.), *The Vibe history of hip hop.* New York: Three Rivers.

Martin, L., & Segrave, K. (1988). *Anti-rock.* New York: Da Capo Press.

Mativat, F., & Tremblay, P. (1997). Counterfeiting credit cards: Displacement effects, suitable offenders, and crime wave patterns. *British Journal of Criminology, 37*(2), 165-183.

Maxfield, M. G., & Babbie, E. (1995). *Research methods for criminal justice and criminology.* Belmont, CA: Wadsworth.

McChesney, R. (2004). *The problem of the media.* New York: Monthly Review Press.

McCorkle, R. C., & Miethe, T. D. (2002). *Panic: The social construction of the street gang problem.* Upper Saddle River, NJ: Prentice Hall.

McCoy, H. V., Wooldredge, J. D., Cullen, F. T., Dubeck, P. J., & Browning, S. L. (1996). Lifestyles of the old and not so fearful: Life situation and older persons' fear of crime. *Journal of Criminal Justice, 24*, 191-205.

McGrath, R. D. (1984). *Gunfighters, highwaymen and vigilantes: Violence on the frontier.* Berkeley: University of California Press.

McQuade, S. (1998). *Towards a theory of technology-enabled crime.* Rochester, NY: Rochester Institute of Technology, Department of Criminal Justice.

McShane, M. D., & Williams, F. P., III. (1992). Radical victimology: A critique of the concept of the victim in traditional victimology. *Crime and Delinquency, 38*(2), 258-271.

Merry, S. E. (1981). *Urban danger: Life in a neighborhood of strangers.* Philadelphia: Temple University Press.

Miethe, T. D. (1995). Fear and withdrawal from urban life. *Annals of the American Academy of Political and Social Science, 539*(May), 14-27.

Miller, D. L. (2000). *Introduction to collective behavior and collective action.* Prospect Heights, IL: Waveland.

Milligan, S. (2003, August 19). Iraqi women recoiling in fear of crime. *Boston Globe.* Available online at http://www.commondreams.org/headlines03/0819-04.htm

Mills, C. W. (1959). *The sociological imagination.* New York: Oxford University Press.

A mixed bag of uniform research. (2000). *School Administrator.* Retrieved December 12, 2004, from http://www.aasa.org/publications/sa/2000_02/white_side_research.htm

Moeller, G. T. (1989). Fear of criminal victimization: The effect of neighborhood racial composition. *Sociology Inquiry, 59*(2), 208-221.

Monkkonen, E. H. (2001). *Murder in New York City.* Berkeley: University of California Press.

Morin, E. (1971). *Rumor in Orleans.* New York: Pantheon.

Mosher, C. J., Miethe, T. D., & Phillips, D. M. (2002). *The mismeasure of crime.* Thousand Oaks, CA: Sage.

Myers, D. J. (2000). The diffusion of collective violence: Infectiousness, susceptibility, and mass media networks. *American Journal of Sociology, 106*(1), 173-208.

Nasaw, D. (1993). *Going out: The rise and fall of public amusements.* New York: Basic Books.

Nasar, J. L., & Fisher, B. (1993). "Hot spots" of fear of crime: A multiple-method investigation. *Journal of Environmental Psychology, 13,* 187-206.

Nelson, B. J. (1984). *Making an issue of child abuse.* Chicago: University of Chicago Press.

Nelson, J. (2000). Introduction. In J. Nelson (Ed.), *Police brutality.* New York: Norton.

Nelson-Rowe, S. (1995). The moral drama of multicultural education. In J. Best (Ed.), *Images of issues: Typifying contemporary social problems* (2nd ed.). New York: Aldine de Gruyter.

Neustrom, M. W., & Norton, W. M. (1995). Economic dislocation and property crime. *Journal of Criminal Justice, 23*(1), 29-39.

Norris, F. H., & Kaniasty, K. (1992). A longitudinal study of the effects of various crime prevention strategies on criminal victimization, fear of crime, and psychological distress. *American Journal of Community Psychology, 20*(5), 625-648.

O'Brien, R. M. (1985). *Crime and victimization data.* Beverly Hills, CA: Sage.

Ogle, J. P, Eckman, M., & Leslie, C. A. (2003). Appearance cues and the shootings at Columbine High: Construction of a social problem in the print media. *Sociological Inquiry, 73*(1), 1-27.

Ohlemacher, T. (1999). Viewing the crime wave from the inside: Perceived rates of extortion among restauranteurs in Germany. *European Journal on Criminal Policy and Research, 7,* 43-61.

O'Kane, M. (1992). *Crooked ladder: Gangsters, ethnicity and the American dream.* New Brunswick, NJ: Transaction Publishers.

Oliver, M. B., & Armstrong, G. B. (1998). The color of crime: Perceptions of Caucasians' and African-Americans' involvement in crime. In M. Fishman & G. Cavender (Eds.), *Entertaining crime.* New York: Aldine de Gruyter.

Orcutt, J. D., & Turner, J. B. (1993). Shocking numbers and graphic accounts: Quantified images of drug problems in the print media. *Social Problems, 40*(2), 190-206.

Ortega, S. T., & Myles, J. L. (1987). Race and gender effects on fear of crime: An interactive model with age. *Criminology, 25*(1), 133-153.

Pain, R. H. (1995). Elderly women and fear of violent crime: The least likely victims? A reconstruction of the extent and nature of risk. *British Journal of Criminology, 35*(4), 584-599.

Pain, R. H. (1997). Old age and ageism in urban research: The case of fear of crime. *Journal of Urban and Regional Research, 21*(1), 117-128.

Parenti, C. (1999). *Lockdown America: Police and prisons in the age of crisis.* New York: Verso.

Parker, K. D., Smith, E., & Murty, K. S. (1993). Fear of crime and the likelihood of victimization: A bi-ethnic comparison. *Journal of Social Psychology, 133*(5), 723-732.

Parnaby, P., & Sacco, V. F. (2004). Fame and strain: The contributions of Mertonian deviance theory to an understanding of the relationship between celebrity and deviant behavior. *Deviant Behavior, 25*(1), 1-26.

Paulos, J. A. (1988). *Innumeracy: Mathematical illiteracy and its consequences.* New York: Vintage.

Paulos, J. A. (1998). *Once upon a number: The hidden mathematical logic of stories.* New York: Basic Books.

Paulson, D. J. (2003). Murder in black and white: The newspaper coverage of homicide in Houston. *Homicide Studies, 7*(3), 289-317.

Pease, K., & Laycock, G. (1996). *Revictimization: Reducing the heat on hot victims.* Washington, DC: U.S. Department of Justice.

Peterson, R. D. (2000). Definitions of a gang and impacts on public policy. *Journal of Criminal Justice, 28,* 139-149.

Pfuhl, E. H., & Henry, S. (1993). *The deviance process* (3rd ed.). New York: Aldine de Gruyter.

Philip, J. C., & Laub, J. H. (1998). The unprecedented epidemic in youth violence. In M. Tonry & M. H. Moore (Eds.), *Crime and justice: An annual review of research: Vol. 24. Youth violence.* Chicago: University of Chicago Press.

Phillips, D. P. (1979). Suicide, motor vehicle fatalities and the mass media: Evidence toward a theory of suggestion. *American Journal of Sociology, 84,* 1150-1174.

Phillips, D. P. (1980). Airplane accidents, murder and the mass media: Towards a theory of imitation and suggestion. *Social Forces, 58,* 1001-1024.

Phillips, D. P. (1983). The impact of mass media violence on U.S. homicides. *American Sociological Review, 48,* 560-568.

Pitkin, T., & Cordasco, F. (1977). *The Black Hand: A chapter in ethnic crime.* Totowa, NJ: Littlefield Adams.

Plait, P. S. (2002). *Bad astronomy: Misperceptions and misuses revealed, from astrology to the moon landing "hoax."* New York: John Wiley.

Polidoro, M. (2002, July/August). Notes on a strange world: Return of Spring-Heeled Jack [Electronic version]. *Skeptical Inquiry.* Retrieved December 12, 2004, from http://www.csicop.org/si/2002-07/strange.html

Pooley, E. (1996, January 15). One good apple. *Time,* pp. 24-26.

Potter, C. B. (1998). *War on crime: Bandits, G-men, and the politics of mass culture.* New Brunswick, NJ: Rutgers University Press.

Powers, F. G. (1983). *G-men: Hoover's FBI in American popular culture.* Carbondale: Southern Illinois University Press.

Radford, B. (2003). Organ theft legend resurfaces in Mexico border slayings. *Skeptical Inquirer, 27*(4), 7-8.

Randall, D. M. (1985). The portrayal of corporate crime in network television newscasts. *Journalism Quarterly, 64*(Spring), 150-153.

Rapping, E. (1992). *The movie of the week.* Minneapolis: University of Minnesota Press.

Ravitch, D., & Viteritti, J. P. (2003). *Kid stuff: Marketing sex and violence to America's children.* Baltimore, MD: Johns Hopkins University Press.

Reiman, J. H. (1998). *The rich get richer and the poor get prison: Ideology, class, and criminal justice.* Boston: Allyn & Bacon.

Reinarman, C. (1988). The social construction of an alcohol problem: The case of Mothers Against Drunk Drivers and social control in the 1980s. *Theory and Society, 17,* 91-120.

Reinarman, C. (1997). *Crack in America.* Berkeley: University of California Press.

Reinarman, C., & Levine, H. G. (1995). The crack attack: America's latest drug scare. In J. Best (Ed.), *Images of issues: Typifying contemporary social problems* (2nd ed.). New York: Aldine de Gruyter.

Reuter, P. (1984). The (continued) vitality of mythical numbers. *Public Interest, 75,* 135-147.

Reynolds, A., & Barnett, B. (2003). America under attack: CNN's visual framing of September 11. In F. Y. Bailey & S. Chermack (Eds.), *Media representation of September 11.* Westport, CT: Praeger.

Richardson, J. T., Best, J., & Bromley, D. (1991). Satanism as a social problem. In J. T. Richardson, J. Best, & D. G. Bromely (Eds.), *The satanism scare.* New York: Aldine de Gruyter.

Ritzer, G. (1995). *Expressing America: A critique of the global credit card society.* Thousand Oaks, CA: Pine Forge Press.

Ritzer, G. (2001). An introduction to McDonaldization. In G. Ritzer, *McDonaldization: The reader.* Thousand Oaks, CA: Pine Forge.

Ro, R. (1996). *Gangsta: Merchandising the rhymes of violence.* New York: St. Martin's.

Robinson, M. B. (2001). McDonaldization of America's police, courts, and corrections. In G. Ritzer, *McDonaldization: The reader.* Thousand Oaks, CA: Pine Forge.

Rogers, N. (2002). *Halloween: From pagan ritual to party night.* New York: Oxford University Press.

Rome, D. (2004). *Black demons: The media's depiction of the African American male criminal stereotype.* Westport, CT: Praeger.

Ronson, J. (2002). *Them.* New York: Simon & Schuster.

Root, W., & De Rochemont, R. (1994). *Eating in America: A social history.* New York: Ecco Press.

Rosenbaum, D. P. (1991). The pursuit of "justice" in the United States: A policy lesson in the war on crime and drugs? In D. J. Loree & R. W. Walker (Eds.), *Community crime prevention: Shaping the future.* Ottawa: Minister of Supply and Services Canada.

Rosenbaum, D. P., & Lurigio, A. J. (1998). *Prevention of crime: Social and situational strategies.* Belmont, CA: Wadsworth.

Rosnow, R. L., & Fine, G. A. (1976). *Rumors and gossip: The social psychology of hearsay.* New York: Elsevier.

Rountree, P. W. (1998). A reexamination of the crime-fear linkage. *Journal of Research in Crime and Delinquency, 35*(3), 341-372.

Rountree, P. W., & Land, K. C. (1996). Perceived risk versus fear and crime: Empirical evidence of conceptually distinct reactions in survey data. *Social Forces, 74*(4), 1353-1376.

Russell-Brown, K. (2004). *Underground codes: Race, crime and related fires.* New York: New York University Press.

Sacco, V. F. (1990). Gender, fear and victimization: A preliminary application of power-control theory. *Sociological Spectrum, 10,* 485-506.

Sacco, V. F. (1995). Media constructions of crime. *Annals of the American Academy of Political and Social Science, 539*(May), 141-154.

Sacco, V. F. (1998). Evaluating satisfaction. In J.-P. Brodeur (Ed.), *How to recognize good policing.* Thousand Oaks, CA: Sage.

Sacco, V. F. (2000a). Crime waves. In C. Bryant (Ed.), *The encyclopedia of criminology and deviant behavior.* Philadelphia: Brunner-Routledge.

Sacco, V. F. (2000b). News that counts: Newspaper images of crime and victimization statistics. *Criminologie, 33*(1), 203-223.

Sacco, V. F. (2003). Black Hand outrage: A constructionist analysis of an urban crime wave. *Deviant Behavior: An Interdisciplinary Journal, 24,* 53-77.

Sacco, V. F., & Ismaili, K. (2001). Social problems and the undefended border: The case of Canada and the U.S. In J. Best (Ed.), *How claims spread: Cross-national diffusion of social problems.* New York: Aldine de Gruyter.

Sacco, V. F., & Macmillan, R. (2001). Victimization and fear of crime: Re-thinking a classic controversy from a criminal event perspective. In R. F. Meier, L. W. Kennedy, & V. F. Sacco (Eds.), *The process and structure of crime: Criminal events and crime analysis.* New Brunswick, NJ: Transaction Publishers.

Sacco, V. F., & Nakhaie, M. R. (2001). Coping with crime: An examination of elderly and nonelderly adaptations. *International Journal of Law and Psychiatry, 24,* 305-323.

Sacco, V. F., & Silverman, R. A. (1982). Crime prevention through mass media: Prospects and problems. *Journal of Criminal Justice, 10,* 257-269.

Sampson, R. J., & Raudenbush, S. W. (1999). Systematic social observation of public spaces: A new look at disorder in urban neighborhoods. *American Journal of Sociology, 105*(3), 603-651.

Sampson, R. J., Raudenbush, S. W., & Earls, F. J. (1997). Neighborhoods and violent crime: A multilevel study of collective efficacy. *Science, 277,* 918-924.

Sasson, T. (1995a). African American conspiracy theories and the social construction of crime. *Sociological Inquiry, 65*(3/4), 265-285.

Sasson, T. (1995b). *Crime talk: How citizens construct a social problem.* New York: Aldine de Gruyter.

Savelsberg, J. J., King, R., & Cleveland, L. (2002). Politicized scholarship? Science on crime and the state. *Social Problems, 49*(3), 327-348.

Scheider, M. C., Rowell, T., & Bezdikian, V. (2003). The impact of citizen perceptions of community policing on fear of crime: Findings from twelve cities. *Police Quarterly, 6*(4), 363-386.

Scheuer, J. (1999). *The sound bite society: Television and the American mind.* New York: Four Walls Eight Windows.

Schlesinger, P., & Tumber, H. (1993). Fighting the war against crime: Television, police, and audience. *British Journal of Criminology, 33*(1), 19-33.

Schlesinger, P., Tumber, H., & Murdock, G. (1991). The media politics of crime and criminal justice. *British Journal of Sociology, 42,* 397-420.

Schlosser, E. (2001). *Fast food nation: The dark side of the American meal.* Boston: Houghton Mifflin.

Schoenberg, R. J. (1992). *Mr. Capone.* New York: William Morrow.

Shaw, D. L., & McCombs, M. E. (1977). *The emergence of American political issues: The agenda-setting function of the press.* St. Paul, MN: West.

Sherman, L. W., Gottfredson, D., MacKenzie, D., Eck, J., Reuter, P., & Bushway, S. (1997). *Preventing crime: What works, what doesn't, what's promising. A report to the United States Congress.* Retrieved on December 12, 2004, from http://www.ncjrs.org/works/wholedoc.htm

Shermer, M. (1997). *Why people believe weird things: Pseudoscience, superstitions, and other confusions of our time.* New York: Freeman.

Shibutani, T. (1966). *Improvised news: A sociological study of rumor.* New York: Bobbs-Merrill.

Shichor, D. (1997). Three strikes as public policy. *Crime and Delinquency, 43*(4), 235-241.

Silberman, C. E. (1978). *Criminal violence, criminal justice.* New York: Vintage Books.

Skogan, W. (1986). Fear of crime and neighborhood change. In A. J. Reiss, Jr. & M. Tonry (Eds.), *Communities and crime.* Chicago: University of Chicago Press.

Skogan, W. (1990). *Disorder and decline.* New York: Free Press.

Skogan, W. G. (1995). Crime and the racial fears of white Americans. *Annals of the American Academy of Political and Social Science, 539,* 59-71.

Skogan, W. G., & Maxfield, M. G. (1981). *Coping with crime: Individual and neighborhood reactions.* Beverly Hills, CA: Sage.

Smith, M. D. (1987). Changes in the victimization of women: Is there a new "female victim"? *Journal of Research in Crime and Delinquency, 24,* 291-301.

Smith, M. R. (2001). Police-led crackdowns and cleanups: An evaluation of a crime control initiative in Richmond, Virginia. *Crime and Delinquency, 47*(1), 60-83.

Sotirovic, M. (2003, March). How individuals explain social problems: The influence of media use. *Journal of Communication,* pp. 122-137.

Sparks, G. G., & Ogles, R. M. (1990). The difference between fear of victimization and the probability of being victimized: Implications for cultivation. *Journal of Broadcasting and Electronic Media, 43*(3), 351-358.

Spector, M., & Kitsuse, J. I. (1977). *Constructing social problems.* Menlo Park, CA: Cummings Publishing.

Spitzberg, B. H., & Cadiz, M. (2002). The media construction of stalking stereotypes. *Journal of Criminal Justice and Popular Culture, 9*(3). Retrieved December 12, 2004, from http://www.albany.edu/scj/jcjpc/index9.html

Stanko, E. A. (1985). *Intimate intrusions: Women's experiences of male violence.* Boston: Routledge & Kegan Paul.

Stanley, M. S. (1996). School uniforms and safety. *Education and Urban Society, 28*(4), 424-435.

Stark, S. D. (1987). Perry Mason meets Sonny Crockett: The history of lawyers and the police as television heroes. *University of Miami Law Review, 42,* 229-283.

Steffens, L. (1931). *The autobiography of Lincoln Steffens.* New York: Harcourt Brace.

Steffensmeier, D., & Harer, M. D. (1999). Making sense of recent U.S. crime trends, 1980 to 1996/1998: Age composition effects and other explanations. *Journal of Research in Crime and Delinquency, 36*(3), 235-274.

Stinchombe, A. L., Adams, R., Heimer, C. A., Scheppele, K. L., Smith, T. W., & Taylor, D. G. (1980). *Crime and punishment—Changing attitudes in America.* San Francisco: Jossey-Bass.

St. John, C., & Heald-Moore, T. (1996). Radical prejudice and the fear of victimization by strangers in a public setting. *Sociological Inquiry, 66*(3), 267-289.

Stolz, B. A. (1985). Congress and criminal justice policy making: The impact of interest groups and symbolic politics. *Journal of Criminal Justice, 13,* 307-319.

Stolz, B. A. (2002). The roles of interest groups in U.S. criminal justice policy: Who, when and how. *Criminal Justice, 2*(1), 51-69.

Sullivan, R. (2004). *Rats: Observations on the history and habitat of the city's most unwanted inhabitants.* New York: Bloomsbury.

Surette, R. (1998). *Media, crime and criminal justice.* Belmont, CA: Wadsworth.

Surette, R. (2002). Self-reported copycat crime among a population of serious and violent juvenile offenders. *Crime and Delinquency, 48*(1), 46-69.

Taylor, R. B. (2001). *Breaking away from broken windows: Baltimore neighborhoods and the nationwide fight against crime, grime, fear and decline*. Boulder. CO: Westview.

Taylor, R. B., & Covington, J. (1993). Community structural change and fear and crime. *Social Problems, 40*(3), 374-397.

Taylor, R. B., & Hale, M. (1986). Testing alternative models of fear of crime. *Journal of Criminal Law and Criminology, 77*(1), 151-189.

Tefertiller, C. (1997). *Wyatt Earp: The life behind the legend*. New York: John Wiley.

Thoits, P. A. (1989). The sociology of emotions. *Annual Review of Sociology, 15,* 317-342.

Thurman, Q., Zhao, J., & Giacomozzi, A. (2001). *Community policing in a community era: An introduction and exploration*. Los Angeles: Roxbury.

Tittle, C. R., & Grasmick, H. G. (1998). Criminal behavior and age: A test of three provocative hypotheses. *Journal of Criminal Law and Criminology, 88,* 309-342.

Toby, J. (1995). The schools. In J. Q. Wilson & J. Petersilia (Eds.), *Crime*. San Francisco: ICS Press.

Tuchman, G. (1978). *Making news: A study in the construction of reality*. New York: Free Press.

Tudor, A. (2003). A (macro) sociology of fear? *Sociological Review, 51*(2), 238-256.

Tunnell, K. D. (1992). Film at eleven: Recent developments in the commodification of crime. *Sociological Spectrum, 12,* 293-313.

Tunnell, K. D. (1998). Reflections on crime, criminals, and control in newsmagazine television programs. In F. Y. Bailey & D. C. Hale (Eds.), *Popular culture, crime, and justice*. Belmont, CA: West/Wadsworth.

Turner, P. A. (1993). *I heard it through the grapevine: Rumor in African-American culture*. Berkeley: University of California Press.

Turner, W. W. (1993). *Hoover's FBI*. New York: Thunder Mouth Press.

United States: The logic of irrational fear: The sniper, risk and public reaction. (2002, October 19). *The Economist, 356*(8295), 4.

Victor, J. S. (1993). *Satanic panic: The creation of a contemporary legend*. Chicago: Open Court.

Wachs, E. (1988). *Crime victim stories: New York City's urban folklore*. Bloomington: Indiana University Press.

Wade, C., & Tavris, C. (1990). Thinking critically and creatively. *Skeptical Inquirer, 14*(4), 372-377.

Walker, S. (2001). *Sense and nonsense about crime and drugs: A policy guide* (5th ed.). Belmont, CA: Wadsworth.

Walters, R. (2003). *Deviant knowledge: Criminology, politics and policy*. Devon, UK: Willan Publishing.

Warr, M. (1980). The accuracy of public beliefs about crime. *Social Forces, 59,* 456-470.

Warr, M. (1985). Fear of rape among urban women. *Social Problems, 32*(3), 238-250.

Warr, M. (1990). Dangerous situations: Social context and fear of victimization. *Social Forces, 68*(3), 891-907.

Warr, M. (1992). Altruistic fear of victimization in households. *Social Science Quarterly, 73,* 723-736.

Warr, M., & Stafford, M. C. (1983). Fear of crime: A look at proximate causes. *Social Forces, 61,* 1033-1043.

Weed, F. J. (1990). The victim-activist role in the anti-drunk driving movement. *Sociological Quarterly, 31*(3), 459-473.

Weed, F. J. (1995*). The certainty of justice: Reform in the crime victim movement*. New York: Aldine de Gruyter.

Welch, M., Fenwick, M., & Roberts, M. (1997). Primary definitions of crime and moral panic: A content analysis of experts' quotes in feature newspaper articles on crime. *Journal of Research in Crime and Delinquency, 34*(4), 474-494.

Welch, M., Fenwick, M., & Roberts, M. (1998). State managers, intellectuals, and the media: A content analysis of ideology in experts: Quotes in feature newspaper articles on crime. In G. W. Potter & V. E. Kappeler (Eds.), *Constructing crime: Perspectives on making news in social problems*. Prospect Heights, IL: Waveland.

Welch, M., Price, E. A., & Yankey, N. (2002). Moral panic over youth violence: Wilding and the manufacture of menace in the media. *Youth and Society, 34*(1), 3-30.

White, G. F. (2001). Home ownership: Crime and the tipping and trapping process. *Environment and Behavior, 33*(3), 325-342.

Will, J. A., & McGrath, J. H. (1995). Crime neighborhood perceptions, and the underclass: The relationship between fear of crime and class position. *Journal of Criminal Justice, 23*(2), 163-176.

Williams, F. P., & Akers, R. L. (2000). Worry about victimization: An alternative and reliable measure for fear of crime. *Western Criminology Review, 2*(2). Retrieved December 12, 2004, from http://wcr.sonoma.edu/v2n2/Williams.html

Williams, H., & Pate, A. M. (1987). Returning to first principles: Reducing the fear of crime in Newark. *Crime and Delinquency, 33*(1), 53-70.

Wilson, J. Q., & Kelling, G. L. (1982). Broken windows. *Atlantic Monthly, 249*(3), 29-38.

Wilson, W. J. (1987). *The truly disadvantaged*. Chicago: University of Chicago Press.

Wilson, W. J. (1996). *When work disappears: The world of the new urban poor*. New York: Knopf.

Winsberg, M. D. (1993). Are crime waves in the United States regional or national? *Journal of Criminal Justice, 21*, 517-520.

Woodiwiss, M. (2001). *Organized crime and American power*. Toronto: University of Toronto Press.

Wright, J. P., Cullen, F. T., & Blankenship, M. B. (1995). The social construction of corporate violence. *Crime and Delinquency, 41*(1), 20-36.

Yin, P. (1980). Fear of crime among the elderly: Some issues and suggestions. *Social Problems, 27*(4), 492-504.

Yin, P. (1982). Fear of crime as a problem for the elderly. *Social Problems, 30*(2), 240-245.

Zawitz, M. W., Klaus, P. A., Bachman, R., Bastian, L. D., DeBerry, M. M., Jr., & Tyler, B. M. (1993). *Highlights of 20 years of surveying crime victims*. Washington, DC: Bureau of Justice Statistics.

Index

About the Author

Vincent F. Sacco is Professor of Sociology at Queen's University in Kingston, Ontario. His research and teaching interests relate to the study of crime and popular culture as well as public perceptions of and reactions to crime. His more general approach to criminology emphasizes the study of "criminal events" and investigates why some people are more likely to be victimized by crime than are others; when and where crimes occur; and why the police, lawmakers, and members of the general public think about crime the way they do. He has published several books, including *The Process and Structure of Crime: Criminal Events and Crime Analysis* (2002, with L. W. Leslie; in the series Advances in Criminological Theory), and *The Criminal Event: Perspectives in Time and Space* (2nd ed., 2002, edited with R. F. Meier and L. Kennedy).